Wildlife in the Garden

Wildlife in the Garden

How to Live in Harmony
with Deer, Raccoons, Rabbits,
Crows, and Other Pesky
Creatures

by
Gene Logsdon

Expanded Edition

Indiana University Press
Bloomington and Indianapolis

This book is a publication of

Indiana University Press
601 North Morton Street
Bloomington, IN 47404-3797 USA

http://www.indiana.edu/~iupress

Telephone orders 800-842-6796
Fax orders 812-855-7931
E-mail orders iuporder@indiana.edu

© 1983, 1999 by Gene Logsdon
An earlier version of this book, *Wildlife in Your Garden,*
was published in 1983 by the Rodale Press,
Emmaus, Pennsylvania.

Illustrations by Frank Fretz
Interior book design by Linda Jacopetti

The paper used in this publication meets the minimum
requirements of American National Standard for Information
Sciences—Permanence of Paper for Printed Library
Materials, ANSI Z39.48-1984.

Manufactured in the United States of America

Library of Congress Cataloging-in-Publication Data

Logsdon, Gene.
    Wildlife in the garden : how to live in harmony with deer,
raccoons, rabbits, crows, and other pesky creatures / by Gene
Logsdon. — Expanded ed.
        p.   cm.
    Includes index.
    ISBN 0-253-33562-0 (cloth). — ISBN 0-253-21284-7 (pbk.)
    1. Gardening to attract wildlife. 2. Garden ecology. 3. Wildlife
pests—Control. 4. Garden pests—Control. I. Title.
QL59.L64   1999
639.9′2—DC21   99-10784

1 2 3 4 5   04 03 02 01 00 99

Dedicated to the good people of Lower Gwynedd and Upper Gwynedd Townships of Montgomery County, Pennsylvania, who made my nine years of living there so pleasant and memorable and who became the models for the composite characters in this book living in the only slightly fictional "Gwynnedde Township."

Contents

Preface   xiii

Chapter 1. Points of View   1

Chapter 2. Thinking Eco-logically   9
The Food Web of a Bluebird   12
Keeping Wildlife Records   15

**Chapter 3. Maintaining a Home for Wildlife:
The Basic Steps**   21
Bees and Their Hives   22
Plants for Wildlife   25

Chapter 4. Housing for Wildlife   39
Smith's Reasons for Sheltering Wildlife   40
Housing for Birds   46
Bird Feeders   54
Shelter for Other Animals   57

Chapter 5. Water: Wildlife Catalyst   60
Backyard Birdbaths and Pools   66
Permanent Pools   67
Plants for Pools and Marshes   69
Other Water Life   73
Stocking a Pool   77

Chapter 6. A Butterfly Sanctuary 84
Beautiful Moths for the Backyard 87
Butterfly Beauties 90
Food Plants for Butterflies and Moths 92
Other Worthwhile Insects 97

Chapter 7. The Most Misunderstood Wildlife 102
Skunks 105
Snakes 107
Bats 111
Owls 112
Vultures 115
Hawks 118
Spiders 118
Wasps 120
Leeches 122

Chapter 8. Human Use of Nature's Food Web 125
The Widow Lady's Niche in Nature 128
Wild Plant Remedies 132
Mushrooms and Other Fungi 133
Berries and Nuts 136
Wildling Recipes 141

Chapter 9. Watching Wildlife 145
Sounds of the Wild 146
Tracks 148
Stalking 153
Building a Blind for Viewing Wildlife 155
Optical Aids for Wildlife Observation 160
Photography 164

Chapter 10. When Wildlife Overpopulates 169
Smith Learns How Smart "Dumb Animals" Can Be 170
A Shocking Solution to Raccoon Raids 173
The Great Neighborhood Deer Controversy 177
The Deer Problem Solved, Sort Of 179
Protecting Young Trees 181
Plants Deer Won't Eat, Sometimes 184
Good Fences Make Good Wildlife 187

Chapter 11. Other Wildlife Restraints 195
Rat Controls 195
Controls for Other Wild Animals 201

Traps   205
Guards, Shields, and Barriers   208
Repellents and Scare Devices   209
Sounds That Deter Wildlife   211

**Chapter 12. Adventures with Wildlife
in the Backyard**   215
Adventures with Birds   217
The Caretaker Gardener   225
Deer Stalker   230
Fate of the Raccoon   231
The Human Animal in the Wild Backyard   234
Wildling of the North   236

Appendix: Useful Lists   240
An Annotated List of Wild Mammals   240
Select Trees, Shrubs, and Vines for Wildlife   249
Food Plants for Caterpillars of Desirable Butterflies
    and Moths   252
Select Nectar Sources for Butterflies   254
Favorite Beetles for the Backyard   255
Characteristics of Edible Wild Mushrooms in the Yard   257
Edible Wild Nuts   259
Edible Wild Fruits   260

Index   265

Smith's Neighborhood in Gwynnedde Township

1. Smith's home and
   wildlife area
2. White's home
3. Brown's home
4. Widow Lady's home
5. Beekeeper's home
6. Dumb Farmer's farm
7. Friends' Meetinghouse
   and cemetery
8. St. Gwendolyn College

9. shoe factory
10. train station
11. Wissahickon Creek
12. Frog Run
13. pond
14. Dumb Farmer's old barn
15. Wandering Creek

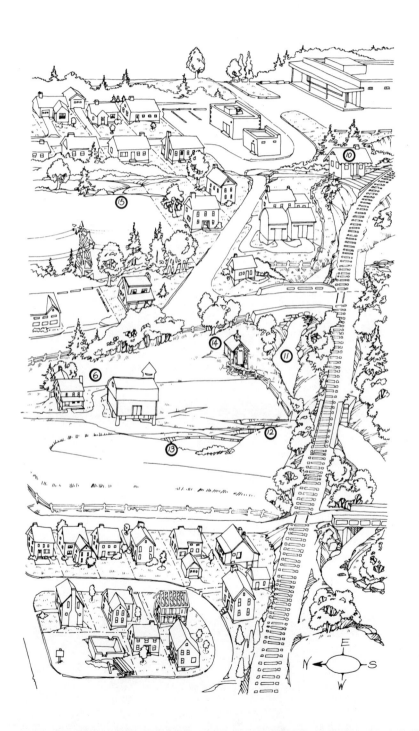

Preface

It almost frightens me to realize that it has been sixteen years since this book was first published under a slightly different title, *Wildlife in Your Garden*. And that the slightly (very slightly) fictional setting for the book was inspired by events that occurred as much as ten years before that, when my wife and I and our two small children were pioneering what has become known as urban farming in lovely Lower Gwynedd Township in Montgomery County, Pennsylvania, just north of Philadelphia.

In the late 1960s and early 1970s, Montgomery County was in (at first) slow transition from an almost idyllic rural area to a major metropolitan suburb. It amazed me to realize that electricity had come to this area of grand homes, golf courses, country clubs, ambitious housing, and commercial development—and still a few horse and livestock farms—just twenty years earlier, that in so short a time a rural culture at least three centuries old with much older European roots had all but vanished. Our backyard still showed the grassed-over dead furrows from the days when it was plowed with horses. Old barns, abandoned orchards, sagging fences, decaying springhouses, ungrazed pastures, a closed-up blacksmith shop at Springhouse still cluttered with nineteenth-century tools, amazingly wild patches of forest, an abandoned gristmill just down the road from us, a hitching rail still in place at the train station, country inns over a century old,

including the old Gwynedd Inn, where the owner still served a free
meal of venison during deer-hunting season, all shaded the glare of
encroaching urbanization with a rural charm and comeliness.

Purely by geographical accident, we were thrust into a situation that would become much more common in later years. As we
ventured into our suburban farming activities on two acres, we discovered that wildlife was burgeoning to awesome population levels. A
century of serious commercial farming had held wildlife in check
(perhaps too much so), limiting wildlife habitat through crop cultivation and livestock grazing. Hunting and trapping, traditional rural
pastimes, also were a factor. In the current transition to urban development, the land ceased to be cultivated and grazed, and it grew up
in brush and weeds and tall grass. Wildlife heaven. When the houses
did come, their owners surrounded them with a diversity of landscaping plants and trees that also encouraged more wildlife. Factories
coming to this area were so intent on preserving natural aspects of the
township that they landscaped quite large areas around them with
"wildlife areas," including lovely preserved woodland and ponds.

There followed a virtual population explosion of those forms
of wildlife that benefit from close human habitation, namely those
species gardeners consider to be "pests" but that non-gardeners love to
watch from their breakfast windows. The people moving into this
wildlife haven did not understand population dynamics (even overly
protective wildlife experts did not understand much, and naturalist
E. O. Wilson endured years of criticism before he was vindicated for
pointing that out). Furthermore, ex-urbanites were already so far removed from the old traditions of hunting that many considered killing an animal immoral. It was plain to see that a conflict was looming, not only between humans and wildlife but between humans who
sought to control wildlife populations and those who did not think
that necessary. The problem would become especially acute because it
mirrored a deeper, more troubling vexation: Should human population be controlled?

And so to this book. And so, as the wildlife problem grows
more acute every day, to its replenishing. Today, thousands of
"Gwynedde Townships" are coming into existence, and so universal
is wildlife (and human?) overpopulation that slowly, slowly, humans
of different beliefs are beginning to agree that "live and let live" is a
gross oversimplification. While some wildlife becomes endangered,

even extinct, other forms, from Canada geese to whitetailed deer, have become not just pestiferous, but from a modern point of view, a menace. How do we strike a proper middle ground in our "live and let live" philosophies? The question is a most difficult one, especially for a human culture that is only slowly gaining ecological literacy.

I have attempted to address that question in this book in my own way. I have updated the first edition, adding some new information not available sixteen years ago, and correcting some obvious errors. I have also added more "fictitious" storytelling to include community conflicts about wildlife that had not much existed sixteen years ago. The change in the title is my effort to indicate to the reader that this is not just a book about how to protect gardens from wildlife. This is a story of people I've known (now fitted with fictitious names) and how they have learned that living harmoniously with wildlife occasionally means becoming a predator themselves. The title *Wildlife in the Garden* seems to me more appropriate because it suggests more human involvement in the predator-prey relationships by which the biological food chain succors all life. We are all wild creatures and, as poet Gary Snyder likes to point out, humans are the wildest of all.

Wildlife in the Garden

Chapter 1

Points of View

From his hiding place inside the overturned flowerpot in Smith's garden, Toad dozes with one eye open. Toad's scientific name is *Bufo americanus,* just as Smith's is *Homo sapiens,* but neither Toad nor Smith attaches much importance to the niceties of scientific accuracy. Toad's list of important matters scarcely extends beyond the length of his tongue, with which he can reach out swift as lightning and catch bugs that fly within range. His repose even now, during his daylight siesta, is deceptive. Smith, down on all fours watching him, does not even see the sudden stab of the tongue when it comes, only that a hapless fly, hovering near the inscrutable toad, suddenly disappears.

Toad accepts the presence of the man as a shadowy movement on the edge of his consciousness—a movement that is not translatable into food. Three years ago, when he first found the garden to be a veritable gold mine of food, Toad hid from the man-movement, digging quickly backward under the handy garden mulch. Now he has become as accustomed to Smith as he is to the movement of trees in a sudden gust of wind, and if he flees at all, it is merely to hop under the closest leaf or scoot farther back into his precious flowerpot lair. On warm nights, he even hops along the man's pathways to the house, where there are bugs aplenty drawn by the porch light and where, from a faucet, water drips to moisten his skin—the toad's way of drinking.

The other boundary of Toad's world is formed by the swampy bit of woodland that comprises the back half-acre of Smith's two-acre lot. There, in the temporary pool of water with which spring rains fill the tiny swamp, he was born—one of thousands of eggs his mother deposited in long, jellylike strings in the water. In woodsy soil on the higher ground nearby, Toad comes in the fall to spend the winter, digging backward into the soft ground, retreating deeper before the advance of frozen earth. Then, moving back upward as the soil thaws, he emerges early in the first fitful warm days to be about his business. Now that he is five years old, of breeding age, he does not head immediately for the garden, eating bugs on the way, as he did as a younger toad. Instead, he returns to the water of his birth, which cradled him as a tadpole. From his throat then comes rapturous song belying the ugliness of his demeanor, the song Smith awaits with almost as much eagerness as the female toads who are drawn by it to mating.

The mating season over, Toad hops to the garden by slow stages down the hedge that separates Smith's land from neighbor White's. It is Toad's predilection for the shady bower of the hedge and the strip of wild grass and weeds that Smith allows to grow on his side of it (mowing the grass high but once a year in mid-August) that has saved his life on numerous occasions. As a wee bit of a toad fresh from the tadpole waters, he was hidden by the tall grass and hedge from would-be enemies: hawks and owls. As an adult, seldom preyed upon because of the whitish liquid that exudes from his skin in times of grave danger—a liquid that fiercely burns mucous membranes of attackers—Toad's most serious enemy is the lawn mower. Under the hedge or in the unmowed grass, he is safe from it, too.

Smith's world, or his view of it, developed at the far end of the food chain that binds him to Toad, is necessarily more complex. Smith and Toad share the marsh, hedge, garden, patio faucet, and an interest in insects. But what is the whole world to Toad is only a focal point or beginning for Smith. He views his garden as a patch of land within a network of neighboring gardens, each a part of the human habitat forming a neighborhood of homes occupying land that was previously a brushy, second-growth woodland, which previous to that was a farm (the old dead furrows of once-plowed fields are still clearly visible in the mowed part of his backyard). Before that, the land had been virgin forest covering a ridge-to-valley slope. It in turn was part of a series of ridge-to-valley slopes radiating northwest from the mouth of the Delaware River like so many giant waves frozen in red laterite soils, pushing away on to the foothills of the Appalachian Range. Each valley between its ridges has its small creek to drain off the excess water of rain and snow. Each small creek flows into a larger one, the Wissahickon, which empties into the Schuylkill River, which flows into the Delaware, and the Delaware into the Atlantic Ocean.

Smith's world view is not only not like Toad's, it's not like some of his neighbors', either. White, next door, sees his world, his habitat, not so much in biological and geological terms as within an intellectual framework of intentional, man-inspired boundaries and institutions. White would say he lives in a suburban development in Gwynnedde Township, in the county of Montgomery, in the metropolitan area of Philadelphia, in the state of Pennsylvania, in the United States of America. Unless his attention is deliberately drawn to it, White does not see the natural divisions of the land into valley and ridge interlaced by stream and river, clothed in trees or grass. What he recognizes is a place interlaced by streets and highways demarcating subdivision and shopping center, blurring older institutions of farm, village, and city.

When Smith and White are not vying to grow the larger tomato, they sometimes argue about their views. (They argue about many things, but their disagreements all arise from this basic difference.) Smith tells White that by ignoring biology in favor of the convenience of lines that appear only on maps, White will inevitably conclude that biology is unimportant and, finally, that it is an unnecessary consideration in planning human habitats. Smith takes great satisfaction in summing up his argument by saying that when the well-being of toads and birds is ignored, next the well-being of man himself will be ignored. To which White replies sarcastically that one need not consider toads when dividing all of Gaul into three parts. And that is why, Smith answers as from a pulpit, Gaul does not remain divided into three parts but seethes every so many generations with war. Toad, from his flowerpot, listens intently to the arguments but has nothing to add.

Because of Smith's view, he spends far more time than he should, probably, raising vegetables and peering into the eyes of such creatures as toads. He seeks to reconnect his mind to an earlier, earthier kind of *sapiens*. Toad is not in his garden simply as a result of the chancy causations of nature, but by Smith's deliberate planning.

Learning that a single toad can demolish 15,000 insects and slugs in a season without half trying, Smith carefully planned the amphibian's continued residence in his garden. He stuck the flowerpot on its side in the dirt under the rhubarb because he had read that most amphibians like to sit with their sides closely in contact with a burrow or hole in which they hide from the hot sun. In dry weather, Smith lets the faucet drip for Toad. For Toad he leaves the strip of lawn next to the hedge unmowed, even though the wild lawn also protects Garter Snake, Toad's most common natural enemy. Such is the irony of ecology, for Garter Snake is also Smith's other Assistant Manager of Slug Exterminations.

That there are toads enough for Smith as well as for White and Brown, on the other side of Smith, and for who knows how many other nearby gardeners, is Smith's handiwork, too, at least indirectly. The little marshy woodland at the rear of his property would long ago have been drained, filled, and occupied by a house or two if Smith and the Beekeeper who lives behind Smith's place had given in to the continual

Toad in His Flowerpot

pressure from developers. Though the offer is always good, Smith demurs, preferring to keep his own bit of private wilderness. If he sells, he often says, likely as not he would soon spend the money traveling to faraway wilderness spots, which, he has sadly learned, are less private and peaceful than his own backyard. And, having the marsh, he decided to make the most of its temporary spring pool. From the Dumb Farmer's pond over the ridge, he scooped two bucketfuls of fertilized toad eggs and dumped them into his pool. With a half hour's pleasant work, he started a new colony of toads that could last forever.

Brown has almost as much trouble seeing the world from Smith's viewpoint as White does. Brown smiles bemusedly at Smith's tiny wildlife sanctuary, believing its very size limits its possibilities too much. Brown sees each man's property as an independent unit, disconnected from the others. What happens on his place, he thinks, has little bearing on the land around him. It is not clear to him that Smith's little marsh is, from the standpoint of the biological food chain, *his* little marsh, too. He is not aware that the valley floodplain below him and the woodland on the ridge above him (both not feasible for housing and so left accidentally in a semiwild state) contribute significantly to the diversity and number of insects, birds, and mammals that populate his lawns and garden. He does not appreciate the wonderful diversity of plant life that humans bring to their subdivisions, nor the contribution toward ecological balance that diversity brings with it. The Dumb Farmer (who calls himself that because, as he puts it, he's so stubborn that he is the last man in the township still operating a commercial farm there) keeps his land in grain and hay meadows and thereby contributes other forms of habitats, with blessings for Brown that the latter does not realize.

One of the chief blessings is that the hay meadows provide most of the honey for the Beekeeper's nearby hives, and as a result, the Beekeeper's bees increase and pollinate neighborhood orchard and garden plants, including Brown's apple trees, of which he is inordinately proud. Brown rides the commuter train to Philadelphia every day but never notices the wildlife cover along the railroad right-of-way. He does not realize, either, that the cemeteries in the community, especially the ancient one at the Friends' Meetinghouse, preserve huge, centuries-old trees with hollow segments of branch and trunk in them large enough for great horned owls and other cavity-nesting birds and animals. He does not know that the old stone barns, still lovingly

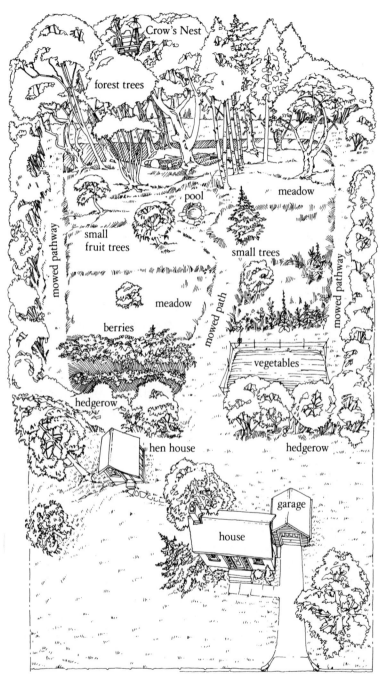

Crow's Nest

forest trees

meadow

pool

small
fruit trees

small trees

mowed pathway

mowed pathway

meadow

mowed path

berries

vegetables

hedgerow

hen house

hedgerow

garage

house

Smith's Wildlife Area

preserved on some of the older homesites in the neighborhood, house three of man's best pest controllers: bats, barn owls, and even a pair of screech owls (which normally nest in tree hollows). Brown is proud of a local factory less than a mile away that preserves many acres around it in woodland and meadow, plus three small lakes that geese and ducks frequent, but he does not realize that the factory owners' sensitivity to nature benefits the natural life of his whole neighborhood.

So, Brown is constantly surprised when deer walk impudently through his backyard, when ring-necked pheasants dust in his flower beds, when raccoons rattle his garbage cans, when he discovers that he can garden organically in his backyard, something he could not do at his previous home, which was located in a region of intense monocultural farming. He finds it hard to believe that Smith identified 92 species of birds in his garden sanctuary in one year and thinks it amazing that Smith found an opossum in his hen-house egg nest one morning. "Why, to hear you tell it," he says to Smith wryly, "there's more wildlife in our backyards than on my home farm in Illinois."

Brown speaks closer to the truth than he knows. Like most of the other people in Gwynnedde Township, he would be surprised to learn that his area quite possibly does have more wildlife than an intensively farmed, rural, midwestern township of similar size. The reason can be given with one word: habitat. Despite its comparatively high human population and numerous subdivisions, towns, shopping centers, and industrial parks, Gwynnedde—like hundreds of other suburban areas slowly changing from farm country to city—has many more places where wild animals, birds, and insects can live than, for example, a Corn Belt township in central Illinois, even though the latter has only a fraction of Gwynnedde's human population. Most of the woodland and pasture of that township in Illinois have been stripped away in favor of endless seas of corn whose rows barely give way—and only grudgingly—to roads. The farmsteads in such a township are often nearly bereft of landscaping—perhaps some wide, often-mowed lawns, and a few stark trees, with the corn shouldering nearly to the buildings themselves. Gwynnedde, on the contrary, appears from the air more as woodland than subdivision.

What humans have done, simply by landscaping their homes with a large variety of trees and bushes, is to create an urban forest. Between subdivisions and behind roadside developments lie many once-farmed acres going back to woodland, a mecca for wild animals. Ridge tops, where bedrock is too close to the surface to encourage housing because of septic tank limitations, remain in brush, pasture, gardens, orchards, and tree groves. Creek valley floodplains are left to nature, some of them on old estates still supporting the original forest that was lumbered but never cleared and cultivated, with many large old trees remaining. Unlike country roadsides in much of the rural Midwest, which are regularly mowed and/or sprayed with herbicides, secondary roadsides in Gwynnedde grow up in brush, berries, and bird song. In addition to railroad rights-of-way, power lines, although ugly and obnoxious to look at on the horizon, preserve wide swaths of insect, bird, and small animal habitat. In some sections, there are pastures or garden spaces. A few remaining horse farms and fields of cultivated grains increase the plant diversity of the township's open space. Several country clubs provide more. Next to the factory with its trees and lakes is a college, its extensive grounds providing still more habitat for wildlings and pleasing landscape for man. If the human occupation of the area could stabilize at current levels, if the people became consciously aware of the many simple things they could do to increase wildlife habitat even more, and if the pollution of the Wissahickon would be stopped, the township could easily become a wildlife paradise as satisfying to humans as any wilderness promises to be. Surprisingly few animals are frightened away to the "real" wilderness by man. Give wildlings their proper habitat—food and shelter—and they will live next to man quite handily.

Much too handily, Smith will let you know. He is not quite sure whether the pleasure of watching pheasants dust in his garden makes up for the hair-raising experience of reaching sleepily into a hen's nest for eggs and grabbing instead a surly opossum. "Be glad it wasn't a skunk," Brown said philosophically.

Chapter 2

Thinking Eco-logically

. . . I believe my great backyard sphexes [cicada-killer wasps] have evolved like other creatures. But watching them in the October light as one circles my head in curiosity, I can only repeat my dictum softly: In the world there is nothing to explain the world. Nothing to explain the necessity of life, nothing to explain the hunger of the elements to become life, nothing to explain why the stolid realm of rock and soil and mineral should diversify itself into beauty, terror, and uncertainty. To bring organic novelty into existence, to create pain, injustice, joy, demands more than we can discern in the nature that we analyze so completely . . . The equation that can explain why a mere sphex wasp contains in his minute head the ganglionic centers of his prey has still to be written. There is nothing below a certain depth that is truly explanatory. It is as if matter dreamed and muttered in its sleep. But why, and for what reason it dreams, there is no evidence.

Loren Eiseley, "Coming of the Giant
Wasps," *Audubon*, September, 1975.

9

When you consider which plants, insects, and animals you ideally would like to share your backyard garden with, you think immediately of the most beautiful and beneficial creatures—perhaps bluebirds, luna moths, fiery searcher beetles, barn owls, bluegills, and foxes. You reject "ugly" or "harmful" creatures—pine voles, rosy apple aphids, starlings, and hognose snakes. This kind of thinking, perfectly logical when applied to a totally man-made environment like a house, won't work when applied to nature. You can select and reject, to a certain extent, what enters your house: furnishings, pets, appliances, and friends. But you can't choose between "friends" and "enemies" in a natural setting. The owls and the foxes must have the voles to dine on. The bluebird enjoys rosy apple aphids. The voles eat the luna moth pupae in their cocoons.

Even these simple observations about the food chain, or food web, as ecologists prefer to call it, in no way approach an accurate notion of the complicated interdependency of living things. Nature is a tremendous banquet table at which sits the eating being eaten. If each eater ate only one other species, then the human mind could map out some logical and more or less easy-to-follow graph of what was going on, but such is not usually the case. The Everglade kite (*Rostrhamus sociabilis*) is a bird that lives almost exclusively on the apple snail, and the sharp-tailed snake (*Contia* spp.) lives on slugs, but most creatures eat a variety of other creatures, including in some cases, as with the praying mantis, its own kind. Snakes eat frogs and birds, among other things. Some bullfrogs and some birds eat snakes. Snakes, frogs, and birds eat spiders and wasps. Spiders eat wasps and wasps eat spiders. Crows will rob nests of other birds but, strangely enough, often will not molest nests close to their own. Foxes normally will avoid skunks, but when hungry enough, a gray fox has been known to climb a tree and drop upon a skunk from above. Meanwhile, within each of these creatures another food web is interacting: Parasites, along with bacteria and other microorganisms, interrelate with their hosts and with each other.

All this competition for survival depends upon causally unrelated factors such as favorable weather, the absence of which can have a greater effect on the population of any segment of the food web than the predator-prey process. Weather is an unpredictable phenomenon. So is, in any particular instance, wildlife road kill. Such factors introduce the element of chance into an already terribly complex system. Chance is not a concept that either the logician or the scientist cares to account for in his deductions. But an ecologist must try. He brings to his imperfect science a unique vision. He must seek truth eco-logically, rather than logically. He must seek explanations that transcend the cause-effect relationships the human mind uses to understand reality. For example, the human mind learns how a motor works by considering causal relationships. The battery "causes" the spark, which "causes" the gasoline vapors to burn and explode, which "causes" the piston to move, which "causes" the crankshaft to revolve, which "causes" the transmission to turn the wheels. Aha, says the human mind, now I understand how a piston engine works! And, for practical purposes, there is understanding. Equipped with that kind of knowledge alone, says the Dumb Farmer, "the dumbest teenager in town can keep a car running long enough to get to his girl friend's house. It's a matter of sheer logic."

Such cause-effect, logical thinking isn't nearly as helpful in trying to "fix" a natural environment. What "causes" an apple? Sunlight and water? The tree it grows on? The man who plants the tree? The apple seed? The soil it grows in? The nutrients that feed it? The microorganisms that break down the nutrients into a form the tree roots can use? The mycorrhizal fungi that allow the roots to absorb the nutrients? The pollinating bee? The bluebird that eats the aphids that would otherwise have withered the branch before the apple formed? Photosynthesis? Plant tissue? Protoplasm? Evolution? God? Philosophers have tried to overcome this "logical" problem by defining various kinds of causes, such as essential cause, first cause, approximate cause, instrumental cause, and so forth. But labeling causes does not help us to understand the apple, much less how to repair a damaged environment. In fact, long ago mankind unconsciously admitted the limitations of causal knowledge applied to the real world with the classic joke: which came first, the chicken or the egg? The question is unanswerable within a logical, causal framework.

Cause and effect are, of course, at work in the food web—or what we humans consider to be cause and effect. The process is not simply linear, however, as we suggest by using the phrase "food chain," nor is it even geometric, as when we say "food web." The interaction is explosive, implosive, exponential, and simultaneous, and therefore four-dimensional. As skilled as we are in marshaling numbers in our computers, the food web defies adequate programming. Introduce the factor of chance, and the computer can only run simulations. For example, if you kill a pair of mice in your house, the computer can quickly tell you not only how many millions of mice you theoretically "caused" not to be born in the next 50 years, but also how many of that number would have survived, given a "normal" mouse environment. What is normal? It is possible that by killing one pair of mice in your house, you allowed another pair to produce more healthy offspring than the two pairs would have produced together, if a shortage of food or habitat prevailed.

Attempts are being made to subject the food web to mathematical analysis in hope of finding keys to unravel the complexities of predator-prey interactions. Biologists such as Joel E. Cohen of Rockefeller University (*Food Webs and Niche Spaces*) are pioneering methods of reducing complex food web information into simple one-dimensional "interval graphs" that can be plotted on straight lines. Then they further convert the data into tables that can conveniently be fed into computers for analysis. Results are interesting to trained ecologists, although backyarders without backgrounds in mathematical analysis will have difficulty understanding the graphs, much less using the information practically in their gardens.

The Food Web of a Bluebird

Consider, for example, the bluebird and how to convert its small food web domain to meaningful analysis. About 80 percent of its food is insects, worms, and other small creatures. It also eats some wild fruit and weed seeds. Its predators—squirrels, raccoons, opossums, and skunks—mostly take young birds and/or eggs. The eggs, incidentally, are usually light blue, though they can be white. Some hawks and the great horned owl will eat adult bluebirds occasionally. The starling kills nestling bluebirds if it can get its head far enough into the nest. The house sparrow drives out the bluebirds and builds its own nest on top of the bluebird eggs. The larvae of a bloodsucking fly, hatching in the bluebird's nest, can kill young bluebirds, too. Though rarely, lice and mites may be troublesome enough to cause nestling mortality.

While availability of food and nesting sites are the main problems for bluebirds, they also must contend with adversities somewhat incidental to their food web. Bluebirds enter stovepipes or downspouts and die when they can't get out. They used to enter the aeration flues of old-time tobacco-curing barns, become trapped, and starve. Thousands of songbirds, bluebirds included, die during their migration, colliding with TV power boosting towers, tall buildings, monuments, and other structures jutting into the sky.

A bluebird mother may lay three eggs or seven or any number between. She may raise one brood or two, sometimes three. If she dies, the male may raise the hatched chicks. Or, he may not. Where there are no tree hollows to nest in, the bluebird adapts to holes in old corner posts of farm fences. When the old fencerows are bulldozed away, as commonly happens now, the bluebird may not be able to find suitable nesting sites at all. To Smith's surprise, though, one bluebird in his backyard ignored prevailing scientific theory and nested in a very un-bluebird type of box. The back of a conventional bluebird house had rotted away, making the nest more attractive to birds that nest on open shelves, such as phoebes and robins. Yet, this bluebird raised two broods on the shelf without being the worse for wear.

In the face of such complexities (and the enumeration above hardly brushes the surface), what chances are there to practice an *exact* science of ecology? As Smith explained while he erected yet another bluebird house on his property, "My bluebird houses are prayers of faith and hope, not acts of scientific certitude. Faith will save nature long before science will."

Perhaps. Science pursues knowledge about nature in several ways. In its early days, science mostly involved identifying and classifying. Then researchers went on to study individuals and their parts in great detail, applying the knowledge gained to manipulate nature or to develop new products, all for the seeming benefit of man. Ignored, or at least often overlooked, in the process were the interrelationships between individuals and their environment, the study of which is called ecology. Overlooking these interrelationships, scientists then assumed that by understanding individuals and their parts, they could understand adequately the whole of the environment—the communities of plants and animals and the soil, water, air, and weather they depend on for survival. Such science easily spawned TV towers that kill thousands of birds annually, or developed a toxic chemical like DDT.

Identification and classification are essentially a logical process of deduction and induction. Smith sees in the woods, for example, a black furry creature with a white stripe down its back and a bushy tail, rooting up a yellow jacket nest. Only one creature fits that description—the common skunk. Therefore, the creature must be a skunk, scientific name, *Mephitis mephitis,* which freely translates into "a godawful smell." Applying the knowledge gained from studying individual skunks and their parts led scientists to conclude that the odor of *M. mephitis* is not only nasty but amazingly enduring. If the cause of the bad odor could be separated from the cause of the endurance, then the skunk oil might make a good base for perfumes. And, indeed it does!

But the deduction and induction by which this kind of knowledge is acquired have limitations in all science, especially ecology. Deduction and induction can guide a person to build a proper "scientific" bluebird house, but whether a bluebird will actually nest in the house is another matter altogether. In the case of the skunk, deduction and induction can help one take skunks apart to make fur coats and perfumes but won't help a bit in putting together used skunk parts into a living skunk again.

For ecology, and really for all science, there is another kind of thought process that transcends deduction and induction, that is based more upon a vision than it is upon logically deduced or induced facts. This vision is aware of the sacredness of the life principle running through all living things, existing elusively beyond the most powerful microscope, extending to all living creatures, and possessed by none of them individually. The life of the tree from which the apple falls extends to the life of the soil; to the life of the bluebird that nests in the tree; to the life of the yellow jacket that eats the fallen apple; to the life of the skunk that eats the yellow jacket; to the life of the whole backyard that is linked biologically to the next backyard, extending at last to all living creatures. The fallen apple, though pronounced dead, teems with all kinds of creatures turning that deadness back into nutrients that will spark new life in plants and animals and begin again the long, slow, interwoven journey back through the explosive, implosive, cascading web of life. In a very real sense, no creature loses life, but instead is constantly reabsorbed into other forms of life. Real death can come only through a final, fatal disruption of the food web itself. This is the vision, the place of ecology: to witness and defend the sacredness of the natural web of life. It is a vision that is neither totally scientific nor religious, but one that combines both the pragmatism of the former and the solace of the latter. There is a way in which we can live forever, says the ecologist, if we will but preserve the inviolability of the web of life.

Keeping Wildlife Records

In becoming a backyard wildlife manager, you will probably proceed as the earliest scientists did. You will learn to identify the living creatures and plants in your yard. You might begin the way the typical birdwatcher begins. Some birdwatchers even play a game that could be called "I Can See and Identify More Kinds of Birds Than You Can." It's a game of one-upmanship. White plays it remarkably well for having learned it from Smith only recently. White grew tired of what he took to be a certain overbearing manner in Smith. Smith got in the habit of leaning over the hedge that separates their yards and saying, "I just saw the most beautiful bird in the world. A Blackburnian warbler." White would roll his eyes, having no idea what a warbler was, much less whether Blackburn was a town in Vermont or an English lawyer. But when, in the fourteenth installment of Smith's "most beautiful bird" orgy, he came up with what he called, syllable by syllable, "pro-thon-o-tar-y warbler," White could tolerate his feelings of inadequacy no longer. "It's not enough I have to try to grow bigger tomatoes than he does," he grumped to his wife, "but now, by God, I've got to see prettier birds."

The following spring, White was ready. When Smith started into his vernal litany with "there's nothing more beautiful in the world than . . ."—choosing this year to let "yellow-bellied sapsucker" roll trippingly off his tongue, White cut him short. "Oh, I don't know," he replied, leaning on his hoe and yawning. "Yesterday I had a cerulean warbler, a rose-breasted grosbeak, and an indigo bunting in my binoculars all at the same time. Now that's something to see." It was Smith's turn to mutter under his breath for three days.

Many birdwatchers eventually pass beyond mere identification of birds. Instead of rushing off to inform other birdwatchers that he had seen a scarlet tanager in the oak tree for the fourteenth consecutive year (ho-hum), Smith finally asked himself, "What is that bird doing up in oak trees all the time?" From that point on he ceased being a mere birdwatcher and became an amateur ecologist. Instead of simple bird lists, he now began to keep "food web lists," upon which he charted not only the identity of a bird, animal, insect, or plant under observation, but what each one ate and what ate it. He learned these facts both from personal observation and also from books. Eventually he started cataloging his finds on 4×6-inch cards with predators and prey listed in separate columns under the identified species. Below is what one of Smith's first cards looked like:

Eastern Bluebird: *Sialia sialis*

Food Sources	Parasites	Predators
insects (all kinds)	blowfy larvae	raccoon
wild fruit	(*Protocalliphora*)	squirrel*
weed seeds	lice	starling
	mites	snakes
		house sparrow*
		(takes over nest)

Food Sites Observed:

orchard
edge of woods

Professional ecologists would prefer that Smith give the scientific names for all species, but Smith believes that kind of information is not usually necessary to manage his backyard wildlife. (He included the genus of the blowfly, *Protocalliphora*, because it was given in the book he was reading.) His method is to list under the species he is recording all the prey, predators, and parasites he can learn through reading, and then to put an asterisk beside the ones he observes in action on his property. He wishes he could buy cards like this already made up for common wildlife. Then he could just score them as he observes particular predator-prey interactions of his wildlife area,—a record of his prowess as an amateur ecologist just as a life list of birds is a record of a birdwatcher's proficiency.

An ecologist might fault Smith on another aspect of his file cards. Scientists would like predator-prey relationships recorded in greater detail. On the bluebird card, specific kinds of insects eaten should be listed, not just a general insect category. Where possible, an indication of the quantity of food eaten ought to be given, and perhaps a little more description of the dining site beyond merely "orchard" or "edge of woods." Smith agrees that he should be more specific regarding insects, but he rarely sees the bugs his bluebird swallows. As for quantity of food, he says he can keep track of the rough number of birds and rats the great horned owl brings to her nestlings if he takes the time, but who can count rosy apple aphids going down a bluebird's throat at any time?

A file of food web cards covering the more common life forms you encounter in your garden environment is not just a scorecard. The information can be marvelously helpful both in teaching you to think ecologically and as a guide to managing wildlife in your backyard. Each card represents a tiny strand of the food web. As your file grows, so does your awareness. Some species are more beneficial than others. If you can make a choice, you know which to choose. You also begin to wonder: How many thousands of cards would I have to compile before I covered the entire food web of just one backyard?

While you are learning humility, you also learn about real life—perhaps your first education in a very important aspect of existence: survival. As you fill out card after card, as you observe day after day, you begin to think in terms of interrelationships. Mother Nature loses her image of maternal gentility in your eyes. Instead of visualizing a bluebird sitting on a post simply reflecting the sky on her back, as the poet might say, your mind's eye sees her poised there ready to pounce on a bug, while a starling waits in a nearby tree for a chance to raid the bluebird's nest. Your dream of peas growing in next spring's garden includes a rabbit just waiting for you to leave the pea patch while a hawk waits for the rabbit to make one false move.

You also learn that while the food web in its entirety is mind-boggling, little segments of it are quite simple and straightforward, recurring in set patterns that are as faithful as night following day. If you look hard, some of the wild trillium blossoms every spring will be inhabited by little crab spiders (*Misumenops* spp.), which do not spin webs but still catch bugs attracted to the flowers. The legs and foreparts of the spiders are colorless and translucent, hard to see even for a bug when it's approaching with nectar on its mind.

Smith has a sort of trick he plays on visitors, a trick he learned from keeping food web cards. Walking in his little woodlot in June, he will point at certain small, brown-topped bracket fungi growing on dead limbs fallen from trees. "If you look under that mushroom over there," he tells a child, "you'll find a little beetle the size of a ladybug with a back as brown as the mushroom." The child, alive to mystery, rushes to examine the fungus. Sure enough, the beetle is there. The child is awed. Smith looks wise and keeps walking. He doesn't know the name of either the fungus or the beetle, but only that the two are always together in June.

Smith keeps cards on such observations anyway, using his own made-up names for the creatures involved until he learns the proper names. He agrees that such a practice might give a straitlaced biologist fits, but for his own personal purposes, "brown bracket beetle" is perfectly clear. To mollify the scientist, he has photographed the beetle on the fungus, and a slide of it is cross-referenced to his card. In fact, photographing interrelationships in nature has become the most excit-

---

32   cs 67, 68, 69
American Toad: *Bufo americanus*

Food Sources   *Predators*

caterpillars (tent*, gypsy moth   lawn mowers & automobiles*
  larvae*)   hognose snakes (*Heterodon*)
slugs*   other snakes, esp. of tadpoles
mosquitoes   hawks, esp. Broad-winged
bees   leeches (of tadpoles)
flies (house*, tachinid*, blow*,   water beetles (of tadpoles)
  bot*)   owls, esp. great horned owl
locusts, crickets*, grasshoppers*   Garter snake worst enemy of
worms (cutworm*, earthworm*,   young toad
  cabbageworm*)
beetles
snails
newts
aphids
leafhoppers

Food Sites:

vegetable garden
lawn
patio under night light

ing part of his backyard wildlife hobby (see Chapter 10, Watching Wildlife), and he hopes someday to have slides for every card in his file. He likes to pretend his hobby is leading to hitherto unknown discoveries, and quite possibly it might. He believes, for example, that the "brown bracket beetle" is eating not the "brown bracket fungus" but other tiny mushroom-eating insects. So far, he hasn't caught the beetle in the act, however. You can see why Smith's wife has a hard time getting him out of the backyard for some away-from-home diversion. Smith has more diversion in his wildlife acre than he can handle. He says that he will die long before his file of food web cards is complete.

As he learns more, Smith's cards have become more sophisticated. Now he has them cross-referenced to a file of color slides, *cs 1, cs 2,* and so on. He tries to give more detailed information about the prey and predators involved with the wildlife he's seen (as indicated by the asterisks on his cards). But he insists that, as in the case of Toad, his favorite garden inhabitant, naming every species of insect devoured would be too much work for his purposes and beyond his current level of knowledge.

If Smith learns more information relative to the food web activities of the card's subject, he uses the other side. On the back of Toad's card, for instance, he recorded, "When attacked and near death, a toad exudes a whitish liquid that burns severely wherever it touches mucous membranes. Thus, a dog or a fox rarely ever pursues a second toad, and this explains why toads are not heavily preyed upon by larger animals." A second entry reads, "Toads eat only moving, living prey." And a third, which is Smith's own deduction, says, "Toad is an AAA wildling, my highest rating for backyard benefit, because it seems to eat far more pest bugs than beneficials. Its few predators (other than neighbor White and his lawn mower, of course) are otherwise beneficial to the garden, too."

Chapter 3

Maintaining a Home for Wildlife: The Basic Steps

The Beekeeper practices good habitat management for wildlife, although he doesn't think of it that way. He only knows that he takes good care of his bees. Because his bees are essentially wild creatures, not domesticated like the Dumb Farmer's cows, the Beekeeper takes care of them by submitting to their wild ways, not forcing them to adapt totally to his convenience. Any attempt to reduce artificially the diversity of plant, insect, and animal life in hope of simplifying the honey production business soon backfires. Kill pest bugs indiscriminately with toxic sprays and you kill bees, too. Practice monocultural farming and gardening, and the bees lose the diversity of plants they need to gather nectar throughout the whole growing season. If bee activity decreases, so does pollination.

So, by definition, the Beekeeper assumes the attitudes of an ecologist as well as those of a wildlife manager. He must assure the bees of an environment that provides all of the building blocks of good habitat: food, water, cover or shelter, adequate territory or space, and a proper house in which to live. Since the Beekeeper has only tenuous control over most of these building blocks as they apply to his bees, he becomes involved in all the varied pulsations of the dynamic food web of nature. Bees teach their keepers respect and gentleness, not just for the bees themselves, but for all life. That respect brings with it a gentle-man's psychology, the psychology of fitting in. The Beekeeper did not suddenly decide to muscle or buy his way into the honey business. He first invited in the bees. That is, he looked around his homestead and saw orchard trees full of blossoms; he saw, across the fence, the Dumb Farmer's fields of blooming alfalfa and soybeans; he noticed the nearby water in the Dumb Farmer's pasture pond and the marsh pool in Smith's backyard; he observed the dizzying variety of flowers, ornamental bushes, gardens, and fruit trees in the surrounding suburban development; he remembered that his old stone barn's south wall blocked harsh winter winds and was shaded in summer by two linden trees and one black locust, both good trees for honey. He looked at his environment and realized that it was a perfect place for bees. Only then did he decide. He fitted his desires into nature's patterns.

Bees and Their Hives

Even the modern beehive bows to the bee's ways. With the older hollow-log, "bee-gum" hive, the beekeeper usually had to destroy the bees to get the honey. It became obvious even in the 1800s that such destructive extraction didn't really pay, so various experimental hives were built that incorporated movable frames. The hope was that perhaps bees might be trained like cows or pigs to adapt to something more convenient to men. But success awaited a discovery. Finally, a minister in Philadelphia by the name of Langstroth discovered through long hours of patient observation (the first necessity in learning to maintain a wildlife habitat) what came to be known as the principle of "bee space." Bees, he observed, allow a fixed space between their combs—just over ¼ inch, but not quite ⅜ inch. In all the hives he examined, this space was maintained no matter how convoluted the comb. When Langstroth placed movable frames of full comb in a box hive closer to each other than that spacing, the bees glued the frames together with propolis. If he moved the frames farther apart, the bees built extra rows of cells in the space. Other beeways inside the hive proved to be critical also. For example, a ¼-inch space needs to be maintained between the top of one box of frames and the next box above it.

The Beekeeper, pointing all this out to visitors, likes to draw one of his "homilies," as he calls them, out of his bee veil. (Visitors, he explains, must listen to his homilies as payment for a tour of his bee yard.) "Here's a case where beekeepers did what food producers generally say they can't do—afford to make a change that costs more,

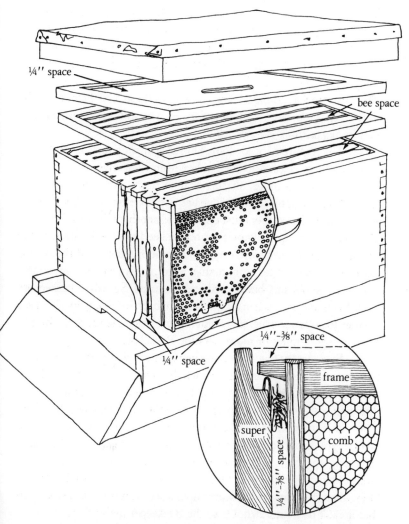

1/4″ space

bee space

1/4″–3/8″ space

frame

super

comb

1/4″ space

1/4″–3/8″ space

Bee Space in a Man-Made Bee Hive—The 1/4- to 3/8-inch space between frames in this hive allows beekeepers to remove honey without destroying the hives.

rather than less, money," he says in his surprisingly high yet majestic voice. "They adopted the new Langstroth hive even though it was a whole lot more expensive than a bee-gum stump. Now, you take farming and all the erosion it's causing. We're cropping this country with bee-gum philosophy. Extracting the crop while destroying the soil."

The Beekeeper relishes the idea of his bees as thieves. "They steal honey for me from all the neighbors," he says. The neighbors don't mind. Because the bees pollinate plants as they gather nectar, tomatoes, squash, melons, and beans in backyard gardens produce more than the gardeners can use. Backyard fruit trees droop with heavy crops. The Dumb Farmer's soybeans produce 5 bushels more per acre than they otherwise would, if you can believe the university researchers who look into such things. "And sometimes those 5 bushels are all the profit in the crop," says the Dumb Farmer, who wants to inform anyone who thinks farming is easy.

The requirement for some kind of spatial privacy, important to some wildlings, applies to bees only within their hive. Outside, bees will roam up to 3 miles, sharing that territory amicably with other hives of bees, so long as no strange bee tries to enter their hive to steal honey. But the Beekeeper must understand another way bees view their territory. No one quite knows yet how a bee fixes the location of the hive in its tiny brain before it goes off gathering nectar. If the hive is moved less than 3 miles or more than 3 feet, the worker bees invariably return to the old site, bewildered and confused. So, when beekeepers move hives at night (when all the bees are back inside) to another area in order to pollinate other plants, they must be sure to move the hive to a new range, 3 miles or more, says the Beekeeper.

Bees are not at all concerned about privacy from humans, however, as some wild animals seem to be. They will live and work in a glass hive inside a human dwelling. If man or beast gets in their way or threatens the hive, the bees respond with their stingers, but they don't move away after the encounter, the way a pileated woodpecker or a quail might do if its nest were disturbed by humans. Curiously, even in defending the hive against an undesirable presence, bees have two kinds of stings. One is a warning—a slap rather than a real haymaker. Only when truly angered or scared does a bee plunge its stinger so deep that it can't be withdrawn. Or so the Beekeeper insists.

Many wild animals establish a territory during nesting into which, of their own species, they allow only their mates. Ecologists think such behavior is a survival instinct assuring a particular family enough food to raise the young. The theory is difficult to prove, and science does not know just how a cardinal, for instance, decides how much territory it will defend, or if the boundaries are precise. Some birds, such as mockingbirds, have such a well-developed sense of territory that they try to keep even birds of other species out of their territory. So vigorous is a mockingbird in its defense of its territory from predators that it will attempt to chase cats away, too, whether close to the nest or not. The cat sits on the ground pretending to be totally oblivious of the angry, diving bird, which as a result becomes bolder with each attack. One dive too close and the seemingly uninterested cat leaps like a spring suddenly uncoiled, snatching the hapless bird from the air.

The Beekeeper says that the best bird to have nesting in the orchard is the kingbird, because, while it doesn't eat much fruit itself, it won't allow other birds in its territory. Smith, who reads voraciously (too much, according to White), thinks he has the Beekeeper on that one. "But kingbirds eat bees," he says, rather primly. The Beekeeper nods, unfazed. "But only the slow drones and the older workers who are about ready to die anyway."

The seclusion essential to a wildling's sense of well-being is generally overemphasized. Wild animals that flee at the sight of man will, when his back is turned, set up housekeeping under, in, or on his house. Wildlings seem to fear the human eyes—the fixed stare—and quick, furtive human motion, especially of the hands. With slow motion and a downcast eye, a human can entice a hungry bird to eat out of his hand. Good food, with wild animals as well as with men, can break down the barriers to domestication. The Dumb Farmer tells that one evening after milking his cows, he noticed a strange cat drinking the milk he had poured into the cat dish outside the stable. Taking a closer look, he saw that the strange cat was actually a skunk. Subsequently, a whole family of skunks (which lived under his repair shop, as it turned out) dropped by for their evening milk. "They hung around all summer, causing no trouble, having apparently reached some sort of understanding with the cats," he says.

Plants for Wildlife

In applying the lessons of habitat manipulation, the backyarder must consider more angles than the Beekeeper, who has eyes only for his bees—but not so many more. In the unexplored vastness of ecological science, you can be comforted in your lack of knowledge by realizing that the truly beneficial environment for one species of wildling almost necessarily means a good environment for all of them, since all are bound together in the food web. Furthermore, while the building blocks of habitat divide nicely on paper, in nature they more often are locked intricately together. You don't need to know all the parts to take advantage of their benefits. Establish a natural community of plants, and you will automatically supply the food, housing, cover, and territorial requirements of many butterflies, birds, and beasts you know little or nothing about. Add water (see Chapter 6, Water:Wildlife Catalyst), and you're in business.

Nevertheless, the first consideration is not deciding which specific plant species to grow, logical as that may seem. Lists of plants that attract wildlife are easy to come by in gardening and conservation publications (and more are found at the end of this book—see Appendix, Select Trees, Shrubs, and Vines for Wildlife). After you study these lists, your choices normally boil down to those that grow well in your soil and climate, many of which will come by their own wild ways to your backyard. More important than the actual choices of plants are the principles of maintaining in a more or less stable form the plant community you do establish, whatever the species.

Plant communities are not naturally as stable in nature as they appear to be. At all times an evolution, or more accurately, revolution, of plant succession is in progress. Shade-tolerant plants constantly shade out ones that need more light. A meadow abandoned by the mower or grazing animals quickly grows up in "weeds," and tall grasses, which are soon superseded by low bushy growth or brush, followed by sun-tolerant, short-lived pioneer trees, which are finally replaced by maturing forest trees. Where rainfall is not sufficient to support forests, the culmination, called a climax, may be prairie grasses, as in the Great Plains.

The climax is not really stable. The large old trees of a climax forest die and fall. The opening to the sun left by the fallen giants invites low-growing plants to start again the process of plant succession. Or lightning may strike a forest tree, and if an ensuing fire burns out acres of climax forest, the whole process starts up once more in the ashes. In fact, fires, along with windstorms are tragic in small forest preserves now, mainly because our virgin forest areas are but a fraction of what they once were, having been depleted by lumbering. In pristine nature, fire is the chief renewer of plant succession, and plant succession provides areas of mixed habitat with far more niches for wildlife than does a climax forest. Wildlife thrives best along what ecologists call "edges," the borderlands between successive plant communities— where meadow and brush meet, where brush and small pioneer trees meet, where pioneer trees and maturing forest meet.

The dynamic change and shifting locales of plant succession are not readily observable to the casual, passing eye. But compress meadow, brush, small trees, and forest into one comparatively small wildlife area in a backyard, and nature's dynamic propensity for change is readily apparent. Having assigned specific areas to each of the four plant communities, you can't just let them "go wild." The meadow would soon become thicket, thicket would change into brushy woodland, and brushy woodland into forest. Without the large expanses of true wilderness, you simply don't have room to allow for such shiftings. You try, and it is a continuing struggle, to stabilize the four plant communities and their "edges" in fixed locations. Or, in smaller yards, you plant trees, and as they mature, you take advantage of the plant successions on your land as they happen over time.

In the backyard habitat, lawn becomes the wild meadow. The Indians kept vast acreages of eastern prairie in meadow by burning the dead grass off every fall, which killed trees and brush that would otherwise have gained a foothold. The backyard manager accomplishes more or less the same feat by mowing, and by manually digging out some unwanted plants that mowing won't control. For a wild meadow, how much mowing is required is still somewhat of a question. The art of maintaining a wild meadow instead of a bluegrass lawn is still in its infancy. One mowing in late summer is a must. In most cases, a mowing in midsummer and another in early fall is better. But proceed with great sensitivity. A mowing later than early fall will prevent beautiful wild flowers, such as the wild aster, from blooming. Mowing too early in summer will weaken spring and early summer wild flowers, eventually causing them to die out. Time midsummer and early fall mowings to control the weedy annuals you want in the meadows. You do not want to have too many. Some of the desirable ones are wild carrot (Queen Anne's lace), mullein, milkweed, and yarrow. Two mowings, a month apart at any time, will control thorny bushes like blackberry, and tree seedlings. For most mowings, you should cut the growth no lower than 6 to 8 inches, which means you'll probably need a scythe or a sickle bar mower, since most ordinary rotary lawn mowers can't be set that high. Occasionally, a lower cutting may be necessary; if certain less desirable weeds become too dominant, you may have to cut the meadow back to lawn periodically and let it begin the stages of plant succession all over again.

Smith has experimented considerably with his little meadow. He has it divided into six parts, each treated differently, the six parts rotated to different treatments every third year. Two meadows are mowed only every other year to a 6-inch height; of these, one is mowed in July, and the other is mowed in late October. Two other meadows are mowed twice a year to a 6-inch height; one of these is mowed in July and late August, and the other is mowed three weeks after the first meadow's cuttings. Another plot is mowed once a year in July to a 6-inch height, and the final plot is mowed every week or so as conventional lawn, 2 to 3 inches in height. In this way, the butterflies and bees are guaranteed the greatest continuous diversity of plants the soil and climate can provide without letting the meadow shift into a community of bushes.

Another way to handle a wild meadow is to allow sheep to graze it lightly, in combination with prudent summer mowing. Not many backyarders can do this, but where appropriate, much mowing time can be saved. Graze no more than one sheep per half acre (three sheep per acre is average stocking rate in the eastern half of the country). To preserve the wildlife character of your backyard, try Mouflon sheep, which are no more domesticated than buffalo, though far more manageable. They have some advantages over domestic sheep, anyway. The Mouflon mother can take care of her young without too much help from you, even to the extent of being rather fearless of dogs. Mouflons are not as susceptible to various sheep problems, particularly internal parasites, especially if stocked at the light rate suggested. The fleece is fine-fibered and excellent for spinning.

Before you plant anything in your meadow, wait to see what volunteers over a few years of little or no mowing. You might be quite pleasantly surprised. The comings and goings of unexpected plants can be as entertaining and instructive as the passage of wild animals across your meadow. With the arrival of different plants will come a flurry of extravagantly beautiful butterflies and spiders, making you wonder why you spent all those Saturdays mowing lawn.

You should try very hard to avoid the growing of some meadow plants altogether. At the top of your list of noxious pests put the Canada thistle (*Cirsium arvense*). Butterfly enthusiasts often list it as a butterfly attractant because it is a good source of nectar and a larval food for some butterfly species. Also, goldfinches eat the seeds and use the thistledown for their nests. Smith once mentioned in an offhand way to the Dumb Farmer that he was going to plant some Canada thistles to attract painted ladies. Usually the Dumb Farmer is impressed

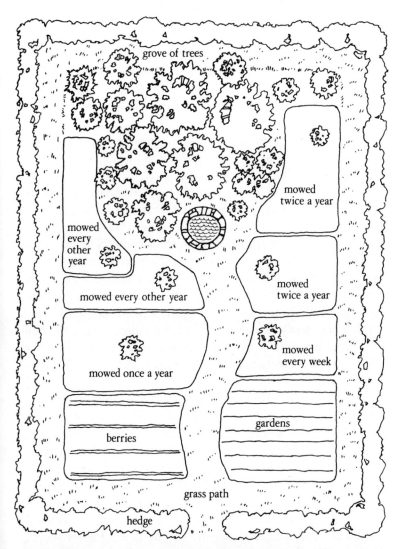

Smith's Mowing Patterns in his Meadow Area—Smith changes his mowing schedule every third year, rotating cuttings of the six plots. The plots cut twice a year are mowed at a three-week interval from each other. The plots that are mowed every two years are cut back to 6 inches.

with such announcements, but this time his face began to contort and quiver in such a way that Smith could not determine whether the man was about to laugh or cry. "The painted lady is a butterfly," Smith added hurriedly, thinking perhaps it was the name that had sparked the Dumb Farmer's twisted grimace. "I don't care who she is," the Dumb Farmer replied, his lips still quivering. "She don't deserve to lie down on a bed of *those* blasted things."

Canada thistle, which comes from Europe, not Canada, spreads by both seed and root, a characteristic of the worst weeds. Few plants are more tenacious in a meadow. Patches of them blot out grass and clover. Trying to walk through them is only a little nicer than walking barefoot over hot coals. Roots grow so deep that herbicides seldom kill them unless applied many times. If continued long enough, frequent mowing will finally force a patch to die out. But in a wildlife area, frequent mowing is something you want to avoid.

If you and your butterflies can't be happy without a thistle, plant the bull thistle (*Cirsium vulgare*) instead. It is a bigger, stouter, even more prickly thistle, but it is a biennial, putting down one big taproot that does not cause it to spread into everlasting patches. The bull thistle has a large, attractive blossom for bees and butterflies, and seeds and down for goldfinches. Eastern field sparrows and eastern song sparrows will choose the base or low branches of this thistle for a nest. Both the tiger swallowtail (*Papilio glaucus*) and the black swallowtail (*P. polyxenes asterius*), splendidly radiant butterflies, suck nectar from the bull thistle. If a plant seeds too many of its progeny around it, which it surely will, you can control them by severing their taproots an inch or two below the root crown.

Some weeds that spread only by seeds also can be too troublesome for a meadow. Burdock is a taprooted biennial, but its large rhubarblike leaves smother all growth around it, resulting in a solid stand of burdock with burrs in the fall that cling irritatingly to clothing. Don't let it get a solid foothold in your meadow. Cut the root 2 inches below the crown. The Beekeeper says that in the dark of the moon in September, the large-rooted plants can be pulled out of the ground easily. (The smooth, year-old roots can be sold in pharmaceutical markets for their medicinal properties.) The Dumb Farmer snorts, "Yeah, they'll pull out in the dark of the moon—if it rains a gullywasher first and loosens the soil."

The next step up the ladder of plant succession, a shrubby area,

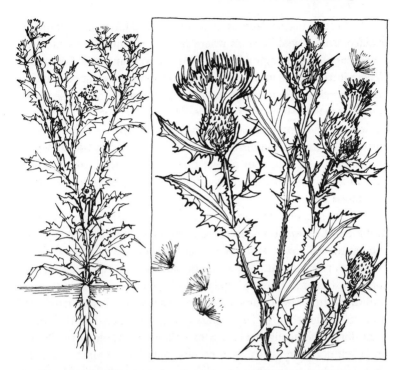

Bull Thistle—The long, single taproot of bull thistle makes it preferable to the Canada thistle, which can spread uncontrollably.

should also be present in wildlife areas. A thicket as usually found in nature is difficult and impractical to maintain in the backyard. Instead, plant a hedge where the thicket and brush plants can be kept in some semblance of order. The logical place for the hedge is at the borders of the sanctuary, where it doubles as a shield of privacy for shy animals.

A wildlife hedge can consist of conventional hedge plants like barberry, and it can be pruned to a close, dense, uniform wall of green. For the optimum benefits to wildlife, the hedge should be composed of many different kinds of plants, some of which should not be pruned regularly. Some of these plants can be maintained at a height of 8 feet or more, higher than a normal hedge, and better for birds. With many kinds of fruiting bushes, pruning should proceed as one might prune raspberry plants in a row; that is, make sure that one plant does not overcrowd another, and where appropriate, prune out old growth entirely in favor of new shoots.

Certain hedge plants often recommended for hedges should be avoided around wildlife areas where very strict control measures are inappropriate. Although wildlife love it, don't plant multiflora rose. Where it can escape into woodland or meadow, it is most pestiferous and, in fact, is illegal in some states now. Multiflora spreads by seed and root. Not to take a back seat to any weed for notoriety, it also can spread by tip rooting. It grows dense and impenetrable until native hardwoods thrust up through it and shade it into oblivion. That may take 50 years. If you want a rose in your hedge, the American wild rose is much meeker and more attractive. If you want a big crop of rose hips, plant the rugosa rose.

The school of educated inexperience that persuaded the United States Soil Conservation Service to recommend multiflora rose years ago has turned now to autumn olive as its favorite wildlife food plant. But when planted near open woods or old pastures, autumn olive can spread just as quickly and overpower native growth just as savagely as multiflora. In a way, autumn olive is even worse. It grows a trunk too thick to be chewed up by large rotary mowers that make short work of multiflora. Think long and hard before planting autumn olive. On the dry, cold, northern plains, autumn olive may have a place, but even there, its close native relative, silverberry or wolfberry (*Elaeagnus commutata*), is better adapted and provides some fruit and protection for animals.

If you are fortunate enough not to have Japanese honeysuckle (*Lonicera japonica*) overrunning your place already, do not plant it, although it is good wildlife cover and a fair food source for birds. It smothers out most other vegetation it encounters except multiflora rose. There are at least 20 other honeysuckles that do not spread so viciously and serve just as well for wildlife, if not better. Trumpet honeysuckle (*L. sempervirens*) is hardier, produces more berries, and in addition, draws hummingbirds and beautiful sphinx moths to drink nectar from its red blossoms.

The hedge may not be the most desirable place for fruiting vines like trumpet honeysuckle. The more rampant growers—certainly wild grape, bittersweet, and woodbine, all superb wildlife food and cover—run all over a hedge, eventually weakening or killing the shy growers and making hedge-pruning an exercise in agony. A better place for such vines is among your tree groves, next to trunks the vines can grow up into, as nature intended. While wild grape, and conceivably other strong growing vines, can eventually kill a tree, you can easily avoid this happening in a small wildlife habitat. Allow one vine per tree to grow for several years, and if it becomes unruly and threatens the life of the tree, cut it off where the vine attaches to the lowest limbs and let another shoot climb back up again. This practice will induce better fruiting, too.

Bramble berries, particularly blackberries, would seem theoretically to be ideal hedge plants, protectively thorny and very productive of fruit. However, in a sunny hedge location, blackberries, and sometimes raspberries, grow so vigorously that they are difficult to keep under control. An ideal place for such berries is in a glade of partial sun within your wooded area. If you walk through natural woodland, you sometimes find a patch of brambles with a more or less well-defined border. If you look up to the sky, you will see that an opening among the tree limbs is letting in just enough sunlight to spark the brambles' growth, yet the patch is limited to a specific area by the surrounding shade. If you have such an opening in among your trees, this is the spot for blackberries. They will be held in some semblance of control without your labor.

As you prune your hedge, keep a sharp eye out for tree seedlings. White ash is particularly troublesome. The seedlings, even when very small, will not pull out and will grow rapidly above the hedge, shading out humbler bushes. A spade knifed about 4 inches into the soil to sever the seedling root is the best way to handle them. Maple seedlings, which tolerate shade, will also come up through the hedge, but they are shallow rooted and pull out easily by hand when small. Many small, pioneer-type trees, like locust, thornapple, birch in its native regions, and sassafras, will volunteer readily under a hedge. Some bushy trees that bear fruit or nuts, like chokecherry, hazel, and black haw, can sometimes be pruned like bushes and incorporated into the hedge. Even wild black cherry, which normally grows into a large forest tree, can be whacked back to hedge height each year, eventually forming a gnarled dwarf of a tree. In the long run, however, trees in the hedge become troublesome and are best grown elsewhere.

The small trees, which form the third plant community in succession, between brushland and large climax forest, can be grown apart either as orchard trees, as individual trees, or as border to the larger forest trees. A backyard fruit orchard serves the purpose quite well, especially if wild fruit trees like papaw, persimmon, and Juneberry are included. Avoid toxic sprays in the orchard, however, in favor of the fullest complement of insects possible. Nature will balance pest populations enough so that you will get at least half a normal crop. Or, if a tree dies because it couldn't survive without spraying, you are being well advised by nature to try a different variety.

Don't prune out all the dead wood. Such wood draws insects that woodpeckers dine on, and the holes the birds hammer out to get them can become bluebird nests later. Don't be too neat. Under the trees (and hedges, too) allow leaves to linger and rot. The duff of decomposing organic matter is a paradise for worms, insects, and insect larvae that delight birds like towhees, brown thrashers, and wood thrushes. Be slow to destroy all of the tent caterpillar nests, especially in wild fruit trees that are not much harmed by the worms (wild cherry, for example). In the early stages of a caterpillar colony, the worms are too small to be very destructive, and by the time they grow up, a yellow-billed or black-billed cuckoo may come along and finish them off before you have to do it yourself. If your birds are slow to eat them, you can always burn the caterpillars out later, when they return to their tents at night.

Where the small trees form a border to woodland forest trees, the chief maintenance chore is making sure the lesser trees continue to get full sunlight. If the large forest trees grow out over them or seedlings of forest trees grow up among them, the smaller trees will diminish and eventually die out. On the other hand, you will have to be constantly alert for seedlings of the smaller trees coming up in the nearby meadow. Some spread by seed, some by seed and sprout. If the large forest trees are too close to the smaller trees and will inevitably shade the latter out, some of these sprouts or seedlings can be spared to grow up to replace their parent trees.

Maintenance of the large forest trees consists mainly of controlling seedlings that will grow up beneath them to take advantage of every smidgen of sunlight reaching the forest floor. To make walking easier, you may want to cull out these younger trees as they come up, by mowing them once a year. Judiciously save a tree here and there as eventual replacements for the big trees. This type of maintenance is not practical in a large area (over 3 acres), and in that case, you can allow the young trees to grow. They eventually crowd each other out, and the survivors block the sunlight that gets through the big trees away from the forest floor, eventually opening up the woods for easy walking.

In a small wildlife area, it is advisable not to think about harvesting any wood for firewood or any other purpose (although if the woodland is over 2 acres in size, you can compromise and cut perhaps as much as half of the available wood without curtailing wildlife activity much). The more dead snags and hollow trunks there are, the more wildlife you'll see. When a tree falls, the log becomes home for many worms, insects, and animals and, as it rots away, adds considerably to the fertility of the soil. It is an excellent practice, in fact, to bring a few old logs into a planned wildlife area if none are there. Some very interesting forms of wildlife depend on rotting logs. The large, ferocious-looking stag beetle lays her eggs in them. When red-spotted newts are in their second stage of life, as land-based red efts, these red-orange, lizardlike animals hide and hibernate under logs in the forest. Meeting one in your wildlife habitat is better than any day at the zoo.

If the fallen log is hollow, it will attract almost all of the smaller wild mammals. But save all hollow log pieces of less than 10 to 12 inches in diameter for making birdhouses. None are cheaper or easier to make, nor more effective (see Chapter 5, Housing for Wildlife).

Prunings from the hedge and lopped-off and wind-fallen tree branches can all be heaped into brush piles. Many small birds love brush piles where they can flit to safety from cats and other predators. Rabbits, ground squirrels, chipmunks, and groundhogs also flock to brush piles. If you don't care to lure any more rabbits into your yard, build brush piles up off the ground, still inviting to the birds, but hardly safe harbor for rabbits (see Chapter 5, Housing for Wildlife).

In fact, a tiny wildlife area may have one potential advantage over a large expanse of wilderness. Because you have compressed the edges of the plant communities closer together than generally found in nature, and because you have introduced a greater variety of plants than one customarily finds in such a small area, you should attract more wildlife per square foot than you might find in a state park or national forest. Smith insists that the only wild animal found in denser populations in state parks than in his backyard is man himself.

Some trees and plants have special roles relating to wildlife. Hummingbirds gather the fuzzlike material on the underside of sycamore leaves and the fluff from willow catkins for nesting material, just as goldfinches use the cottony parachutes of dandelion seeds (after eating the seeds) to line their nests.

Conifers, generally speaking, do not produce as much food to support wildlife as do deciduous trees. Wild birds and animals that do feed on conifers (primarily on seed cones), and also the insect community living on conifers, usually require rather large expanses of forests and are not frequently seen in backyards, except where such expanses are close by. Nevertheless, almost all local wildlife will make use of backyard evergreen trees of whatever kind—pine, spruce, fir, cedar, hemlock. These trees become preferred nesting sites for hedge-loving birds even where the trees grow singly, and their dense foliage keeps many birds from freezing to death in winter. White pine in particular provides seed cones that are eaten by many birds and small mammals. In the West, juniper and pinyon pine provide almost a complete menu for bird, animal, and in some past civilizations, human communities. The heavy branches of spruce reaching clear to the ground shield out snow. They make tentlike houses for birds and animals where some food, in the form of insects in the ground or on lower branches, is available even in blizzard sieges. Cones hanging high on the tree through winter are another source of food for winter-embattled birds, like the red-breasted nuthatch.

Some winter food is valuable because it does *not* taste very good to birds, at least not before it freezes thoroughly. Thus, some persimmons, bittersweet, haw apples, and other fruits you see hanging well into winter do not usually appeal to migrating birds. Yet in late winter and even early spring, these berries provide starvation food for the stay-at-homes. Some wild persimmons, of course, are more delectable than others, and the raccoons will strip the better ones early, given the chance.

Weed seed is the normal "grain" for birds and grazing animals. That's the main reason why weedy fencerows are such a boon to wildlife out in the country. Grass and clover seeds are also excellent food "grains." Garden crops allowed to go to seed help, too. Smith found an added benefit from this practice. When lettuce would go to seed, enough seeds remained to start a volunteer crop the next spring long before he could cultivate a crop outdoors, and at the same time that he could get a crop going in his cold frame. For some reason, the overwintered seeds germinated faster and endured cold, spring weather better than any plants he tried to start. So, he no longer starts lettuce in the cold frame. Nature does it for him in last year's garden.

Lacking the right kind of backyard environment to let weeds go to seed, you can achieve much the same arrangement by planting what wildlife specialists call a food patch—domestic grains that will provide overwintering seeds. If you intend to feed birds regularly (that is, every day), a food patch might be unnecessary and might even lure birds away from your feeder. But if you are going to be gone for long periods (like to Florida), a food patch may well ensure that your birds will still be around when you get back.

Recommended mixtures of seeds vary with geographical and climatic area, but in general, grain sorghum, cane sorghum, sunflower, buckwheat, millet, and corn are preferred food patch grains, along with Korean lespedeza in the southern and middle sections of the country. (You can contact your local state wildlife agents for specific regional recommendations if you want the very latest word on the best food patch seedlings.) The lespedeza is not too hardy in the North and is used because hordes of migrating blackbirds, which might eat up everything else, even in a several-acre food patch on a game farm, do not feed heavily on lespediza seeds. Stiff-stemmed plants are preferred in the North so that the grains will not be completely buried, even after heavy snows.

In most cases however, a well-developed backyard wildlife habitat will have enough weed seeds to make a food patch unnecessary. A good compromise is to overseed early vegetable gardens with buckwheat, clover, or annual rye grass as the vegetables mature and to allow late, unharvested vegetables to go to seed, along with those late, seldom-pulled weeds. (In the North, plant buckwheat *before* July 10 so that it has time to make seeds before winter.) This makes for a sloppy-looking garden in the fall, but your birds will think it beautiful. Late-planted rape, kale, and parsley provide greens into winter for many birds who, just like humans, need vitamin C.

Nearly every plant that grows supplies some food or cover for some species of wildlife. If the foliage or fruit itself does not provide food for birds and animals, the insects attracted to it will. Therefore, it is almost presumptuous to draw up lists of "best plants for wildlife," at least from the standpoint of the wildlife. Any well-rounded mixture of grasses, weeds, flowers, vegetables, fruits, vines, shrubs, and trees will provide an ample menu for wildlife diets. But many of the plants that produce great quantities of food or the thickest, safest, and densest foliage for cover and nests are difficult-to-control, rampant growers. Or they're exotic, nonnative species that either can't compete with the native plants or will dominate and crowd out the natural mix of plants that is the foundation of a good variety of wildlife. As mentioned before, multiflora rose and autumn olive are the two classic examples of the latter. Though with great effort both might be controlled in the small backyard habitat, the birds will carry the seeds far and wide into woodlands and meadows. There, in a few years, these plants can seriously hamper the growth of the natural plant community, until forest trees grow up to dominate and shade out these exotic pests. The birds may thrive, but neither man nor beast can walk through a meadow or woodland taken over by multiflora rose or autumn olive.

Chapter 4

Housing For Wildlife

Smith was fuming. He hoed furiously away at the purslane, muttering loudly, as was his habit when fuming. "No wonder we can't make any headway in ecological understanding," he growled at the cabbages. Toad, cowed by such peevishness, backed farther into his flowerpot home. "Even the president of the United States doesn't understand ecology." The cabbages remained astutely apolitical and noncommittal.

What had brought on Smith's frustration was a well-meaning remark that the president (Ronald Reagan at the time) had made. The president had urged the nation, in the interest of saving oil, if not heating bills, to clean up the woodlands, "since we have permitted a lot of dead trees to accumulate, which are harmful to the woodland ecology." That remark, Smith told the onions, as he weeded his way down another row, was as shameful a show of ignorance as Richard Nixon's announcement that he did not know what a soybean looked like. It was even more reprehensible. "Admitting ignorance," Smith said, winking at the brown thrasher, "might be inappropriate for a president but could do no harm and might encourage a little honesty in Washington. But to instruct 225 million people that dead trees were bad for the environment when exactly the opposite was true . . ." Smith's voice trailed off. The brown thrasher nodded, perhaps in sympathy, perhaps just to see what was under the leaves he was scratching in.

The president's remark did have one good ecological effect, however. Smith was not usually the type of person who would make trouble for anyone, least of all his neighbors. But now he resolved to resist their blandishments. He would *not* cut down the dead oak tree in his backyard, no matter how much social pressure they applied. While it may seem strange to a later generation, in the suburbs in 1982 it still took some courage to leave a dead tree standing or a plot of lawn unmowed. The typical American saw a threat to the general security in such deviant behavior. Or perhaps, as Smith liked to believe, the specter of the dead snag reminded them of death, an inordinately fearful subject to mid-twentieth-century Americans.

Smith's neighbors all thought they had a good reason for vetoing Smith's dead tree. Brown, on his left, thought it might harbor insects that would attack his own healthy pin oaks and apples. White, on his right, declared that the blamed thing was going to fall over on his $300 grafted copper beech. The Widow Lady was afraid it would topple over someday and crush poor Smith himself, for whom she had taken a motherly concern. Even the Beekeeper, who normally sided with Smith in these kinds of neighborhood arguments, believed the dead and hollow trunk would lure a hive of wild bees, which might then transmit some disease to his domestic bees. The Dumb Farmer, who agreed with President Reagan on all economic matters, grieved over the wasted firewood the dead and rotting tree represented.

Smith fought back. He proved to Brown that the rotting tree could contain few insects of clear and present danger to live trees, and that the dead tree drew woodpeckers that ate the insects and drilled holes in the tree, used not only for their own broods but later by other nesting birds as well. Moreover, the woodpeckers flew over on Brown's apple trees and ate overwintering codling moths hiding under the bark. With a tape measure, he proved to White that if the tree fell, it would not reach White's property. Smith assured the Widow Lady that he had plenty of insurance. He asked the Beekeeper why wild bees, surely in the neighborhood anyway, had not already contaminated his hives. And for the Dumb Farmer, he unleashed his sermon on the necessity of dead trees.

Smith's Reasons for Sheltering Wildlife

One-third of all the birds and mammals that live in the forest need dead trees for nesting, feeding, and roosting, he told the Dumb Farmer, who tried to appear properly chastened throughout the entire speech. The dead wood also supports a whole world of fungi absolutely essential to life. Without dead wood rotting back into the soil, there would be a net loss of fertility. Rotting leaves couldn't replace it all. One study indicated that burrowing creatures such as chipmunks and salamanders, which use dead logs for shelter, help disperse the spores of mycorrhizal fungi in the rotting vegetation that live tree roots need, to absorb the nutrients released by the rotting process. The study suggested that without wood rats, flying squirrels, and other lovers of dead wood and hollow trees, there might not be a healthy forest at all.

If all the old trees were removed, Smith pointed out sternly, most wildlife would be removed, too. According to an article by Peter Steinhart, "Leave the Dead" (*Audubon* magazine, January, 1981), an Arizona study showed that cutting all the dead ponderosa pine out of a given forest area eliminated 50 percent of the wildlife, including most of the woodpeckers and swallows. The red-cockaded woodpecker is almost gone from parts of Louisiana where it was once common, because not enough dead and dying pines remain. The mountain bluebird is on the decline because of lack of hollow trees for nesting sites. In Europe, experiments demonstrated that the prevalence of certain forest diseases was directly related to lack of dead and dying trees needed for nesting places. With nesting boxes installed in sufficient numbers, bird populations built up again and controlled the bugs that caused the diseases.

The Dumb Farmer did not really disagree with Smith, except to say that the latter painted too grim a picture. Snags—totally dead trees—provide cavities for birds, bees, and squirrels, true enough. But, he pointed out, leading Smith by the nose through his woods, the absence of such trees did not mean *utter* catastrophe. Old trees, still years away from death, but with partially hollow trunks or hollow limbs, provide more housing for birds than snags do. "And safer, too," he said. "Completely dead trees fall down pretty soon, nests and all."

The old-fashioned farm, the Dumb Farmer went on to say, makes a better housing development for birds and wild animals than the forest does. In the farm woodlot, trees are cut selectively, not by clear-cutting, so that instead of an even-aged tree "crop," as the paper companies like to put it, trees of all ages from young sprouts to old skeletons are continually present. The wood thrush can build her nest in the fork of a young ash, the nuthatch in the hollow limb of an otherwise healthy white oak, the squirrels in the large cavity of an old but live beech.

The farm fields provide habitat and housing for a wholly different band of birds that the forest cannot support: the meadowlark and bobolink in the grass of permanent pastures; ducks and geese on the edge of the farm pond; bluebirds in holes in old fence posts; quail and pheasant in the hayfields; killdeers in the bare ground of last year's cornfield. The crumbling old barn at the far end of his place, a leftover from a long-ago homestead, is a veritable wildlife hotel. A barn owl nests in the cupola above the roof. Bats hang at rest in the 2-inch space between the double purlins supporting the roof rafters. At one corner, where joist, joist header, sill plate, and mow floor meet to form a boxlike enclosure, a pair of screech owls live, entering and exiting through a hole under the eaves where an exterior wall board rotted away. Pigeons still fly in and out of the dovecote openings in the upper barn wall and nest on the ledges formed by the framing above the main doors. Raccoons have made a den among a few hay bales put in the barn years ago and never used. The coons share the hay with a hive of bumblebees. Barn swallows plaster their nests on the huge beams of the lower level where once the cows were stabled. A family of skunks have tunneled under the foundation at one end of the barn, woodchucks at the other end. Some rats and mice find haven in the old barn, although their days are not easy—the skunks prey on the mice; the owls on both rats and mice, and the waste grain that once supplied their food has long since run out. A pair of milk snakes live in a crack of the old stone foundation, preying on mice, too.

In the farm's woodpiles and rock walls, chipmunks live. Once, on a flat rail of a rail fence the Dumb Farmer keeps up for sentimental reasons, a mourning dove built her sloppy nest and hatched her brood. In the Dumb Farmer's repair shop, a wren nested in a tin can nailed by its opened top to the wall.

In a niche on top of the rock wall of his old springhouse, under the eave, phoebes raise a family every year, wetting the mud-plaster out of which they form their nest in the spring water. Perhaps strangest of all, a pair of nuthatches took a liking to the enclosed soffit on his house

Dumb Farmer's Barn—The decaying barn on the Dumb Farmer's land shelters a variety of wildlife, including owls, pigeons, raccoons, barn swallows, skunks, and chipmunks.

and, finding a hole into it, nested inside. Building the nest, the two little birds carried literally hundreds of strips of hickory bark into the cavity, apparently in an effort to decrease the space inside to a more nuthatch-like room. The strips were about 3 inches long each and 1 inch wide. At the hole, the nuthatch would grab the strip by the end with its beak and push it through the hole ahead of it. If the strip was too wide, the bird would discard it or occasionally peck away at it until it fitted.

As for the Dumb Farmer's main argument for more optimism about the future of wildlife in the face of encroaching civilization (that is, if humans would just use their heads), he saved it until last and delivered it on a cold day in January. "Lookee up there on my chimney," he said to Smith. "See those birds up there around the opening? They're enjoying the heat from my wood-stove fire. They stay warm and use less calories to do it. In spells of real cold weather, chimneys can mean the difference between their deaths and survival. If you pay attention, you'll see birds roosting on chimney tops in winter all over the township."

Cities sometimes offer more housing opportunities for wildlings than the countryside, the Beekeeper pointed out, getting his oar into the discussion. Heaven knows the rock dove, alias the pigeon, has found the city more to its liking than the country. Pigeons have become so numerous that their droppings deface buildings, sidewalks, and occasionally human beings. Because of man's peculiar ambivalence toward animals, neither the cursers of pigeons nor their feeders ever think that the solution to their problem, or the justification for their feeding, is to eat the excess population, said the Beekeeper. Squab is a delicacy, he insisted, and pigeons are able to reproduce every 28 days, with the hen incubating a new clutch while the male feeds the first until the young can fly on their own.

Getting squab from city pigeon nests is easier said than done, though, since the birds nest so often in inaccessible places, high up in the gingerbread decorations of towers, turrets, battlements, and statuary of classic Gothic and neo-Gothic architecture. Nature has an answer for that, too, however. Peregrine falcons, though rare due to pesticides and loss of habitat, find the high canyons of city buildings as amenable as the steep cliffs and palisades of their natural homes. And the pigeons are such easy pickings. Also, the rare Cooper's hawk will swoop in occasionally from some ridge forest at the city's edge and grab a pigeon lunch.

Killdeers have decided that nesting on flat tar paper roofs in cities is as tolerable as on the bleak bare soil of an April cornfield, and on the roof, no tractor and plow will come along to destroy the nest. Chimney swifts colonize the large chimneys of old-fashioned city buildings everywhere, as they have for centuries. Raccoons make a good living raiding city garbage cans at night, retreating to sylvan park areas by day, with never a worry about coon hunters on their trail. Deer are moving into cities in increasing numbers, and in some city environments, hunting is permitted to reduce their numbers. The gorgeous red house finch, a native of the Southwest, seems to enjoy the company of humans. Released in eastern city areas, it is thriving and so far has not proved to be a pest (which does not mean that it won't be in the future). Wildlife experts believe the numbers and varieties of birds in cities would be much greater now were it not for the ill-advised introduction of the obnoxious house sparrows and starlings, which love the environment of humans, but drive out other bird species that could and would live the city life.

One of the strangest success stories in bringing wildlife species into a city environment is the case of the European wall lizard in Cincinnati, Ohio. A small boy, so the story goes, smuggled two of the lizards through customs on his way back from Italy with his parents. He released the lizards back home in Cincinnati along a limestone cliff wall, the very environment the lizard likes best. The little reptiles are now slowly spreading, to the guarded delight of scientists. The reason? The lizards are harmless little creatures whose favorite food is fresh cockroaches.

As for Smith's dead tree, the outcome of the neighborhood discussion was a compromise. Smith could keep his dead snag, the Dumb Farmer agreeing that one dead tree per 2 acres was not going to cause a calamity in the firewood market or the national economy. Smith agreed that half a dozen big old trees still alive but with decaying inner parts, were better than one or two completely dead trees. So, it was ecologically forgivable for the Dumb Farmer to cut his snags down and heat his house with them and warm the chimney-top birds at the same time. And everyone agreed, even White, that Smith, without a large enough wildlife area to support more than a couple of big old trees with hollow nesting sites in them, was altogether correct in putting up as many birdhouses as he had a mind to. They all hoped he might even get ambitious enough to install a few birdhouses on their properties.

Housing for Birds

In birdhouses, the simplest and cheapest are the best, which is true of hardly anything else in this old world. Smith collects hollow limbs and logs on hikes or from woodcutters. Since a hollow log has very little wood in it for firewood, woodcutters are usually glad to save him the smaller ones they come across. Smith saws each hollow log into a length appropriate for the size of the bird he has in mind, nails a piece of board to the top and bottom of the cut piece, drills a hole of the proper diameter about 3 inches from the top, and the birdhouse is ready to be installed in a tree or on a post. Because the house looks like an abandoned woodpecker hole, the birds are drawn to it more readily than to a house of sawed lumber.

The roof board ought to extend out over the entrance hole to reduce chances of rain getting inside the nest. The bottom board should be a bit wider than the diameter of the log piece if the house is to sit on a post, so that there is room to nail, screw, or bolt it down securely. Ideally, the post should be of metal so that squirrels and cats can't climb it, but a wood post with a metal sheath at least 1½ feet long will stop animal predators as well.

To install it in a tree, set the birdhouse on a limb, then wire it securely to the tree trunk. Place pieces of scrap lumber between the wire and the tree at four evenly spaced intervals around the trunk, so that the wire does not become embedded in the trunk as the tree grows. On a growing tree, the wire will have to be loosened and rewired every other year, or it will break as the tree trunk expands. Be sure the house is not tipped upward, but rather slightly downward, so that rain cannot fall into the entrance hole.

Ventilation holes in this kind of birdhouse usually are not necessary, since the roughness of the construction leaves cracks between the roof board and the bottom board and the house. If there are no cracks, several ⅜-inch holes at the top and one drainhole at the bottom might be advisable, especially for a nest on a post out in the open, not protected by shade or the trunk of a tree.

Smith leaves the largest hollow logs he can commandeer in lengths as long as he can handle—up to 8 feet—and places them more or less haphazardly on the ground under the trees of his wildlife area. He stocks about four this way, and when one rots away, he replaces it. Almost any wild animal will take temporary shelter in hollow logs, and various salamanders and snakes live and hibernate under them. Usually, the logs become festooned with fungi. Whether or not any of these natural phenomena do take place on or in his hollow logs, Smith likes to point out that they make wonderful benches to sit on and meditate.

Many books give specific measurements for birdhouses, but birds are not all that fussy and do not always nest where they are supposed to. Phoebes will ignore an open-sided box built for them and build a nest perched precariously on top of a porch light nearby. Wrens have been known to occupy a compartment of a purple martin house.

Small birds will live in nesting cavities made for larger birds, if the larger birds don't force them away. So the purpose of making small entrance holes to birdhouses is to keep large birds out. Of the cavity-nesting birds, the wren can squeeze through a hole with only a ⅞-inch diameter, but a 1-inch-diameter hole is better, since even that is too small for birds that would drive out the wren—the starling and the house sparrow. A hole of 1⅛ to 1¼ inches will stop sparrows and starlings but will accommodate chickadees, titmice, nuthatches, downy woodpeckers, and Carolina wrens, which can barely squeeze into the holes used for smaller wrens. Swallows, bluebirds, and hairy wood-peckers need a 1½-inch entrance hole, which unfortunately is large enough for house sparrows also. To discourage the sparrows (but not necessarily keep them out entirely), never put a perch on the birdhouse, set the birdhouse no more than 5 feet off the ground, and restrict the entrance hole to a 1⅜-inch diameter, which is easier for a bluebird to squeeze through than for a sparrow. Also, sparrows are not drawn to a hollow-log house as readily as to a house of sawed lumber.

All the small birds will nest in a cavity space of 4-inch diameter or more. The depth of the hollow—the distance between entrance hole and floor—should be 8 to 10 inches, although the birds have some say in the matter; no matter what depth you allow in construction, they will build up nest material to varying heights inside. If the eggs or hatchlings are too close to the entrance hole, a starling can stick its head inside and kill them. Or a raccoon can reach in with its paw and grab them. Thus, it is better to make the box a little deeper than most instructions call for. The rough, irregular sides of the hollow log will enable the young nestlings to scramble up and out when they are ready to fly, even if the nest is unduly deep by birdhouse blueprint standards.

The red-headed woodpecker and other woodpeckers of that size need about a 2-inch-diameter hole, as does the crested flycatcher.

Unfortunately, starlings get through a 2-inch hole, too, but red-headed woodpeckers can be fearless defenders of their territory and drive the starlings away. Other cavity-nesters of similar size are not so courageous. The flicker takes a 2½-inch hole and a 7-inch diameter cavity, 18 inches deep. Starlings avoid the flicker. There is, in fact, a difference of opinion among wildlife watchers as to the harm actually done by starlings to other birds. Smith says that in the battle for tree holes, squirrels, bees, flickers, red-headed woodpeckers, and starlings all seem to get along quite well. Irving Petite says in his book *The Best Time of the Year,* "I lived with starlings morning, noon, and until twilight without ever seeing one of them take another bird's egg; the only shells they carried were those they carried out from their own nests." Furthermore, tree swallows have been observed raising a brood in a nest built, used, and vacated by starlings.

The saw-whet owl and the purple martin need an entrance hole of 2½ inches, and both like a chamber of 6 inches or more in diameter. The screech owl and sparrow hawk, both excellent mousers (though the latter is fond of grasshoppers above all), need an entrance of 3 inches and a cavity with a 12-inch diameter or more and a 9- to 12-inch depth from entrance to floor. Wood ducks take a 4-inch hole and barn owls a 6-inch hole; both like a lot of space—at least a 12-inch-diameter hollow log, or 10 by 18 inches in a nest box of sawed lumber. Houses for these larger birds are best made of lumber, as it is difficult to handle large log pieces or to cut a large hole in them.

When hollow logs aren't available, any piece of straight-grained log can be split apart for a birdhouse. Carefully split away the four barked slabs, use the squared middle for firewood, and nail the four slabs together again to make a hollow log. If firewood pieces aren't available, you can build one out of sawed lumber, using the same measurements above, changing the 4-, 6-, 7-, and 12-inch-diameter cavities to 4-, 6-, 7-, and 12-inch-square cavities.

There are many designs for birdhouses, but the best one suits all birds—a simple rectangular box with a slanted roof, the back board extending far enough below the box to provide a place to nail or screw the box to a post, a building, or a tree. The top can be hinged for easy

Plans for a Sawed-Lumber Birdhouse—The dimensions given for this birdhouse are those for a bluebird. They can be changed to sizes appropriate for other birds.

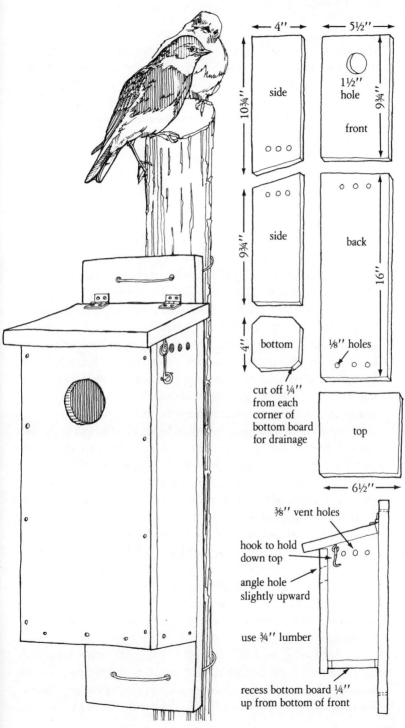

side

4″

10¾″

○ ○ ○

9¾″

side

○ ○ ○

4″

bottom

cut off ¼″
from each
corner of
bottom board
for drainage

5½″

1½″
hole

front

9¾″

○ ○ ○

back

16″

⅛″ holes

○ ○ ○

top

6½″

⅜″ vent holes

hook to hold
down top

angle hole
slightly upward

use ¾″ lumber

recess bottom board ¼″
up from bottom of front

49

opening and cleaning, since all birdhouses should be cleaned out in late winter or early spring. Provide a hook and screw eye on the side to latch the hinged top securely closed. You can also attach the roof with wood screws and simply remove the screws at cleaning time as you would with a hollow-log house. Painting is not necessary but will add life to pine and other woods that deteriorate over time when exposed to the weather. Use white latex exterior paint or some other paint that contains no pentachlorophenol or other possibly toxic preservatives. Do not paint the inside of the box.

Although martins will nest in very elaborate houses, simple ones will work just as well. A row of hollow gourds or plastic bottles with properly sized holes, suspended from horizontal arms attached to a post at least 12 feet but preferably 16 feet off the ground, will suffice.

The most difficult part of making a purple martin house is getting it hoisted up on a post to an adequate height. Two telescoping metal posts work best. The lower post, about 9 feet in length, is set 3 feet into the ground permanently with concrete packed around it. The post that slides inside it (1 ¾-inch post inside a 2-inch post) should be about 10 feet long, with appropriate holes near its base and near the top of the bottom post so that when it's extended, a bolt can be slid through the holes to hold the house up. A flange on top of the post will provide an easy way to attach the birdhouse. For most homeowners, it is prudent to buy posts especially made for purple martin houses.

Birdhouses for bluebirds should be set more or less in an open area with trees nearby, such as at the edge of a lawn or meadow. Wren houses will draw inhabitants just about anywhere around the house or garden. For woodpeckers, nuthatches, and tree swallows, a woodland tree is best, preferably at the edge of the grove. A box for wood ducks should be close to or above water; for screech owls, it should be in the woods, perhaps at the edge of an open area. Owl nests in trees ought to be at least 15 feet from the ground; boxes for the other birds can be somewhat lower, but not below 6 feet, generally speaking. Bluebird houses can be as low as 3 feet from the ground to discourage house sparrows. If a bluebird house is placed that low, though, a wide metal plate should be attached to the post under the house to keep cats from leaping up.

Open-sided houses—shelves, so to speak, with roofs over them—can be built for robins and phoebes, not to mention the ubiquitous house sparrow. Grackles and orchard orioles have some-times, though rarely, been known to adapt to a man-made shelf in a

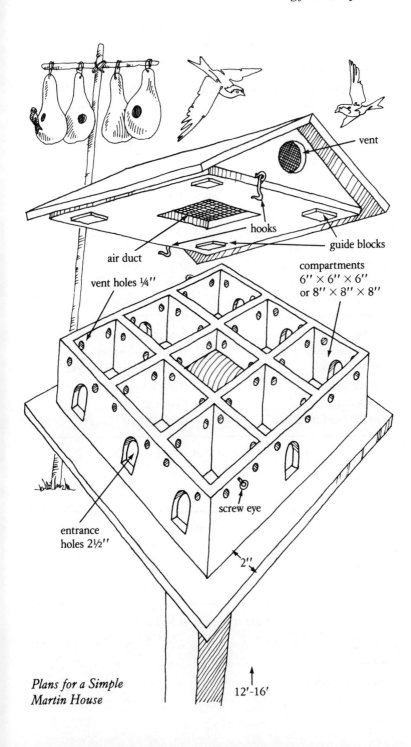

vent

hooks

guide blocks

air duct

compartments
6'' × 6'' × 6''
or 8'' × 8'' × 8''

vent holes ¼''

screw eye

entrance
holes 2½''

2''

*Plans for a Simple
Martin House*

12'-16'

protected spot. A partial list of species that will adapt to bird boxes or other man-made contrivances follows:

Birds and Their Choice of Man-Made Shelter

Cavity

eastern bluebird
mountain bluebird
western bluebird
black-capped chickadee
Carolina chickadee
chestnut-backed chickadee
mountain chickadee
brown creeper
wood duck
red-shafted flicker
yellow-shafted flicker
crested flycatcher
American goldeneye
sparrow hawk
purple martin
hooded merganser
red-breasted nuthatch

white-breasted nuthatch
barn owl
saw-whet owl
screech owl
yellow-bellied sapsucker
starling
cliff swallow
tree swallow
violet-green swallow
plain titmouse
tufted titmouse
downy woodpecker
hairy woodpecker
red-headed woodpecker
Bewick's wren
Carolina wren
house wren

Cavity or shelf

house finch
house sparrow

Shelf

mourning dove
purple grackle
barn swallow

Shelf or open-sided box

phoebe
robin
brown thrasher

Putting up boxes does not mean that the wildlife-lover will automatically lure more birds to his backyard. The more boxes there are, however, the better are the chances. Researchers have learned that most cavity nesters will pick a box in an area where there are several to choose from rather than only one. Most birds will not nest close to others of the same species. This is particularly true of bluebirds, which normally maintain about 100 yards between families. But they seem to like the extra nest boxes.

A male wren may fill one box with twigs, then his mate might come along and choose a different box nearby for their home. Since wrens need less territorial space than bluebirds, another female wren may take up quarters in the first house the male prepared. He will service both of them quite readily.

Patience brings rewards unimagined. Smith put bluebird houses throughout the neighborhood, and to his chagrin, the only house occupied so far is the one on White's place. White, who thinks Smith is a wee bit looney about his wildlife sanctuary, goes out of his way to brag about "his" bluebirds, teasing Smith unendingly. "You see," he says, "if you would throw a few chemicals around over there in your organic acre, you'd get some bluebirds, maybe." And then he goes on his way, whistling exultingly between his teeth.

Smith got even with him. Finding a 3-foot length of hollow log with a cavity diameter of nearly 10 inches and a ready-made hole of nearly 3 inches where a limb had rotted out, he wired it up about 20 feet in a hickory tree (nearly falling off the ladder in the process). For two months he made daily visits to the box. One evening, sure enough, as he cocked his head sideways and peered cautiously around the tree, there was a screech owl, its head cocked sideways out of the entrance hole, peering cautiously down at Smith. Smith smiled and slipped quietly away. That winter he did not wrap his little fruit trees in protective screening against the mice. He would take a chance. The venerable ornithologist Edward Howe Forbush had written that owls living in boxes near his orchard had rid him of a mouse problem. So Smith would try it, knowing that White would be watching.

Whether the screech owls did their job or whether some other control was in effect, only nature knows, but mice did not gnaw Smith's trees that winter. White, always observant, mentioned in March that Smith had forgotten to wrap his trees. "The mice probably played hell with them," he said condescendingly. "Oh no," said Smith, his eyes sparkling with satisfaction. "No damage. You see, the screech owls kept the mice under control."

"Oh yeah," replied White sarcastically, "and the big bad wolf ate my grandmother, too."

"You mean you haven't seen my screech owls?" Smith countered in mock surprise. He led the scoffing White back past the unmolested fruit trees, up to the hickory with the nest box in it. As if on cue, the owl stuck its tufted ears and sanguine little face out of the hole for White's edification. White had very little to say for two months.

If a thick evergreen grove or hedge is not available for winter bird protection, a grouping of thrown-away Christmas trees, either piled or set decorously in the snow, makes a good substitute. Cornstalks from the sweet-corn patch, bound into bundles and set up into a shock, or along both sides of a row of tender thornless blackberries to protect the berry plants from winter injury, make an ideal winter bird shelter.

Bird Feeders

Feeding the birds, at least in winter and spring, will make any bird housing development much more successful. For his own enjoyment, Smith found that the best place to feed birds was directly outside the kitchen window from which he views the world while eating breakfast. In short order, the birds became unafraid of the humans on the other side of the window, and very close and interesting observations could be made by both parties. It has not escaped the nuthatch's notice that Smith waves his arms wildly only when the house sparrows take over the eating station, and so he stands by, dashing quickly in for a sunflower seed when the sparrows retreat before the flailing arms. On his part, Smith has recorded a pecking order among his birds that is observed most of the time. The red-headed woodpecker is king, able to chase away even the jaunty blue jays. Cardinals bow to both woodpecker and jay. Titmice and song sparrows stay on the ground below the feeder where the larger birds do not bother them much.

The finches are generally fearless, especially the house sparrow (which is really a finch), and merely move aside when the larger birds come to eat, rather than fly away as do the more timid downy woodpeckers and nuthatches. The purple finch will not take a back seat to either the goldfinches or the house sparrows. Starlings will not come close to his window for reasons Smith cannot explain, and so they do not dominate the feeding station and scare other birds away as others who feed birds report. He has also learned that chipmunks do not necessarily hibernate, as the books say, but come out in the coldest weather for a stray seed under the feeder. The tamest bird is the black-capped chickadee, which flits along just above Smith's head when he makes his winter rounds of the wildlife sanctuary, hoping for a handout. Squirrels have not as yet climbed up the deck to his window feeder, but if they did, he'd put the feeder on a steel post, or a wood one with a 1½- to 2-foot metal sheath, so that neither they nor cats could climb it.

Smith's feeder is an old, shallow pan with holes in the bottom to let out rain, secured to the deck railing by one roofing nail. He does not even have a roof over it. A few feet away, he hangs a used, mesh grapefruit bag full of meat fat. Much more elaborate feeders can be purchased or made, but Smith sees no need for improvement. Even a roof over the feeder would be of only minor help, since the snow would still sweep in under it and bury the birdseed, forcing him to uncover it. On the question of expensive bird feeders, Smith replies with one of his oft-repeated sayings: "A fool and his money are soon parted."

The typical bag of birdseed is not a very wise buy, either. As with all things commercial, humans find a way to cheapen products even when cheapening is unnecessary. Most birdseed mixtures are heavy on grain sorghum seed, which birds do not like very much. Unless very hungry, they throw it out of the feeder to get at the sunflower seeds. Also, sunflower seed mixtures are now heavy on the small black variety rather than the large grey-and-white-striped variety. Birds much prefer the latter. If possible, buy the grey-and-white-striped sunflower seeds only, even if you have to pay more. Instead of sorghum seeds, feed cracked corn, which is hardly more expensive and provides more energy to the birds. Suet (meat fat) and the larger sunflower seeds are all the feed some winter birds need, but the addition of cracked corn will feed others. For finches, you can add the expensive niger thistle seeds if you wish, but it's not necessary. The finches will do quite well on sunflower seeds. A finch gets one in its beak and rolls it around until one side of the hull comes off (as if by some twist of magic). A second or so later, the bird spits out the rest of the hull, then crumbles and swallows the kernel. Goldfinches will sometimes hold a seed with one foot against the perch they are standing on, and deftly peck the kernel out.

Peanuts are another excellent winter food for birds. Feeding them peanut butter is all right, although the Beekeeper believes it is too sticky for birds. Experts disagree. But what passes for peanut butter these days has a lot more in it than ground peanuts, and none of these other ingredients have much nutritional value.

The Widow Lady, who lives behind Smith's wildlife sanctuary just north of the Beekeeper, deserves to be called the All-Time Champion Bird Feeder. The Beekeeper claims that she spends $10 for her own food per week and $30 for the birds. Hardly a tree in her yard does not hold either a birdhouse or a cylinder of hardware cloth crammed with suet—meat and fat scraps she gets free at Ed and Kate's Corner Grocery at Gwynnedde Station. She saves up ears of corn the Dumb Farmer lets her pick up from his field after harvest, and wedges them behind the loose bark of shagbark hickories for jays, cardinals, and squirrels to snack on. She grows a little plot of wheat in her garden, which she binds into sheaves and then, through the winter, flails out for grinding into her own flour. After flailing out the wheat from the sheaves, she hangs them over the clothesline for the birds to peck out any unthreshed grains. She gathers and cracks out the meats of hickory nuts, walnuts, and butternuts for herself. But any shells that contain particles of nuts too tedious to get out she puts in the bird feeder, and the birds finish the job with their little beaks. Squash seeds, milk clabber, boiled rice, old biscuits, bread and cake crumbs, lettuce and cabbage leaves too far gone for salads, rotting apples, grapefruit halves, all go to the birds. She even sprinkles a little table salt in a corner of the feeder along with some fine poultry grit. For hummingbirds, she puts sugar water, or sometimes honey from the big jar the Beekeeper gives her every year, in tiny medicine bottles and hangs them out in bushes with red and yellow ribbons tied around them.

"If you want hummers," she says, full of bird lore when a guest shows interest, "plant red and orange flowers. Trumpet vine is good. Salvia is the best. Once they get used to the sugar-water feeder, they will stay around."

The Widow Lady has the only occupied martin house in the neighborhood. She is the only bird feeder who has seen a bluebird at her feeder. And chickadees eat out of her hand.

"Oh, it's nothing, really," she says. "Just takes a little patience."

What is the best bird to have about? Without hesitation she answers, "The wren." The wren sings cheerfully all summer long, eats insects but no fruit, likes the company of humans, will drive other birds, except the martin, from its territory. "If both live in your garden," she promises, "you will have few bugs and rarely a bird to eat your fruit."

Shelter for Other Animals

Brush piles, as mentioned earlier, make excellent bird and animal attractants. If you desire a brush pile for the birds but not for rabbits and woodchucks (the latter will invariably dig burrows under the brush), pile brush on a raised platform. Set four cement blocks or similar-size wood blocks on end to form the four corners of a square or rectangle. Lay a stout limb across each pair of uprights and then pile the brush on them. With about 2 feet of open space under the brush to

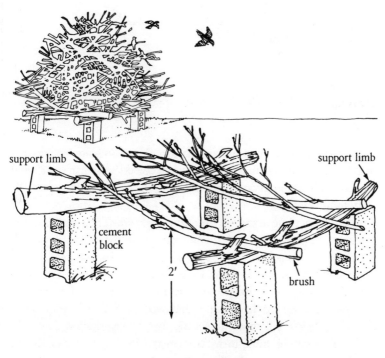

support limb

support limb

cement block

2'

brush

Brush Pile for Birds

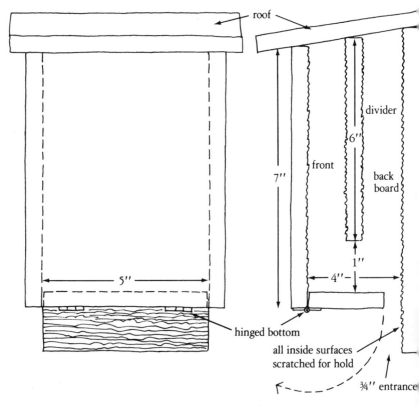

Plans for a Bat Box

make it accessible to foxes, badgers, dogs, and cats, undesired rabbits and woodchucks will have to go elsewhere for protection. Brush can also be used to build an observation blind in your backyard (See Chapter 10, Watching Wildlife).

Do not remove stumps from your backyard. They often become home for various ants, which then become a significant source of food for pileated woodpeckers. These large, crow-size woodpeckers, which depend on dead trees and stumps for survival, will eventually tear up an ant-filled stump almost as effectively as a stump-remover. If you're not fortunate enough to have a pileated woodpecker visit your yard, perhaps a flicker will appear to eat the ants, its favorite food.

Bats can be lured to wildlife areas with properly-made boxes installed in trees. A simple box with a slanted roof like the birdhouse described previously, with a narrow (¾-inch) slot in the bottom is all that is necessary. As many as 50 bats can crowd into a box 6 inches square and 6 inches high, though a larger box may be better. Measurements are not critical. A box 7 inches high, with an inner cavity of 4 by 5 inches and a dividing board down the middle of the cavity to within an inch or so of the bottom, serves very well. Bats cling to the vertical walls and the dividing board. They prefer narrow, cramped spaces.

Use rough wood to construct the box so that the bats can climb out more easily. Do not put the finished box anyplace where sunlight can overheat it. Actually, a place that receives some morning sunlight can be beneficial to the bats.

Chapter 5
Water: Wildlife Catalyst

One garden pool is worth a thousand plants because, no matter what various foods wildlings eat, they all drink water. When Smith first bought his home and lot years ago, the Beekeeper had gently impressed upon him this basic lesson of wildlife management. The Beekeeper had his reasons. He wanted to save the little seep-spring swamp in the back of Smith's lot just below his own place. He did not trust suburbanites. Too many of them saw a bit of wetland as an eyesore or as so much muck for mosquitoes to breed in, and called on bulldozers to erase them.

It was not the Beekeeper's subtle educational campaign that convinced Smith to save the swamp, however, but a passing remark the old man made when they were sitting under the red maple at the edge of the tiny open pool of water in the marsh. "There's a water boatman," said Smith, pointing at a black, beetlelike bug skittering across the pool's surface, its legs propelling it oarlike through the water. The Beekeeper took his time to reply. "You know," he finally said, "there's another bug ought to be called a 'boatman.' It can't swim like that skatin' bug there, and it can't fly either. But it likes to eat water plants, so it builds itself a boat out of leaves and floats out to them."

Smith gave the old man a sharp look of disbelief. "You're kidding. What's its name?"

The Beekeeper shrugged. "Can't remember."

Back in those days, before Smith knew the Beekeeper well, he might easily have dismissed that piece of information as a droll tidbit of folklore, of which the old man seemed to possess an endless supply. But he checked himself, remembering what had happened on a walk through the ridgetop woods the previous autumn. The two had paused to get their breath after climbing the hill to the ridgetop, and in the interval, they became aware of a faint pattering sound on the leaves around them, as of sprinkling rain.

"It can't be raining," Smith had said. "Clear as a bell out."

"No. T'ain't rain," said the Beekeeper, after listening intently. "The walkingsticks are laying eggs tonight. That's what you hear. Thousands of walkingstick eggs dropping out of the trees."

Luckily for Smith, darkness had hidden his broad smile that night. Reading a book on insects later, Smith learned that the pattering in the woods that night likely *was* caused by walkingsticks—curious insects, brown to green in color, about 4 inches long, looking like branch twigs, but possessing legs and antennae—laying their eggs.

So, at the marsh, Smith did not smile. As soon as he got home, he flipped through his books, scrutinizing the sections on garden pools and water bugs. Sure enough, in James and Louise Bush-Brown's *America's Garden Book*, an unimpeachable authority, he found this passage: "A remarkable insect is the leaf-eating *Hydrocampa propiralis*, which constructs boats from bits of leaves and cruises about the pond."

That information electrified Smith's vision of his place. He knew from then on that his little swamp was going to become the center of his leisure time. If *Hydrocampa propiralis* would deign to visit him, he'd gladly supply it with all the water plants it desired, just for the privilege of seeing it weigh anchor and sail across his pool. And, he began to wonder, if so fascinating a creature existed right under his nose for all of his 52 years, unknown to him, what other marvels awaited his discovery?

The spring that fed Smith's swamp was a weak one, hardly deserving of the name. Water seeped out of a fissure in the underlying bedrock, which was hardly 2 feet below the soil surface at this point. Smith (or rather the Beekeeper putting words in Smith's mouth) theorized that the bedrock formed a sort of shelf under the soil at this location, holding the water as if in a cup of rock until it filled and slowly seeped to the far end of the shelf 50 feet away, where it found its way back into another crack in the rock. Only a very tiny pool of open water stood in the swamp year-round, and even that occasionally dried up in dry weather. But the surrounding ground, an area perhaps 10 by 50 feet, always remained moist, with little mounded hummocks sticking up above the soil surface.

Smith wanted a permanent pool, if possible, large enough to support at least half a dozen fish, a few frogs, toads, salamanders, crayfish, and perhaps a turtle. He decided to dig a hole in the middle of the wetland area 2 feet deep and about 6 feet in diameter. Or rather, the Beekeeper decided that Smith should do that. The Dumb Farmer, who had come over to sit under the red maple with the Beekeeper and watch, concurred in the decision. That was how his granddaddy often "captured" a spring for a cattle water hole, he said.

As Smith dug, his two advisors watched closely, prepared to make any decisions that might be required, on every subject from digging to the proper moment to rest and quaff the contents of Smith's refrigerator. The dirt from the hole could not be just flung into the surrounding swamp, they decided, as that might destroy the fragile boglike ecosystem established there. The mud would have to be carried out to the edge of the swamp, the Beekeeper suggested, wincing at the added work this would put on Smith's shoulders. The Dumb Farmer had an idea: Make a raised, narrow path with the dirt from the pool's edge to the marsh's edge, so that Smith (not to mention the Beekeeper and the Dumb Farmer) could walk to the pool in any weather without sinking into the marsh.

Smith nodded agreement, too winded from the exertion of shoveling to say anything. But he had scarcely dug 6 inches deep around the 6-foot diameter of the evolving pool when the Beekeeper had another idea. The pool ought to have a firm rock wall around it, or else the mud sides would eventually slump and slide back into the hole. Off the trio went in the Dumb Farmer's pickup to the pile of rocks he, his father, and grandfather had patiently gleaned from the fields of his farm. Four truckloads later, Smith was digging again while the Beekeeper and the Dumb Farmer lined the descending hole with rocks. They stair-stepped the wall inward in 8-inch gradations, so that the wall would hold without the need for any skilled layering of rocks, and also so that the pool would have various depths at the edges to accommodate the preferences of different animals and plants. To make room for this kind of wall, the Beekeeper, again wincing for poor Smith, decided to enlarge the overall diameter of the pool to 8 feet.

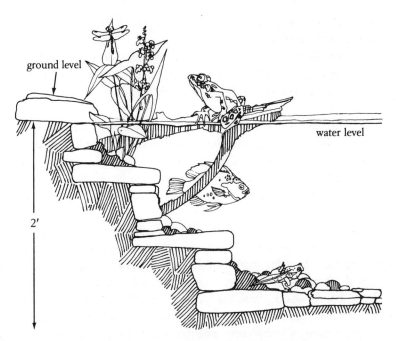

A Cross-Section View of Smith's Pool

Slowly, the pool filled. The Dumb Farmer and the Beekeeper were pleased with their work and bragged about it for years. The pool's water level dropped during summer droughts, but dried up completely only four times in the ensuing years. During such crises, Smith puts the fish—catfish, bluegills, and minnows, mostly—in a barrel by the garage until it rains again. Or, in the case of catfish and bluegills of adequate size, he eats them and restocks with small ones. One severe winter, the pool iced over for too long and killed the fish, but in most years, the spring water keeps the pool warm enough so only 3 inches of ice forms at the most. If snow covers the ice, Smith pushes it off so that sunlight can get through to the oxygenating organisms in the water.

Frogs, toads, salamanders, and crayfish have established their own life routines in and around the pool, and both box turtles and painted turtles come and go. But Smith waits, so far in vain, for the coming of *Hydrocampa propiralis* to eat the leaves of the yellow water lily or the arrowhead plants he grows in pots set in the pool. One day, he watched a kingfisher drop like a rock from a dead branch of the red maple into the pond, smacking the surface with a splashy clap and emerging from the spray with a minnow in its beak. He thinks maybe that was better than seeing *H. propiralis.*

"But that old Lazybird will take all your fish now that he's found them," the Beekeeper pointed out. Smith shrugged. More minnows he can always buy. Seeing a kingfisher catch one was a thrill beyond purchase.

Backyard springs like Smith's are not exactly rare in the Piedmont areas of the Appalachian range from Maine to Georgia, and across the central states to the Mississippi from Pennsylvania through West Virginia, southern Ohio, Indiana, Illinois, Kentucky, and Tennessee. The patient house-hunter can usually find a place so adorned. In fact, generally speaking, you'll find springs almost anywhere in hilly country, just as a natural bit of swampy wetland can occur almost anywhere on more level terrain. In areas where springs are characteristic, look for them behind the subdivision houses on the edges of a housing development, where the backyards run down hillsides to floodplains or creek valleys—the natural borders of housing developments. These houses on the peripheries of subdivisions often have extra large backyards, since no more houses can be built back into the small drainage valleys. Land in these valleys also becomes a sort of wasteland that can often be purchased or simply used as a kind of neighborhood wildlife area. If springs occur on these hilly backlots, they may be mentioned in the real estate description, or with a hillside seep-spring especially, they may not be mentioned. The prospective buyer thinking of experiencing a wildlife area should examine these backyards very closely.

Much more common sources of natural water for the wildlife area are the creeks that divide housing developments. In Smith's township, hundreds of homes have backyards that end in clear running streams. If the area is properly sewered, these creeks remain relatively unpolluted. Where subdivisions still rely on septic tanks, many of which eventually become overburdened and ooze sewage into the creeks, these streams no longer support much fishlife and are decidedly undesirable for children to play in.

Within walking distance of Smith's place in any direction, small clean streams and their valleys provide strips of elegant wildlife area between the subdivisions. The creeks themselves contain minnows, like the redbelly dace, which watches the surface for floating insects (the male's underside turns red during the spring spawning season).

There are chubs, bullheads, and even bluegills in the deeper pools, not to mention an occasional goldfish released from the captivity of a bowl in a nearby house. Neighborhood children spend long, happy hours playing along the water or wading in it, racing homemade toy boats, building little waterwheels and dams, trying to catch the fish, or simply sitting on the bank as their parents do, daydreaming to the sound of the water rippling by.

As these streams wind their way through their little valleys, the outer bends of the meanderings form high, rather steep banks beyond the grasp of plow, mower, or even bulldozer. Here bloom in the spring a profusion of wild flowers: bloodroot, trout-lily, trillium, quaker ladies, wood sorrel, and violets of various kinds. On the inner bends of the meanders, across from the high banks, lie pockets of rich creek-bottom soil where skunk cabbage, buttercups, Virginia bluebells, and wild iris run rampant. The alternating high banks and low fertile bottomland produce an amazing variety of trees and bushes, too, from small slender dogwoods on the high side to huge beaches on the low side. Other trees include walnut, hickory, red oak, white oak, ironwood, willow, an occasional elm not yet stricken by Dutch elm disease, hawthorn, crabapple, sassafras, box elder, maple, and even frail witch-hazels, their amazing blossoms in February and March easily missed by all but the most observant eyes.

Birds and animals are drawn to the water in fair measure. Raccoons come for fish; opossums hope for a sluggish crayfish or unwary snake. Muskrats look for roots of water plants. Mink follow in pursuit of muskrats. Turtles doze on sunny rocks. Groundhogs come to the water's edge when there is not enough dew to slake their thrist. Overhead, the mourning dove, drawn to water as surely as man is, builds its haphazard nest in a wide crotch of a tree. The Baltimore oriole hangs its intricate, swinging nest high above the water or sometimes over a street nearby, as if a thoroughfare of cement or water were all the same to it. Red-winged blackbirds nest in bushes that bend over the water. When all is very quiet, if such a time ever occurs in a neighborhood full of children, and teenagers with sports cars and motorcycles, the green heron slinks along the creek bank, hungry for minnows. Along the wider valley of the Wissahickon Creek, into which the small streams flow and above whose floodplain even more houses perch, the Canada geese loiter, half tame, so bold in nesting time that they chase horses and riders on the trails through the valley.

Such are the rewards of water for those with the foresight and means to build or buy homes near it. One of Smith's neighbors on the stream below him bought for a bargain a wedge of steep land between road and creek that seemed to offer developers no economic opportunity. The owners built a home perched on deep pylonlike foundations on the hillside, the house jutting out above and almost over the creek. On Sunday mornings, in a quiet breakfast nook overlooking the stream, hardly a stone's throw from a busy road, they can watch the life of the stream to the music of its gurgling water.

Backyard Birdbaths and Pools

Homeowners without access to natural springs or streams can easily put a pool in their backyard. The poorest man can afford a birdbath—a shallow receptacle with 1 to 3 inches of water in it. Place the bath at least 3 feet above the ground, even though birds prefer their baths at ground level. The extra height gives birds a good view of approaching cats. Although a cat can jump higher than 3 feet, it can seldom do so and catch a bird at the same time. Humans never can tell what a cat will do next, but birds usually know. Set the birdbath in a more or less open area to help the birds keep watch, too, but where branches of trees and bushes are close by, at least on one side. The nearness of foliage gives the birds a quick retreat and a sense of security.

The ideal birdbath should be made of cement or pottery for long life. Metal pans rust out, plastic cracks, and rubber may have a coating that dissolves in water and becomes potentially dangerous to the birds. Also ideally, a steady drip of water from a hose gives the bath more appeal to birds. In the absence of a birdbath, a lawn sprinkler probably does the birds more good than it does the lawn. The misting water deters cats, and the birds will stand in it and bathe as they do in falling rain.

With a little more expense and imagination, anyone can have a pool in his yard. Easy ones are made by cutting wooden barrels in half and sinking both halves into the ground. On a hillside, two or more half barrels can be placed one above the other so that water can be made to flow by gravity from the topmost to the bottom. The water then can be pumped back up to the top again with a small, recirculating motor.

Waterfalls from one pool to another are more than just beautiful and musical; the falling water helps oxygenate the little pools so that they might support a few fish, if desired. Very small pools are fine for amphibians. An old sink stuck in the ground can make a good place to put a few frog or toad eggs to hatch. A layer of mud and a floating water plant will help the tadpoles to hide from predators.

To be safe, allow no more than one 6-inch fish per 3 cubic feet of water. It is generally considered wise to allow no less than 50 square feet of surface water and a minimum depth of 18 inches for any pool into which fish are put. In cold climates, a depth of 2 feet is minimum and 3 feet advisable, unless the fish are to be taken out of the pool over the winter. Lesser quantities of water are hard to keep oxygenated, unless you can install an aerator. Also, lesser quantities of water tend to get an overbalance of algal bloom that won't clear up. Do not expect any garden pool to stay crystal clear like a chlorinated swimming pool. A certain amount of cloudiness to the water is a sign of its vitality, evidence that the microorganisms that form the basis of the food web in the watery environment are present in abundance.

Low-cost pools that are simple dug-out holes, cushioned with sand, and then lined with tough flexible plastic liners, seem most popular for garden pools today. Rocks are laid around the top edge of the plastic to hold it in place and make an attractive edging for the pool. Plastic liners are somewhat fragile, however; they tend to deteriorate in sunlight and become very brittle in cold weather. They puncture easily when children and dogs decide to jump into the pool, an event to be expected as surely as night follows day. A preformed, rigid, fiberglass pool is better, although costlier. Choose fiberglass pools that are more or less square-shaped at the bottom, like a bathtub, rather than saucer-shaped. Water in shallow, saucer-shaped pools rises and falls in temperature too abruptly between day and nighttime for fish and some water plants to survive.

Permanent Pools

The serious garden-pool lover will want a permanent fixture, pleasing to the eye. He or she will be wise, then, to choose concrete. It is wise, also, to hire an expert to do the construction, since it is critical that the pool not leak. The footer of the pool must extend below the frost line. Walls and floor should be thoroughly bonded together with steel reinforcing mesh and ⅜-inch reinforcing rod in the concrete. The floor should be of concrete, 6 inches thick, poured over about 6 inches of gravel. The walls should be at least 4 inches thick. It is best to pour the walls and floor at the same time, which requires wood or metal forms the full size of the walls all around. If excavation is done carefully, the outside dirt wall can serve as the outside form for the concrete.

It is possible to avoid forming up the walls. First, pour the floor, and when it is barely half dry, lay up a brick or tile wall 4 inches out from the dirt wall, filling in behind the wall with concrete as you go. If the wall starts to bulge, brace it and let the concrete set up a bit before continuing to build upward. Or, lay the wall up entirely, and when it is solid pour the concrete behind it.

The edges of an artificial pool ought to be constructed so as to provide a ledge where the water is only about 2 inches deep. Here, water-loving plants in pots can be set to provide a place for birds to bathe and amphibians to rest. To build this shallow-water ledge, discontinue building up the walls at a point a few inches below the planned water level of the pool. Place large flagstones on top of the wall—stones that will stick out into the pool as far as possible and also overlap the wall on the other side (see illustration). Indent the wall at this juncture, as shown, and continue up the soil surface, filling concrete behind the wall, and topping it all off with a flagstone coping. The flagstones that stick out into the pool and form the ledge may need to be supported temporarily until the concrete dries.

Put pieces of drain tile in the pool for fish to hide in. Some species of fish, like the channel catfish, may use such places for nesting sites.

Small, spoon-shaped frog and plant pools can be fashioned with concrete without any forms at all. Dig and smooth the excavation, lay down reinforcing mesh and rod, then shovel 4 to 6 inches of concrete over the excavated surface. Mix the ingredients extra dry, so that the concrete doesn't run. Wading and swimming pools can be home-built this way but are practical only in warm climates. In the frost-heaving North, they invariably crack and leak.

Wait three weeks after the cement is dry before filling the pool with water. After two weeks, drain the first water and fill again. The first filling draws out alkalies in the cement that might be harmful to fish.

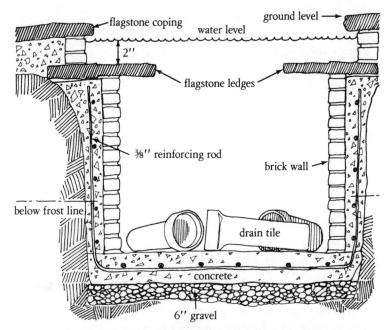

Cross Section of Permanent Pool Construction

Plants for Pools and Marshes

Before stocking water animals in the pool, establish a plant community in and around it. The first plants in your pool will come of their own accord in the form of algae. The water usually turns green with algal bloom. Then, as other microorganisms gain a foothold in the water by consuming the algae, the various life forms balance and the water clears up somewhat.

Begin then to introduce oxygenating plants that can grow in the water. Common weedy ones include bladderwort (*Utricularia vulgaris*), water-weed (*Anacharis canadensis*), fanwort (*Cabomba caroliniana*), water-milfoil (*Myriophyllum* spp.), pennywort (*Hydrocotyle* spp.), water-shield (*Brasenia schreberi*), water-stargrass (*Heteranthera dubia*), and pondweeds (*Potamogeton pectinatus* and *P. natans*). Any of these might arrive in your pool unbidden, and any of them will completely fill the pond, too, if allowed. Controlling them by hand-pulling or by dragging a garden rake through the water is fairly easy to do with a small pool. All these plants have some value as food for other water residents and for waterfowl. Duckweed (*Spirodela polyrhiza*) and water smartweed (*Polygonum* spp.) have food value, too, but need to be scrupulously controlled. Duckweed in particular will soon cover a pool with what looks like flaky green scum.

Water lilies, grown in pots set on the bottom of the pool or on a rock or other pedestal at mid-depth, are most beneficial plants. They provide oxygen and a hiding place for water animals of all kinds. Small frogs sunbathe on the flat, floating leaves. Growing one or two in a pot allows you to keep the lilies from spreading and covering all the water. Both the white water lily (*Nymphaea odorata*) and the yellow water lily (*Nuphar luteum*) are hardy and easy to grow. Both have edible root shoots and leaves.

Mix a rich soil in the pot in which you intend to grow a water lily. Add well-rotted manure or compost. Use a large pot or a small tub—a couple of cubic feet of dirt is about the right amount for a healthy water lily. Place a piece of tuber on the surface of the pot soil (or barely cover it), and submerge the pot at least a foot underwater. It is a good idea to cover the soil in the pot with an inch of gravel to keep the soil from washing out. Hundreds of varieties of water lilies are available from nurseries specializing in water plants (see Appendix, Source Lists). Some are hardy; some are not. Semihardy plants in underwater pots are usually safe through the winter. The pots can be lifted and stored in a safe place during cold weather if you want to be sure.

In the shallow water of the ledges around the pool, arrowhead (*Sagittaria latifolia*) usually does well in pots. Cattails (*Typha latifolia*) will grow there, although they do not seem to like the confines of a pot very much. Pickerelweed (*Pontederia cordata*) can be grown in shallow water quite easily and has a showy blue blossom. All three of the above plants can be troublesome weeds in larger ponds. Many kinds of reeds and rushes will grow in pots in shallow water, too.

Artificial pools generally have dry banks, but a great variety of beautiful wetland plants are possible around pools dug in natural wetlands. Here the marsh-marigold (*Caltha palustris*) and the cardinal-flower (*Lobelia cardinalis*), two of our prettiest native wild flowers, feel right at home. So does the wild blue flag (*Iris versicolor*) on both wet soil and even right in the water.

Smith got a bit carried away in his little swamp. Succeeding with the more common wild flowers, he decided to try some true bog plants. A true bog, technically, is made up mostly of sphagnum moss, with the live plants growing on top of deep deposits of dead ones. A real bog contains water and muck of a very low pH (making the bog very acid), and only plants well adapted to acid soils will grow there—like cranberry. Its water is so acid, in fact, that no common fish species will live in a true bog. Smith's soil tested fairly acid—5.5 pH to 6.0 pH—and cranberries would grow in his "bog" half-heartedly. Most bog plants need a pH of 4.0, so, when Smith tried to grow insect-catching sundew and common pitcher plants or any of the little wild orchids common on bogs, he did not have much luck. Only the semidomesticated strains of pink and yellow lady's-slipper (*Cypripedium acaule*, available from many nurseries) survived in shady spots, but they did not grow as vigorously as they do in their natural habitat. Since sphagnum moss from bogs itself is very acid (unless it has been commercially cleaned), Smith borrowed a trick from herbariums and tried growing sundews and pitcher plants in pots of sphagnum moss with a bit of soil mixed in. He set the pots brim-deep in the marsh so that the moss remained very wet. Sure enough, the plants grew. Peat moss worked about as well and was cheaper, so he later switched to it.

A tamarack tree took easily to the edge of Smith's marsh, but unlike many plants found in association with bogs, the tamarack will adapt to almost any rather acid soil, and it does not require a thoroughly or continuously wet soil. It tolerates somewhat drier conditions just as blue flag tolerates a wet, acid bog, but will grow on almost any moist soil.

In fact, most plants recommended for around garden pools or in wetlands will thrive in any woodsy soil that stays fairly moist in spring. Thus, jack-in-the-pulpit (*Arisaema atrorubena*), bee-balm (*Monarda didyma*), Virginia bluebell (*Mertensia virginica*), the trilliums (*Trillium grandiflorum*), and trout-lily (*Erythronium americanum*), often listed as water-garden plants, require only moist and partially sunny locations but will tolerate slightly more swampy conditions. Joe-Pye-weed and boneset (two members of the *Eupatorium* genus with medicinal value, the former quite showy with pink-purple blossoms) like moist, not wet, soil and an open, sunny location. So do wild asters, spiderwort (*Tradescantia virginiana*), fringed gentian (*Gentiana crinita*), and swamp milkweed (*Asclepias incarnata*)—all beautiful, bee- and butterfly-luring plants.

Snapweed or jewelweed (*Impatiens capensis*) is considered a wetland plant by many gardeners, but this interesting wild plant grows

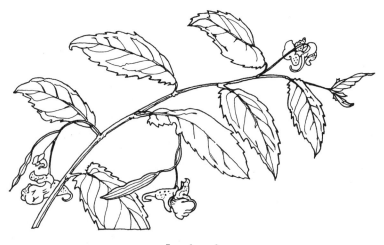

Jewelweed

on any rich, shady soil that retains some moisture throughout the summer. The Beekeeper loves jewelweed because it gives him a chance to pass on old traditions to children. "Lookee here," he'll say when he finds a child and a mature jewelweed pod in the same area. Gaining the child's attention, he will touch the seedpod ever so lightly, and it will snap and fling its seed into the air as if he had tripped some unseen spring on the plant. He also claims that there is nothing better to arrest poison ivy rash than rubbing it with a bruised (crushed) jewelweed leaf. (Once more, Smith found the old man to be right. And the bruised leaves worked soothingly on pain caused by stinging nettles, too.) The lower, orange-spotted petals of jewelweed hold little sacs of nectar that hummingbirds seek out, along with bees, especially the flylike green halictid bee (*Augochlora* spp.).

Some ferns and mosses love shady, moist areas. Smith once made a moss garden in the shade of some spicebushes (*Lindera benzoin*) and a sweet pepperbush (*Clethra alnifolia*), both of which grow well on wet sites. His method of making a moss garden was simple enough. Whenever he found a rotting piece of wood or a rock in the woods with a different kind of moss growing on it, he put it in his moss garden. The Dumb Farmer was not impressed. "Looks more like a moss-covered junkyard, if you ask me," he sniffed. Ferns particularly suitable for wet sites include the sensitive fern (*Onoclea sensibilis*), the ostrich fern (*Pteretis pensylvanica*), the narrow beech fern (*Dryopteris*

Phegopteris), Clinton's fern (*D. clintoniana*), and the berry bladder-fern (*Cystopteris bulbifera*). All prefer moist stream banks.

Few trees, other than cypress and willows, will grow with their roots right in water, and it is not usually a good idea to place trees so close to a garden pool that the leaves all fall into it. Enough leaves will get into the pool as it is, and they will have to be cleaned out occasionally. In wetlands or in swampy, poorly drained terrain, the following trees will thrive: silver maple, red maple, box elder (all of which provide seeds for bird food, particularly the latter in winter); yellow, river, and gray birches; water ash and green ash; sweet gum; cottonwood and largetooth aspen; swamp white oak, pin oak, and willow oak; American linden; balsam fir; white cedar; black spruce and red spruce; and hemlock.

Some other less common trees suitable for wetlands include black alder (*Alnus glutinosa*), American hornbeam (*Carpinus caroliniana*), sweet bay (*Magnolia glauca*), sour gum or tupelo (*Nyssa sylvatica*), buttonwood (*Platanus occidentalis*), and American arborvitae (*Thuja occidentalis*).

Other Water Life

The plants most ubiquitous in watery sites are the tiny, almost microscopic organisms in the pool water itself, which along with equally tiny animal organisms make a sort of nutritious soup in the pool—the beginning of the watery food web that connects the tiniest filamentous algae and diatoms to the largest fish, heron, osprey, and fish-eating bear. Leaves from trees fall into the water and, with other organic matter, decompose, becoming food in the process, for various bacteria, fungi, protozoans, copepods, amphipods, and other minute organisms. At the same time, the decomposition provides fertilizer for algae and diatoms, which in turn are the foods for larvae of dragonflies, caddis flies, mayflies, water beetles, small crustaceans, and myriad other forms of watery life.

Many of these insects can be as fascinating to the wildlife watcher as the well-known larger animals. Although quite common along rivers and around lakes, the golden mayfly is an insect of striking beauty, not only in color but in form, with its amber wings and long, golden, uplifted "tails." Its naiads (aquatic larval form) are an important source of food for fish and for dragonfly naiads. The golden mayfly naiad itself eats diatoms and algae from the bottom mud and underwater vegetation. Adults are eaten by swallows and other birds, and by fish leaping out of the water after them. One wonders if their golden color might not be an aid to the fish in this regard.

Dragonflies together compose a family as challenging and interesting to watch as birds. Some 450 species (including damselflies, which fold their wings above their bodies when at rest, unlike most dragonflies, which keep their wings spread) are known in North America.

Dragonflies and damselflies represent not only one of the most strikingly beautiful families of insects around a pool, but one of the most beneficial, because they are important predators of mosquitoes. Naiads eat mosquito larvae (and the larvae of many other insects), while adults prey upon adult mosquitoes and almost any winged insect they chance upon, capturing them in full flight. Certain of the larger dragonfly naiads capture tadpoles and even small fish. These naiads have a strangely elongated lower lip that they extend with lightning speed to capture prey. Bristles on the lip help pull the prey back into the naiad's mouth. When fully grown, the naiad crawls out of the water, its skin splits, and out comes a dragonfly. Adults mate in midair, the male

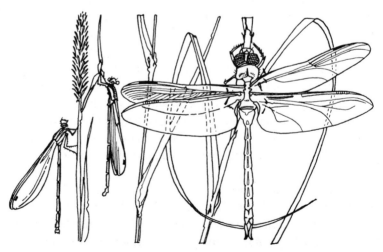

Damselflies and a Dragonfly at Rest—Damselflies fold up their wings when not airborne, while dragonflies spread their wings when resting.

depositing sperm in a chamber on his own abdomen. While he holds the female, she picks up the sperm with the tip of her abdomen.

The largest American species of dragonflies have wingspans over 5 inches long, like the green heroic darner (*Epiaeschna heros*). Even the common green darner (*Anax junius*) has a wingspan of over 4 inches and a length of about 3 inches, with a scintillating green thorax and metallic blue abdomen. The twelve-spot skimmer (*Libellula pulchella*) with its spotted wings, is easy to identify. The half-banded toper (*Sympetrum semicinctum*) with its bright red abdomen, and the white tail (*Plathemis lydia*), with its banded wings and especially the gleaming white body of males, are breathtaking to discover.

Adult caddisflies are not nearly as picturesque as dragonflies, but the habits of their aquatic naiads are most interesting to observe. For self-protection, these larvae build shells or cases around themselves— little houses of leaf bits and twig parts cemented together with saliva glue. A larva drags its little suitcase around with it as it eats algae and grows. When it pupates, it crawls completely inside and closes the end up. Some of the cases look so much like little twigs that they are very difficult to find. Others are tubular or cylindrical in shape, not as big around as a pencil and about ¾ inch long. A colony of them shows up fairly well on the pool bottom, but one alone is hard to distinguish from the other debris at the bottom.

Some caddisflies that inhabit streams do not make cases but construct tiny nets that they stretch across a fast current. Then they eat the tiny bits of plant food that catch in the net. Caddisfly adults are mothlike in appearance but with extremely long antennae. Most are mottled grayish and brown in color.

Another common but intriguing family of water bugs is that of the water beetle. Black, oval whirligig beetles (*Dineutus* spp. and *Gyrinus* spp.), about the size of peas, swim on the water surface at great speed, usually in random circles, preying on insects, mites, and even snails. Their larvae live and pupate in the water. The diving water beetles (*Acilius* spp. and *Dytiscus* spp.) resemble the whirligigs at first glance, but average a little larger size. They're dark green to black, and they prey on other insects including mosquito larvae and larger invertebrates. The diving beetle traps a bubble of air under its forewings (elytra), which it then breathes while underwater for as long as several hours.

The ubiquitous water strider, more often called skater or skating bug, is so light it can walk on the film that normally covers the surface of pool water; hence its colloquial name in the South of "Jesus bug." Striders can communicate with each other by means of the ripples on the film on the water surface. The ripples reflect light that the strider "reads" and reacts to—perhaps turning away from the source of the motion, or going toward it in the case of an insect it wants to eat or a mate it wants to court. A drop of detergent on the water will dissolve the film the strider walks on, and the strider will sink. Entomologists say there are insects that actually excrete a kind of detergent that dissolves the film behind them so that striders cannot pursue them.

Backswimmers (*Notonecta* spp.) swim upside down, as their name indicates, but their bulging eyes allow them to see in all directions just as well. Because they hunt on their backs, they attack the more vulnerable underside of their prey.

The giant water bug (*Lethocerus americanus*), nearly an inch broad and as much as 2⅜ inches long, is distributed throughout the United States, and because of its size, it is an easy wildling to observe. It eats not only insects but tadpoles, salamanders, frogs, and small fish. This huge bug plunges its beak into the hapless prey and injects an anesthetic that numbs and subdues it. The chemical also begins the process of digestion, liquefying the innards of the prey. The bug simply sucks out the body juices, leaving an empty shell or skin. The experience of watching this repulsive consumption in progress can be rather traumatic for the neophyte bug-watcher. Annie Dillard, in her wonderful book *Pilgrim at Tinker Creek*, describes it thus:

> *He was a very small frog with wide, dull eyes. And just as I looked at him, he slowly crumpled and began to sag. The spirit vanished from his eyes as if snuffed. His skin emptied and drooped; his very skull seemed to collapse and settle like a kicked tent. He was shrinking before my eyes like a deflating football. I watched the taut glistening skin on his shoulders ruck, and rumple and fall. Soon, part of his skin, formless as a pricked balloon, lay in floating folds like bright scum on top of the water; it was a monstrous and terrifying thing.... This event is quite common in warm fresh water. The frog I saw was being sucked by a giant water bug.*

Stocking a Pool

In nature, a pond builds a complete food web only slowly. Plants around and in the water diversify in time, each drawing other organisms that directly or indirectly feed on them. But waiting for nature to draw all the fish and animals potentially adapted to a pool may take many years and is chancy at best. How long will it be before a wading bird alights at a new pond with fish eggs on its legs potent enough to hatch and survive? Stocking a man-made pond artificially is the only answer, and it will be successful if attempted with one eye on the natural succession of food web associations. First, plant life in and around the pool is established. Much of this will take care of itself naturally, but it doesn't hurt to move the process along from the very beginning. Thus, a bucket or two of "soup" water from an established pond can be poured into a new pool early on to seed in a rich variety of algae and diatoms. Water bugs can be captured at an established pond and transferred to a new one, although a light over the new pool might easily accomplish the same purpose. Most water bugs can fly and are attracted to light at night.

Whatever forms of life the backyard wildlife manager stocks his pool with, he should be guided by the "safe" rule; that is, transfer native species, those forms of life found in and around ponds closest to him. These species are adapted to his climate, soil, and water and, thus, have a better chance of survival. Foreign, introduced species may not survive at all, or they may proliferate because of a lack of natural controls at the new pond site. Most of our worst weeds and many of our animal pests are the result of introductions from afar.

After plant and insect life are established, one of the next animals to stock is the pond snail, which feeds mostly on decayed organic matter. Next, try crayfish netted from a nearby creek or pond. Crayfish are mostly scavengers, too, like the snails, but in addition they eat insect larvae, worms, snails, other crustaceans, and small fish. Crayfish form a manageable link between these lower species and the higher ones you will want to stock. Fish, frogs, turtles, snakes, water birds, raccoons, and opossums love crayfish. And so does man, since crayfish are diminutive models of lobsters and taste just about like them. In Louisiana, to say nothing of fine restaurants in France, crayfish are a gourmet delicacy. Here's a recipe for crayfish thermidor adapted from

The Conservationist, the official publication of New York State's Department of Environmental Conservation:

Crayfish Thermidor

2 tablespoons chopped onions	1 egg yolk
½ cup button mushrooms, sliced	1 tablespoon white grape juice
2 tablespoons butter	2 cups crayfish, tails only,
2 tablespoons whole wheat flour	cleaned, cut into pieces, and
⅛ teaspoon pepper	cooked (about 3 to 4 dozen
⅛ teaspoon paprika	crayfish)
½ cup light cream	2 tablespoons fine buttered
½ cup chicken broth	cracker or whole grain
½ teaspoon Worcestershire sauce	bread crumbs, dry

Saute onions and mushrooms in butter. Blend in flour and seasonings. Cook over low heat for a few minutes. Remove from heat and stir in cream, chicken broth, and Worcestershire sauce. Bring to simmer, stirring constantly. Simmer 1 minute. Add egg yolk, grape juice, and crayfish. Combine well. Place mixture in individual baking dishes and sprinkle with cracker crumbs or bread crumbs. Bake 5 minutes in a 450°F oven. Use large or medium-size crayfish.

Serves 6

Frogs and toads can be stocked next, if they do not come to the pool of their own accord. The best way to start them is to gather a few masses of eggs from a nearby pond in the spring. Dump them, along with a bucket of the pond's water, into the new pool. The water plants established in your pool should be food enough for the hatching tadpoles, but a bit of fresh meat in tiny pieces can be fed in addition.

Toad eggs are laid in strings of gelatinous material, frog eggs in masses. Toads like 1 to 2 feet of water to develop in; frogs less than 1 foot. Put the eggs close to water plants so that the newly emerging tadpoles can begin to eat immediately. It takes about six weeks from egg to the time the tadpole starts growing legs and another six weeks before it changes to a fully formed tiny toad or frog. Most of them will be eaten by predators before they grow to adulthood. Not all frogs live in water or even stay close to it. The spring peeper prefers trees but comes to water for mating. A tiny frog, less than an inch in size, it has a very large soprano voice and is among the first to herald spring. It can breed in temporary pools of water in the forest. The wood frog likes the forest environment, too, but it is not as apt to be found in a backyard, no matter how many trees are there, because it prefers a fairly large expanse of swamp for breeding. Cricket frogs and chorus frogs frequent grassy wetlands and brushy areas. One year when June rains fell in torrents and created long-lasting pools of water even in his crop fields, the Dumb Farmer thought he heard a flock of strange water birds in the wheat field where 6 inches of water lay below the waving wheat plants. He stalked carefully through the water. No birds flew although the sounds persisted. Finally, he found their origin: little brownish frogs with a streak of greenish yellow down the back and over the nose. Cricket frogs, the Beekeeper said they were, although the sound did not seem much like that of a cricket. Ever after, the Dumb Farmer remembered the incident, telling his grandchildren of the summer that was so wet that frogs bred in his wheat field.

The green frog is most likely to be happy with a garden pool, and it can be captured, if one is fast and stealthy, along almost any creek east of the Mississippi. This shy frog sits on the bank and when almost stepped on, leaps in a high arch into the water, usually with a low cry—*tonk!*—that sounds a bit like the sound of an iron skillet being struck with a heavy wooden spoon.

Leopord frogs are apt to abide in a backyard wildlife area where a plot of meadow is allowed to grow 6 inches or more in height. If such meadows are near creeks or ponds, these frogs wander into them in late summer looking for insects.

Bullfrogs are large enough to supply an occasional meal of frog legs if one has a relatively large pond, 1/10 of an acre or more. As for small garden pools, bullfrogs will usually not stay in them, because such pools won't supply enough food. This may be just as well for the wildlife lover, since voracious bullfrogs might clean out the pool of most of its inhabitants. Bullfrogs eat earthworms, snails, crayfish, spiders, fish, snakes, birds, mice, ants, wasps and other insects, tadpoles, other frogs, even other bullfrogs, and occasionally small turtles.

Frogs and toads are good attractants for higher forms of wildlife. They are important foods for a great many birds, fish, snakes, and turtles. Having frogs in the backyard may be the only way you will have a chance of sometime spotting a heron or other large wading bird.

With frogs about, snakes will come to the wildlife area, an event to rejoice in, not to deplore (see Chapter 8, The Most Misunderstood Wildlife). Of native American snakes that frequent water, only the cottonmouth, or water moccasin (*Agkistrodon piscivorus*), is dangerously poisonous. The cottonmouth inhabits only swampy regions of the southern United States. Snakes in garden pools are almost always harmless water snakes (*Natrix* spp.). Garter snakes (*Thamnophis sirtalis*), beneficial insect eaters, sometimes take a swim. The common blacksnake (*Elaphe obsoleta*), another beneficial snake, is usually seen close to water.

The eastern painted turtle (*Chrysemys picta picta*), the commonest turtle and the one most likely to take up residence in a garden pool, is one of the wariest and quickest of turtles. It seldom strays far from water. A pool with less than 100 square feet of surface space is hardly large enough for turtles, but the decision will be the turtle's. If he or she likes the pool, he or she will stick around. If not, there is little any human can do about it. Smith has hoped for years that the rare bog turtle (*Clemmys muhlenbergi*) might turn up in his marsh, but he'll settle for *C. insculpta*, the more common cousin known as the wood turtle. The wood turtle may yet come, since it wanders far from water in the summer. But the rare bog turtle stays close to the bog it was born in.

Salamanders and newts keep their own counsel, coming and going in their secretive ways. Most begin their lives as frogs do, as tadpoles in pools of water. As adults, they hide in moist places on land—under rocks, logs, or leaves. They eat about the same bill of fare as frogs do, but unlike frogs, they do not sing at all in the spring. One exceedingly interesting but fairly common salamander in the eastern half of the country (although not distributed evenly throughout the whole region) is the red-spotted newt or red eft (*Notophthalmus viridescens viridescens*), the latter name applied to the terrestrial stage of this salamander's life. Its bright vermilion color is reason enough to bring it to your wildlife area. Red efts are easy to catch. Though hardly 3 inches long and not as big around as a finger, their coloration makes them easy to see. They move slowly, having few enemies. The orange-red color warns off potential predators, for the red eft's skin has glands that can give off a neurotoxin painful to its natural enemies. It is quite harmless to man, unless a man is crazy enough to bite into one.

The red-spotted newt—alias, the red eft—is unusual even among salamanders, in that it lives three distinct lives rather than just the two with which most salamanders are content. The mother lays individual eggs on water plants and submerged twigs near the bottom of the pool, which makes the eggs hard to find, even with their gelatinous coating. Within a month, the eggs hatch and the tiny tadpoles live out the summer in the pool, going through the same kind of metamorphosis that other salamanders do, lungs replacing feathery gills, and legs developing. When they leave the water, their yellowish skin has changed to bright orange with a row of black-rimmed red spots along each side. They spend one year or more as land animals, overwintering under logs or stones, patrolling the forest floor in warm weather, eating worms and insects. Then they undergo a third change; the red coloring subsides, except in the spots, replaced by a dull olive hue. Their bodies elongate a bit, and their skins become smoother. Then they return to the water to live their third life.

Without the benefit of the gills they shed as tadpoles, the mature newts must return periodically to the water surface for air. Now they eat grubs, crustaceans, frog eggs, and insect larvae (including mosquito larvae). Spring matings begin in rather ho-hum fashion, a pair of newts locked listlessly and languorously together for about 15 minutes, the affair ending in a great thrashing about. Then, on the bottom of the pool, the male newt deposits spermatophores, which the female walks over and picks up with the lips of her cloaca, the eggs then being fertilized inside her.

Smith always becomes agitated when considering the red-spotted newt. Why, he demands of the Beekeeper, does nature go to such trouble and complexity over a measly 3-inch creature which 90 percent of the world neither knows nor cares about. The Beekeeper shrugs. "I'm not going to worry about it until it grows wings and flies out to eat my bees."

With a high variety of plant and water life established, the pool is ready for fish. Again, the best rule to follow is to go to the nearest creek and seine some minnows. Some are liable not to be real minnows but the fry of larger fish species. All, however, should be native and adapted to your area. Because your pool is small, you can control overpopulation of desirable species and evict undesirable ones, such as rough carp that might be inclined to keep the pool too riled up for the other species. Resist the temptation to stock exotic species, except maybe goldfish (a form of carp), which are hardy and adaptive to small pools. Goldfish do not make good eating, however. If you like the notion of eating a few fish occasionally, bullheads and bluegills will serve your purposes better. Both will quickly overpopulate, so you must be prepared to remove 80 percent of the increase unless your pool is big enough to hold a couple of largemouth bass and a pair of bullfrogs. But even in farm ponds where bass and bullfrogs are stocked, bluegills, bullheads, and most minnows tend to overpopulate. One 6-inch fish per 3 cubic feet of water is about all a small pool can handle without adding oxygen artificially. Even if extra oxygen is supplied, though, overcrowding invariably leads to diseases.

For wildlife watchers with just a tiny pool, minnows of various kinds are the most practical way to enjoy "fish-watching." The Beekeeper told Smith that minnows could be trained to come for food by whistling. Smith didn't believe it, but taking great care to see that he was unobserved, he began whistling before tossing bread crumbs on the water. Sure enough, within six weeks, shrill whistles would bring the fish to the surface, ready for dinner.

One of the most common minnows, perfect for a garden pool, is the chub (*Semotilus atromaculatus*), which grows to a length of 7 inches, and actually is, at that size, quite exciting to fish for with a light fly rod. The black-nosed dace (*Rhinichthys atratulus*) is also common and tolerant of rather poor quality water. It and its cousin, the redbelly dace, are good mosquito-control fish. In a creek in southern Indiana near Smith's boyhood home, a minnow the boys all called the "American patriot" lived in large numbers. Only 2 to 3 inches long, it was colored bright red, white, and blue. Smith has not found it on any fish list yet, and sometimes wonders if he dreamed the whole thing up. He keeps saying that if he ever gets back there again, he will seine some for his garden pool.

There are over 200 species of minnows in North America, some of them very large fish. True minnows have scaleless heads, and no teeth in their mouths but, instead, a few teeth in their throats. Another mark of the minnow is that it has a single dorsal fin supported by less than ten flexible rays.

Watching minnows is most rewarding, not so much because in general they act so much differently from other fish, but because in the wild they are usually more accessible to observation. They work in shallow water near the banks. Chubs, for example, build nests of pebbles, carrying the small stones in their mouths. The female spawns in the nest, and the male fertilizes the eggs, covers them with more pebbles, and then builds another nest. Minnows try to defend the territories around their nests, sometimes grabbing a competing fish and dragging it away. Male fathead minnows will even chase away females of their own species until, finally, a persistent female gets the message across to the busy, prospective spouses.

"Spawning season is a fine time for fish-watching," writes Laurence Pringle in an article, "Just Minnows" in *Audubon*, March, 1982.

If only we were smaller and better adapted to life underwater, then we could pack a lunch and a field guide, slip into a stream, and watch these fertility rites in clear detail. Imagine several species of minnows maneuvering around one nest, the males flashing their bright colors, the water carrying a euphonious chorus of trills, purrs, chirps, and other minnow calls. Emerging from our aquatic field trip, perhaps with a new dace or shiner added to our life list, we would never dream of calling these fishes "just minnows."

Hunkered down beside a little garden pool or a stream at the end of the yard, the backyard naturalist can come very close to this kind of field trip. And maybe he can contribute new knowledge to the field. Pringle relates in his article that a biologist in Michigan once patiently counted the pebbles a 6-inch river chub carried to its nest construction site: over 7,000 in a 30-hour period, traveling an estimated 16 miles in the process!

Chapter 6

A Butterfly Sanctuary

A garden aimed at attracting as many beautiful insects as possible would draw little favorable attention from humans if it were called a dragonfly garden, or beetle sanctuary, or, mercy, a moth retreat. There is only one suitable name for such a place: a butterfly garden, even though many of the other insects that will inhabit it, especially the giant silkworm moths, are certainly as beautiful as any butterfly. Smith believes the luna moth (*Actias luna*) to be as lovely an ornament gracing the airways as any bird. Like other silkworm moths, it is harmless, eating nothing at all during its brief, resplendent adult life. Even the larvae of the prettiest moths—and butterflies—are seldom harmful in the amount of plant foliage they eat.

Not that a harmless and lovely creature like a luna moth cannot be dangerous, Smith will tell you with a twinkle in his eye. Once, a luna moth almost caused his death, as he tells the story. Moths fly mostly at night and butterflies by day, although there are enough exceptions to make that rule a chancy way to distinguish the two. One night many years ago, when Smith was playing third base in a softball game, he happened to look up at the lights behind and above the bleachers to his right. There he saw a pale green luna dancing in the shimmering light, its long tails, like tresses, trailing out below it as it climbed laboriously up the shaft of light toward the bulbs. As Smith gazed raptly at the beautiful moth he had seen only once before, there was the sharp crack of ball on bat, and a sizzling line drive whizzed inches past his eyebrow. He had no time to duck, let alone throw his gloved hand up to catch. Two runs scored, but worse, says Smith, when the dust had settled on the playing field, the moth had disappeared.

Normally, however, watching insects is a safe pastime, and as pleasant as watching birds—perhaps more so. Insects are more approachable, and their life-styles can be studied more easily than those of birds. In the typical backyard, the diversity of insects is greater than that of birds, and with insects, especially the butterflies and moths, one can vary his attention from adult to larva. The caterpillars are often as beautiful as the winged adults.

Insects can be collected, too, without harming the ecosystem. Once moths and butterflies have fertilized and laid their eggs, which they do soon after they emerge, the adults have finished their life work and will soon die anyway. Moths and butterflies can be raised like domestic animals. A few commercial moth and butterfly "farms" have flourished in backyard situations, the oriental silkworm industry being a prime example. That Americans have not succeeded at this type of farming seems to be mostly a lack of patience, for silk production entails tedious attention to detail. Such meticulous detail makes for high labor costs, too.

To draw butterflies and some moths to a wildlife sanctuary requires plants that provide nectar, since this is the only food, other than water, that most butterflies ever consume (see Appendix, Select Nectar Sources for Butterflies). In general, butterflies obtain nectar from many wild weed plants, wild flowers, clovers, and domestic flowers. They are more at home, however, among wild meadow flowers than in the flower garden. Obviously, a sanctuary in which both are grown is better than one or the other.

Nectar flowers attract adults, but that is only half the battle. For a sustainable population of moths and butterflies, larval food—the plants caterpillars eat—must also be included in the sanctuary.

Moths and butterflies live two distinct lives. The worms that hatch from the eggs eat almost continually, shedding skins as many as four times before they pupate. A butterfly pupates inside a hard case called a chrysalis, while most moth caterpillars spin a flexible, papery cocoon around themselves. Some merely wrap a few leaves around themselves, or burrow into the ground instead of spinning a cocoon. In any event, what emerges from a chrysalis or a cocoon is a far different creature from the one that entered it. The change is so complete, and the manner in which it takes place so complex, that the human brain is left with only a frustrating series of whys echoing down the long chain of being. Why does nature go to such lengths to perpetuate these creatures? The mind is left, not with an answer, but with reverential awe.

Smith, for a time, entertained the idea of going into the silkworm business as a hobby. Since he also entertained a thousand and one other bold and romantic projects, this one, too, might never have been put into action. But one autumn day, he spied a row of extra large, long cocoons fastened to a wild cherry tree in his yard. He knew they were cocoons of one of the silkworm moths because of their size, but he did not know which one. He guessed they were cecropia moths (*Hyalophora cecropia*), and that turned out to be correct. The cocoons were heavy and without holes in them. No wasp had parasitized them. If he shook one, he could hear the pupa squirm inside. Chances were good that they would hatch. To protect the cocoons from mice, squirrels, and blue jays over the winter, he decided to put them in a screened box in his unheated garage, where the cocoons would experience normal winter temperatures and humidity.

Over the following months, Smith forgot about his cocoons. Then, one night in June when he flipped on the garage light preparatory to closing the overhead door, he found to his amazement several huge, male cecropia moths fluttering around the outside of the screened box. He could tell they were males because of their feathery antennae. They were wild moths trying to get into his box. Peering inside, he saw why. The moths, some of them females, were emerging from the cocoons. At first it seemed that no moth with a wingspan of almost 6 inches could squeeze out of the narrow purse of the cocoon. Yet, as each emerged, the crumpled, wilted wings began to expand and dry as the moth pumped fluid into them. Fully emerged, the moths sported red-orange bodies, and wings of gray-brownish-purplish, highlighted with rusty orange and white crescents and lines. Near the tips of the wings were dark purplish brown eyespots, glinting on the quivering wings as if alive themselves. Entomologists theorize that the eyespots scare away birds, and examining them, Smith believed it could be so.

Within hours of emerging, the females were heavy with eggs, and when Smith put willow and wild cherry twigs in the cage, the moths deposited a few eggs on them. When seen under a magnifying glass the eggs themselves were beautiful jewels. In a few days, Smith turned all the adults loose except one male, which he kept as a specimen.

The eggs began to hatch shortly thereafter. Smith brought fresh leaves every two or three days. The larvae ate and grew fast. On the fourth day, the worms stopped eating suddenly, turned moist and dark-looking, and shed their skins, which they quickly ate. They then returned to leaf-chomping. A second molt came on the ninth day, a third on the seventeenth day, and a final one on the twenty-third. In two more weeks the caterpillars had reached maturity—magnificent green creatures as big as a workingman's finger, with yellow, blue, and red bristles adorning their bodies.

They stopped eating and began drawing a few leaves around them with their silk, which they spun out of a jellylike substance extruded from a hole in the lower lip. The spun silk hardened on exposure to air. Rolling their heads back and forth, the caterpillars wove webs around themselves that, by the time they were fully completed cocoons contained from ½ to 5 miles of silken thread (depending on which expert is talking). Inside, the caterpillars' cells literally began to dissolve, while the cells that would form the adult moths were activated by hormonal fluid. Thus, the process began by which, after the long winter and spring, the adult moths would emerge.

Smith was delighted. He was well aware that he could never have collected enough silk cocoons to make spinning silk a practical enterprise. But he so enjoyed watching the silkmoth cycle that he continued raising them for several more years.

Beautiful Moths for the Backyard

Most of the giant silkworm moth caterpillars feed on deciduous trees likely to be found in a typical woodlot in the eastern half of the country. The cecropia caterpillar prefers wild cherry and maple but will feed on many other trees. The polyphemus (*Antheraea polyphemus*), even more strikingly colored than the cecropia, feeds in its larval stage on oak, elm, hickory, maple, and other shade trees. The promethea (*Callosamia promethea*), also called spicebush silkmoth (not to be confused with the equally sensational spicebush swallowtail butterfly, *Papilio troilus*), prefers spicebush, as its name indicates, but eats wild cherry and sassafras, too. The luna prefers hickory, walnut, oak, and ash and is sometimes seen flying by day or resting on a low bush in broad daylight. The other silkworm moths are usually seen when they flutter against screens and windows at night, trying to get to the light inside. The Cynthia silkworm moth (*Samia Cynthia*), an introduced species, feeds only on ailanthus and so is likely to be seen only in urban backyards and metropolitan areas where "the tree that grows in Brooklyn" flourishes.

None of the silkworm moths can be fittingly described with words. Even photographs often fail, since the full glory of their colors demands that the light strike the wings at precisely the right angle. (This is also true of butterflies and especially other insects whose colors are lustrous and metallic, such as the larger beetles.) The inability to describe silkworm moth beauty is apparent in this detailed description from *The Audubon Society Field Guide to North American Insects and Spiders,* an inexpensive but good book to help the amateur insect watcher.

> *Body olive-brown with three tufts of white hair on each segment. Wings olive-brown; basal [bottom] half darker with transverse middle bands of pink, white, and black; bold white crescents (lunules) bordered in front with black, behind with yellow. Basal part of both wings has curved, white line bordered with black. Fore wing has small eyespot near tip.*

That's an accurate description, but it simply can't evoke the sensation of awe that looking at one of these beauties can.

The giant silkworm moths are not the only breathtaking beauties a butterfly sanctuary can hold. The very large (up to a 6-inch wingspan) imperial moth (*Eacles imperialis*) is yellow with purple-gray marks. Its caterpillar feeds on all kinds of broad-leaf trees, and even evergreen trees. Chances of seeing one around human habitations are not good, however, because this moth has a real weakness for artificial light. Not only is it attracted, but it seems to hang around even into daylight, when birds spot it easily and eat it. It has, therefore, become scarce in human-populated areas.

Some of the moths known as "underwings" hide their beauty much of the time. At first glance, they are plain, mousy-colored night fliers. Yet their secondary wings, or underwings, when visible, flash with vibrant color. The sweetheart underwing (*Catocala amatrix*) has orange-pink underwings, highlighted by black bands and a white fringe. The mousy color (*Euparthenos nubilus*) of the locust under-

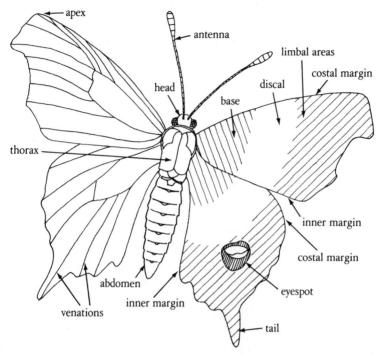

Parts of a Butterfly

wing is offset by underwings of orange-yellow. Both moths are rather common where their caterpillar host plants grow—willow and poplar for the sweetheart, black locust for the locust underwing. But about the only chance to see them is under a porch light at night.

Entomologists have learned that a mixture of sugar water, mashed fermented fruit, stale beer, and a little rum smeared on the trunks of trees will attract many of the night-flying moths. After applying the sweet concoction with an old brush, wait until dark, then approach cautiously with a flashlight. The underwing moths seem to be particularly partial to this bait.

The sphinx moth family contains some eye-catching beauties also. The hummingbird moth, or common clearwing (*Hemaris thysbe*), hovers like its namesake above a flower, uncoils its long tongue, and drinks nectar. Its body is olive green with plum red bands around it. Its wings are reddish brown when the moth first emerges from the cocoon, but the scales soon drop off in flight, leaving the wings nearly transparent. Many wild flowers, particularly wild fringed orchids, depend on moths and butterflies with their long tongues (proboscises) for pollination. The clearwing hovers over a wild, purple-fringed orchid, for example, unrolls its tongue, and thrusts it into the tubelike nectar sac below and behind the flower. Only such a long tongue could reach that nectar. On its way into the nectary, the moth's tongue brushes against a little wad of pollen (called a pollinium) set upon a tiny sticky disk. As the moth withdraws its tongue, the disk attaches to it, and the pollinium is pulled from its anther case. When the moth again drinks from another flower, the pollinium is pushed against the new flower's stigma, and the pollen adheres, pollinating the seed.

Hummingbird moth caterpillars feed on honeysuckle, a prime moth and butterfly larval food as well as an adult source of nectar. Where Japanese honeysuckle is plentiful (and wherever it grows, you can bet it is plentiful), clearwings and other flying insect jewels are apt to be abundant. But plant only the more bush-type honeysuckles that do not spread as pestiferously as the Japanese strain.

Cerisy's sphinx (*Smerinthus cerisyi*) sports beautiful roseblushed underwings, each of which is further adorned with a black and blue eyespot. The caterpillar is bluish green with a few diagonal yellow streaks and a green and yellow "horn" at the rear. Horns on moth and butterfly caterpillars look dangerous but are harmless. Many humans are fooled by them as much as birds are. The horn on a tobacco hornworm (the caterpillar of a large but dull-colored moth), does not sting, despite all folklore to the contrary.

Butterfly Beauties

The ability to scare with Halloweenlike disguises is even more pronounced in the caterpillars of the swallowtail butterfly family—butterflies that are equally as beautiful as the silkworm moths. The large, green caterpillars of the spicebush swallowtail (*Papilio troilus*) and the tiger swallowtail (*P. glaucus*) exhibit big fake eyes on their thoraxes, above their real eyes. On the spicebush swallowtail caterpillar, the mimicry is so faithful that there is a white line through the "pupil" that perfectly simulates the way light is reflected from a real eye. Most days, Smith relies strictly on the scientific theory of evolution to explain nature, but when he looks at the glint in a spicebush

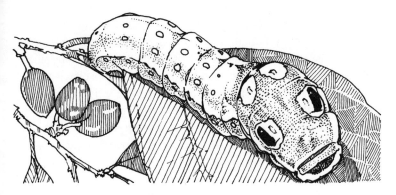

Eyespots and False Mouth on a Spicebush Swallowtail Caterpillar

swallowtail caterpillar's false eyes, he can only shake his head. Those fake eyes, he says, need only one more touch to make the dilemma of man's senses vs. his rationality complete: if only they could wink.

Below the fake eyes is a fake mouth that almost, but not quite, smiles. Near the fake mouth, a tongue snaps out, snakelike, when the worm is disturbed. It is fake, too, in reality a scent organ that can exude a pungent odor to repel predators when false faces fail.

On the other hand, a few caterpillars look so beautiful as to preclude harmfulness, yet they can sting rather painfully. The best example is the saddleback caterpillar moth (*Sibine stimulea*). The moth itself is rather nondescript and harmless, brown and black with several white dots. But the caterpillar is surely the most strikingly dressed worm in North America. Both ends of the caterpillar are plum-brown and the middle section green. Positioned in the center of the green, on the back, is a purplish brown saddle with a white border around it. There is also a white border between the green "blanket" and the two ends. Tufts of hairy bristles on the sides and ends give the worm the appearance of a miniature Scottish terrier wearing a plaid coat. But the side bristles can deliver a painful sting.

The caterpillar feeds on a wide variety of deciduous trees and shrubs, but hardly ever in populations dense enough to be harmful. Some manuals list it as a pest, but there's little justification in spraying this extravagant adornment of nature. Just don't try to pick it up with bare fingers.

The spicebush swallowtail's disguise in its larval stage serves it very well. Its favorite food is the spicebush (or benzoin) of the eastern

United States (*Lindera benzoin*). This mostly woodland bush, which blooms attractively yellow in very early spring, produces bright red fruit loved by wood thrushes. Without its disguise, the caterpillar might long ago have been lost to evolution by way of thrush diet. Butterflies have many ways of fooling birds. Entomologists theorize that the piercing colors some butterflies flash when they open their wings to flee a diving bird tend to surprise and scare the bird. The milkweed butterflies—the monarch (*Danaus plexippus*) and the queen (*D. gilippus berenice*)—need not often rely on such stratagems, however. Because of the bitter milkweed upon which they dine, they are toxic to birds, or at least distasteful enough so that a bird won't eat a second one. The viceroy butterfly (*Limenitis archippus*), a tasty morsel, looks so much like a monarch that birds avoid it, too, if they have tried eating a monarch before. Humans have learned to tell the two species apart easily, but fortunately for the viceroy, birds are slower learners. Monarch butterflies glide with wings at an angle, while the viceroy holds its wings horizontally.

Food Plants for Butterflies and Moths

Milkweed is one of the best plants for a butterfly garden because, like honeysuckle, it provides, simultaneously, larval food for caterpillars and nectar for adults. It is also a host plant for many interesting and beautiful insects besides the milkweed butterflies. The milkweed tiger moth, for example, is timid and silvery brown in color, but its caterpillar, which feeds on milkweed, is densely hairy, with long tufts of black and white hair at each end, and orange hair down the midline. Its unique appearance has earned the larva its own name apart from adulthood as a moth: the harlequin caterpillar.

Several beautiful beetles feed on milkweed, too, notably the red milkweed beetle (*Tetraopes tetraophthalmus*). Identify it by the four black dots on the head and black dots and streaks on its red body. This beetle can make a squeaking sound by rubbing together rough areas on its thorax, but Smith, who has tried to record the sound, says it will never compete with the cricket.

The milkweed tortoise beetle, or argus (*Chelymorpha cassidea*), is brick red or yellow with a translucent border around the edge of its back. There are six black dots on the foremost segment of the thorax (the pronotum). It prefers wild morning glory but eats milkweed routinely, along with other plants. Its most visual characteristic is its ability to stretch its bright red head grotesquely out beyond the pronotum, as if it were a tiny but evil one-eyed ogre.

The dogbane leaf beetle (*Chrysochus auratus*) feeds on milkweed and dogbane and rates as one of the most glamorous of insects— scintillating, metallic green with a metallic gloss of copper, brass, and blue on the elytra. The beetle exudes a foul-smelling secretion that birds seem to find offensive. The milkweed leaf beetle (*C. cobaltinus*) is similar, but not quite as garish, being a glossy dark bluish green on top and bluish black underneath.

Other insects are drawn to milkweed for nectar. Some also feed on foliage or flowers occasionally. The spring azure butterfly (*Celastrina argiolus*), which sometimes appears even before all the snow is gone, may lay eggs in the second generation on milkweed. The caterpillars exude a sweet honeydew that ants crave. The ants then protect the caterpillar from predators. Honeydew-exuding caterpillars of other species actually become guests of ants in their anthills and thus escape predation.

The best milkweed for butterflies seems to be *Asclepias tuberosa*, fittingly known as butterfly-weed. This roadside weed sports a cluster of bright orange flowers and thrives in dry sandy soil. Second best is the swamp milkweed (*A. incarnata*), which grows best in rich, wet soils. Its flower clusters are a dusty rose color. This milkweed is home for yet another leaf beetle, *Labidomera clivicollis*. It resembles a ladybird beetle but is slightly larger, with orange-yellow elytra overlaid with a black X.

Thistles do double duty as larval food and nectar source, too. The large swallowtails, especially the eastern black swallowtail (*Papilio polyxenes asterius*), seek out the purple thistle blooms for nectar. The painted lady (*Cynthia cardui*) uses thistles for larval food.

Hops and nettles are larval food for several butterflies. The common but beautiful red admiral (*Vanessa atalanta*), every gardener's companion, depends in particular on these two plants, as does the hop merchant (*Polygonia comma*). The question mark (*P. interrogationis*), another common but eye-catching species, likes hops and nettles but will also feed on elm, hackberry, and basswood trees. The question mark gets its name from a design on the underside of its wings, which is not easy to see, since the butterfly often rests with wings outspread rather than the characteristically folded, vertical position of most

The Underside of a Question Mark Butterfly

butterflies. Milbert's tortoise shell (*Nymphalis milberti*) feeds on nettles, too.

The butterfly lover should try to include in his tree grove not only the common deciduous trees that attract moths and swallowtail butterflies, but also a few that are not so common. Hackberry supports a whole family of butterflies, some quite showy, like the hackberry butterfly (*Asterocampa celtis*) and its cousin the tawny emperor (*A. clyton*). Unusual snout butterflies (*Libytheana bachmanii*) depend on hackberry, and the tree is the alternate choice not only of the larvae of the question mark, but also of the beautiful mourning cloak (*Nymphalis antiopa*). Sassafras is an alternate host plant for the spicebush swallowtail's caterpillar. Smith's favorite butterfly, the zebra swallowtail (*Graphium marcellus*) feeds in the larval stage exclusively on papaw. Smith grows papaw trees for that reason, but so far, in vain. He believes there are no nearby wild papaws to support a native population of zebra swallowtails that could be attracted to his trees.

Other beautiful butterflies are equally as host-specific. The California dog face larva (*Colias eurydice*) feeds on false indigo and is found only where the climate is favorable to this plant. Larvae of the great purple hairstreak (*Atlides halesus*) eat mistletoe on live oak trees. The rare bright blue copper (*Lycaena heteronea*) depends for larval food on a few buckwheat species that grow wild in southern California.

Sometimes a somewhat rare butterfly increases in numbers because of human fads in plants. A century ago, the pipevine swallowtail (*Battus philenor*) lived mainly on Virginia snakeroot and was seldom seen in backyards. About the beginning of this century, Dutchman's-pipe (*Aristolochia durior*), of the same plant family as Virginia snakeroot, became a popular ornamental. The big, greenish black swallowtail found the plant to its liking and flourished. Now that pipevine is out of favor and seldom planted, the swallowtail has also become scarcer.

Not all butterfly larvae are vegetarians. The caterpillar of the harvester (*Feniseca tarquinius*) eats aphids and scale insects and thus is particularly beneficial in the garden and orchard. It is found most often where alders abound, because the caterpillar seems to prefer aphids on alder. The butterfly is brownish orange above, with purplish brown spots and specklings. As the caterpillar eats aphids, it puts the sticky filaments it draws from the aphids on its back, where they look somewhat like hair. The worm keeps piling on these filaments as it eats, as a disguise and for protection. The harvester ranges over most of the United States and southern Canada, east of the Great Plains.

Every region has its butterflies, no matter how hot or cold the climate. The buckeye (*Precis coenia*) and the gulf fritillary (*Agraulis vanillae*) are southern standouts. The former's larvae feed on snapdragon, monkey-flower, plantain, stonecrop, and other low-growing herbs. The latter larvae feed on the leaves of passion-flower. The checkerspot butterflies (*Chlosyne* spp.) in the larval stage feed on various asters and are found mostly in the northern half of the United States. The alpine butterflies (*Erebia* spp.) overwinter successfully in Alaskan temperatures of $-70°F$ and their larvae live on saxifrages and sedums. The beautiful white and black, red-dotted phoebus (*Parnassius phoebus*) inhabits cold mountains and Arctic tundra and feeds on low-growing stonecrops.

At least one beautiful butterfly is considered a garden pest in the larval stage. The black swallowtail (*Papilio polyxenes asterius*) is revealed by its popular names: parsley swallowtail, celery swallowtail, and carrot swallowtail. Mostly black, with a row of yellow spots across the lower half of the wings, yellow crescents along the lower border of the wings, and blue coloring and two red dots in the middle between the tails, this common butterfly never fails to delight and astonish observers as it alights on clover and thistles, seeking nectar. It is one of the few effective pollinators of red clover other than bumblebees.

The caterpillar is green, with a black head, black bands around each segment, and gold spots sprinkled liberally over the body. Smith allows them to eat carrot tops and some parsley, and swears that in 25 years he has never seen them do any significant damage. Besides, he says, one black swallowtail is worth more than a whole bushel of carrots or a truckload of celery.

One of the enchantments of observing butterflies—besides their variety and beauty—is the possibility of contributing new knowledge to human understanding of them. At least 12,000 species of moths and butterflies flutter in North America (125,000 worldwide), and not all of them have been classified yet. Life histories of some that are classified are not complete. With a few years of spare-time study, a devotee could turn a backyard butterfly sanctuary into a research laboratory, just as did the famous entomologist, Henri Fabre.

Butterflies and moths contribute significantly to plant pollination and are sometimes indispensable. Often, pollination involves an almost unbelievable symbiosis between certain plants and insects in assuring the continued existence of both. For example, the yucca of the Southwest could not reseed itself without the work of a tiny, white-winged *Pronuba* moth. Nor could the moth survive without the yucca. The particular yucca involved blooms at night, usually only one night, but by some mysterious process, on that night the *Pronuba* has emerged from its pupal stage and is ready to lay eggs. The blossom opens, allowing the moth to enter. With a special set of mouth parts (palpi), the moth scrapes together a ball of pollen and carries it to a second plant, thus ensuring cross-pollination. There, it lays its eggs in a hole in the ovary wall of the flower, then climbs down to the blossom (the blossoms hang downward on this species of yucca), and crams the ball of pollen into the stigma at the end of the flower's pistil. If then flies off, its job finished. Since there seems to be no direct benefit to the moth from this final action, science is again faced with a phenomenon that is difficult, if not impossible, to explain by the theory of evolution. The eggs, usually 4 or 5 in number, hatch, and invariably, each worm eats about 20 seeds, leaving just enough to ensure the spread of the yucca.

The tiny wasp that fertilizes the Smyrna fig is another awe-evoking creature. The Smyrna fig is a weird fruit to begin with—its flower actually blooms inside the fig. The little *Blastophaga* wasp can get to it only by crawling through a tiny hole in the end of the fruit. But the wasp does not lay its eggs in the Smyrna fig. Instead, it crawls inside the fig's wild cousin, the caprifig, which does not produce good fruit, only what are called gall figs. The males hatch first, chew out of their respective galls, chew into the galls where the females are hatching, mate, and die. The females scramble out over the male caprifig flowers, picking up a load of pollen, and then fly to the domestic Smyrna fig, which possesses only female flowers. The female wasp crawls inside the Smyrna, looking for a suitable place to lay her eggs, but mysteriously, does not lay them. She flies to another Smyrna and again is not satisfied with the egg-laying conditions there. But the pollen from the wild caprifig pollinates every Smyrna she enters, thus assuring the development of fruit. Eventually, the wasp flies to another caprifig, lays her eggs in the galls, and another generation of wasps is assured. When California growers first brought Smyrnas to this country, the trees produced no figs until caprifigs were planted nearby.

Destruction of habitat endangers many species of moths and butterflies. A few have already become extinct, like the sthenele brown, gone from its locale around San Francisco. The bay checkerspot in the same area is now threatened. Unlike whales and rhinos, which need the support of an international community to survive, butterflies can be saved from extinction by *individuals* who own backyards and gardens and think of these areas as tiny wildlife habitats.

Other Worthwhile Insects

The wildlife sanctuary that sustains butterflies and moths will contain a full complement of beetles, too. Some beetles are "bad" to humans because they eat the plants humans want to eat; some beetles are "good" to man because they eat insects that are "bad" to humans. Be that as it may, there are beetles as beautiful as any butterfly, and as Smith likes to say, quoting the noted entomologist Alexander Klots, they are "unquestionably the outstanding order of insects." (If you doubt that, look at Bernard Durin's lifelike paintings of beetles in *Insects* by Gerhard Scherer.)

Fireflies are one of the most common—and most uncommon—of the beetles. Smith once gathered a jar full of them, or rather persuaded his son and daughter to gather them, then tried to read the newspaper by their light in a dark room. If he held the jar against the paper he could see a word or two. Humans have isolated and identified all the substances involved in firefly light, or believe they have, but have not been able to develop a lighting system from them. If humans do harness "bioluminescence," they will have gone a long way toward solving their energy problem. Firefly light is far more efficient than electric light, as it produces no heat and therefore loses only a minuscule part of energy as compared to the energy lost from artificial lights.

Humans have names for the firefly's magic, but the firefly has the magic. The cells on its sixth and seventh segments contain a fatty substance that produces light when it oxidizes. The cells are called photocytes and the substance, luciferin. Oxygen is transmitted to the luciferin through tiny tubes, and the firefly's nervous system transmits a signal, apparently at the command of the firefly, that activates the process. Three other substances cooperate with the luciferin to turn on the firefly light: magnesium, luciferase, which is an enzyme, and adenosine triphosphate.

As the Beekeeper loves to point out, if one can correctly name these substances in a wise tone of voice, he is considered by the rest of mankind as "learned." But actually, knowing names that humans make up for realities is only the most rudimentary kind of knowledge. It's also arbitrary, because as the number of names increases, scientists are constantly reclassifying and renaming their discoveries. The firefly is obviously better informed, even though it does not know anything at all about adenosine triphosphate, and its intelligence is instinctive rather than rational. The flashes of light it produces are coded messages. Usually the male, flying in the air, is the first to send out what amounts to love calls. The female on or near the ground (the females of some species can't fly at all) returns the message. Scientists have thought, occasionally, that they have cracked some rather complex secret codes between fireflies, but beyond their basic business of signaling each other for mating, little is known for sure. Different species seem to have different codes. And females of cannibalistic species can mimic the flashing code of other species to lure a male to its death!

Firefly light varies in color. *Photinus pyralis,* a common firefly, has a light that tends to be yellowish, while *Photuris pennsylvanicus,* found in the eastern United States, has a greenish light.

Fireflies are beneficial beyond the gift of their teardrops of limpid light over the summer night lawn. Their larvae eat slugs, snails, and various insect larvae. Predatory firefly larvae do not pupate and become adults until their third summer. Then, in one glorious, short-lived fling, they flash off, mate, lay eggs, and die. The larvae overwinter in the ground. They possess the power of bioluminescence also, and are known popularly as glowworms.

Ground beetles are often dull of color, but at least two are both handsome and beneficial. The green pubescent (*Chlaenius sericeus*) is mostly green, as its name indicates, and eats slugs and snails. The European ground beetle (*Carabus nemoralis*) is particularly desirable around the garden, since its favorite food is cutworm. The European is dull black overall, but the hard wings (the elytra) that cover most of its back are violet or greenish bronze, with three rows of tiny pits on each. The pronotum has iridescent violet ridges around front and sides.

Tiger beetles are beautiful and beneficial, too. Humans seldom have to hunt for the shiny green tiger beetle (*Cicindela sexguttata*) because it seems to seek out humans who are walking along the woodland paths it likes so well. Smith always sees one at the far edge of his grove. He has decided that the beetle comes out of hiding because it thinks the human will inadvertently chase small spiders and insects into its grasp. (The barn swallows always follow the Dumb Farmer when he fires up his old tractor and chugs across the meadow. They want to catch the insects that fly up, flushed out by the noise and movement of the tractor.)

The fiery searcher, or caterpillar hunter (*Calosoma scrutator*), is one of the most handsome of large beetles. It eats caterpillars, and so should inhabit any butterfly garden. It especially likes tent caterpillars. Unusual among beetles or any insects, the adult lives up to three years. It ranges over the entire United States. Its principal color is iridescent, greenish gold, with purple and reddish legs and a gold border around the elytra. It can exude a liquid that burns skin, so it's best not to pick it up with bare hands. Its cousins, *C. calidum* and *C. sycophanta,* are nearly as beautiful.

The stag beetles are another family of large, striking insects, dark reddish brown to black in color, and possessing large antlerlike jaws, especially the males. The elephant stag (*Lucanus elephus*), measuring up to 4 inches in length, is especially vicious-looking. The stags can pinch with their wicked-looking mandibles, although rather harmlessly, so are often called pinching bugs. They are beneficial insects because their larvae feed mostly on dead wood, turning it into rich compost to fertilize the forest. The adults eat little or nothing but are attracted to nectar and artificial light. Humans generally see them around porch lights, or next morning on their backs on the patio, where they have fallen, unable to right themselves. Don't step on the seemingly frightful creature. Turn him over so he can escape. To lure from hiding the beautiful reddish-brown stag (*Pseudolucanus capreolus*), set out some fermented sugar water or wine near an artificial light.

The metallic wood-boring beetles (*Buprestis* spp.) are also most beautiful, but like the lustrous Japanese beetle, too pestiferous to rate "favorite" status.

The checkered beetles are small, hardly ever more than an inch long, but they are often brightly colored and are quite beneficial, since the larvae of many species eat bark beetles and grasshoppers. The red-blue *Trichodes nutalli* is one of the prettiest, but as a beneficial its reputation is somewhat checkered, too. Adults prey on thrips and other small insects, and eat pollen. They almost always are found on flowers (east of the Rockies, mostly), where they also lay their eggs. The larvae attach themselves to bees and wasps that visit the flowers, and the latter unwittingly carry them back to the nest, where the worms feed on bee and wasp larvae.

Probably the most beneficial beetles are the ladybugs (family Coccinellidae), without which the world might be overrun with aphids and scale insects. The commonest explanation for the name ladybug, or ladybird, has it that the pious country folk of the Middle Ages dedicated the little beetles to Mary, the mother of Jesus, known then as well as now among Catholics as Our Lady. They wanted to honor the beetles for polishing off an insect invasion in the grape fields. But ladybug beetles were considered sacred long before that and were associated closely with the ancient Germanic fertility goddess, Freya. For all the thousands of years since then, it has been "bad luck to kill a ladybug." Since each of a ladybug's 200 or so larvae can eat 100 aphids a day, sometimes 40 in an hour, and since the adult can wolf down its share, too, killing a ladybug is, indeed, bad luck.

There are many kinds of bright red-orange ladybugs, usually distinguished into species by the number of spots on their back. The bright color is thought to be a warning to predators, since ladybugs can exude an acrid fluid from openings on their legs. Some predators eat them anyway. Adult ladybugs often hibernate together in large numbers in woods, under rocks or leafy debris. These sites should be noted carefully and should be preserved in the backyard sanctuary.

Most butterflies, moths, and beetles are smaller, and therefore possibly not so striking to the eye as the ones described previously. But that makes them no less beautiful to the observant bug watcher. The bug watcher (like the birdwatcher) moves from an interest in the gaudiest and largest butterflies and moths to the smaller beauties, then is taken by spiders, dragonflies, and beetles—the latter sometimes the most resplendently colored insects of all. Finally, as Smith has learned, it becomes impossible to walk across even a lawn without a pleasant distraction coming from the insect world.

Chapter 7

The Most
Misunderstood Wildlife

Fillet of a fenny snake
In the cauldron boil and bake.
Eye of newt and toe of frog
Wool of bat and tongue of dog
Adder's fork and blind-worm's sting,
Lizard's leg and owlet's wing.
For a charm of powerful trouble
Like a hell-broth boil and bubble.

Shakespeare, from *Macbeth,* act 4, scene 1

Human culture has steeped us all in prejudices about certain animals. Many of us have learned to fear without discrimination all snakes, lizards, owls, skunks, bats, vultures, spiders, wasps, and even toads, because they either can inflict possible harm upon us, or simply look as if they could. In folklore and literature, these animals are invariably portrayed as villains, their imagined villainy indirectly encouraging the killer impulse in man to destroy them. Real danger comes from only a very few species of these animals, and that danger is exceedingly exaggerated. Most of these animals are, in truth, not harmful to mankind and, in fact, are extremely beneficial.

Smith and the Beekeeper like to argue about why snakes are so universally feared. Smith believes the response is learned from the culture and is not innate or instinctive. He likes to tell the story about the boy in his boarding school, who carried little ring-neck snakes around in his pocket. One day, to the astonishment of his classmates, he pulled one such snake from his pocket, wrapped it in a piece of bread, and proceeded to bite off its tail.

Actually, Smith points out, the boy was somewhat calculating even in this grotesque display. The little ring-neck snake is accustomed to losing its tail to predators. Upon being threatened in its natural environment, it curls up and turns the orange underside of its tail to clear view. The hungry predator—a hawk, skunk, owl, or even a large frog—snaps at the orange blob, mistaking it for the snake's head. The ring-neck slithers away, minus its tail but still alive.

The Beekeeper does not think human revulsion for snakes is learned from folklore and literature's portrayal of snakes as evil—for example, as the devil in the Garden of Eden—but from an earlier evolutionary period when snakes and other reptiles *were* a great danger to humans. Man first evolved in a warm climate, the Beekeeper declares, proven by the fact that he is nearly hairless. In man's habitat then, there were many more dangerous reptiles than there are today. When humans react to a snake by screaming and running, they react from an instinctive fear, well grounded in ancient practicality. When, on second thought, they come back and kill the snake, they are demonstrating why man survived, while so many of the ancient reptiles did not. Or so the Beekeeper believes.

The Dumb Farmer is no help in the matter. He sides with neither Smith nor the Beekeeper, rather accepting both their arguments as possibilities. Unlike them, though, he maintains that human fear of snakes actually safeguards the animals more than it endangers them, and in any event, he is prepared to use this fear to his own benefit. As the only farmer in the neighborhood, he is looked upon as something of an authority on nature, a fact that privately amuses him. He knows that farmers in general understand very little about the natural world around their farms. Indeed, farmers have been the chief perpetrators of erroneous folklore about snakes: that blue racers chase and attack children; that milk snakes suck milk from cows; that hoop snakes curl up into the shape of bicycle tires and roll down hills; that some snakes stab victims with the sharp end of their tails; that snakes swallow their young to protect them. In this folklore context, owls seen in daylight are a sign of death in the family, frogs generate spontaneously from lumps of mud (a misconception even Aristotle entertained), hawks kill only chickens, and toads cause warts. Many farmers still kill hawks, owls, and snakes and hang them on their fences along the road to boast of their mighty deeds. The Dumb Farmer acknowledges with a wry smile, "They don't know they're killing their best friends." Nevertheless, the Dumb Farmer has found it convenient to encourage human fear of snakes in an attempt to keep the suburban population that surrounds his farm from trampling his crops, breaking down his fences, and causing the kind of thoughtless mischief that some people always visit upon property they have no vested interest in. When trailbikers threatened to turn his woodlot into the Indianapolis Speedway, he popularized the story of the "hanging blacksnakes." From his own past experience, he knew that during the first warm days of spring, the big but harmless blacksnake that lived in the bank of his pond would come out to sun itself and look for a mate. Often it would climb up into a bush or small tree, off the still-cool earth, to take in the sun.

So, the Dumb Farmer called the young reporter from the new Suburban Life newspaper and asked if she would like to see a snake 6 feet long and as big around as his wrist—right here in the tame and tranquil environment of suburban life. The story, complete with a photograph of a huge, vicious-looking snake hanging out of a tree, was one of the most unforgettable articles ever to appear in the paper. In a second photo, there was the Dumb Farmer, the honest, reliable tiller of the soil, staring solemnly into the camera, discussing how blacksnakes often hang in trees, waiting to drop upon unwary passersby, and how they liked nothing better than to choose a spot over a woodland trail, sort of like, well, *exactly* like the eroded trails the motorbikers were chewing into his woods.

The resulting publicity cut down on the number of trespassers using his pond for swimming and fishing without permission, but it was a skunk that by chance solved the Dumb Farmer's trailbike problem. Unlike snakes, the skunk does not try to run away at the approach of a human being. The skunk does not know the meaning of running away, its awful smell allowing it to view the entire world with lofty disdain. It is the Dumb Farmer's opinion that a teenager on a trailbike has a condescending view of the world, similar to that of a skunk. Once astride his mount, his senses of propriety and politeness vanish. He feels justified, even obliged, to ride wherever his wheels can take him, spewing his gaseous exhausts and earsplitting noises rudely upon the rest of creation.

In the Dumb Farmer's woods, trailbiker and skunk met. As could have been predicted, neither felt inclined to step aside. Trailbiker revved and roared. Skunk snorted and spread its tail high and wide in its classic pose of warning. Trailbiker popped a wheely. Skunk wheeled, and the two tiny but potent jets on either side of its anus fired, point-blank. At 5 feet, the first trailbiker was an easy mark. The second, skidding to a halt just 10 feet away, was also within range. A third, stopping just beyond accurate range, received only a drop or two of the potent butylmercaptom, but even that was enough to render bike and rider both exceedingly unsavory company. It was weeks before either of the first two bikes could be ridden without a wave of nausea being felt by their young owners, who lived with that odor for a week, despite numerous scrubbings with tomato juice.

The Beekeeper claims that the incident was not happenstance. He says that the Dumb Farmer planned it all—that's why he was feeding milk to the skunks at his barn. The Dumb Farmer only smiles, mischievously.

Skunks

The skunk is actually a rather peaceful creature. Males are short-tempered in spring when they are looking for mates, but there are many instances on record of humans taking skunks out of traps or removing tin cans stuck on the heads of the curious animals without getting sprayed. De-scented skunks make interesting pets, although they can be somewhat surly when their daily routines are changed. The only real danger from a wild skunk is that it can carry rabies and can transmit the disease by biting other animals, such as cows. Such incidences are rare, but they can occur.

Counterposed against that one drawback (and remember, man's best friend, the dog, is much more likely to pass rabies on to humans) are the skunk's many beneficial qualities. The naturalist Earnest Thompson Seton said, "Every skunk is the guardian angel of a garden acre." Skunks eat a wide variety of food, including yellow jackets, snakes, and mice, but mostly they dine on insects and insect larvae. A study of 1,700 skunk stomachs showed that the contents were over half insects and larvae, the rest being mainly mice and earthworms, with some turtle eggs, fruit, grain, and birds. The skunk loves Japanese beetles and will gorge on gypsy moth caterpillars, two very good reasons why the little black and white furbearer should be encouraged.

Skunks are clean animals, building a new nest for every litter. They never get their spray on themselves, although the Dumb Farmer says that the young, playing rough and tumble among themselves like a bunch of kittens, sometimes get carried away and inadvertently emit a bit of odor. When Mother leads her family out for a night of hunting, the young follow single file behind her in a most endearing way. Should one wander off the track, it easily becomes lost, since skunks do not see well at any distance. Then it whines and cries like a baby until Mother fetches it back in line again.

Skunks going about their business of hunting food will pass very close to a human standing quietly, without sensing the person's presence, or paying any attention if they do notice. David Brendan Hopes, in a March, 1982, *Audubon* magazine article, "I Heard the Skunk Sing," tells of sitting on one end of a log while a skunk made a nest at the other end, humming contentedly as it went about its task.

Skunk fur is beautiful and goes in and out of fashion for fur coats. Black skunk fur used to be called Alaskan sable in the trade. The white stripe down the back and over the forehead of the common skunk (*Mephitis mephitis*) varies in width and length. The less white in the

Skunk and Young

pelt (and, therefore, the more black), the more valuable it is considered. Two other varieties of skunks live in the Southwest—the hooded skunk (*Mephitis macroura*) and the hognose skunk (*Conepatus leuconotus*). The latter is quite rare.

Snakes

Snakes, like skunks, are pets to some people, phobias to others. But of the many species in the United States, only a few are dangerously venomous, and even bites from these snakes are rarely fatal. How many snakebite deaths do you hear of? Rattlesnakes (*Crotalus* and *Sistrurus* spp.) are the most widely distributed of the venomous snakes. Copperheads and cottonmouths (*Agkistrodon* spp.) range more southerly, copperheads most often in upland habitats from the mid-South to the lower North, and cottonmouths residing in southern swamplands. Although people rarely die of rattlesnake bites, much less from those of copperheads or cottonmouths, all three must be considered dangerous. Complications from the bite of a rattler are exacerbated if the bitten person panics and runs for help. Try to stay calm and walk or call for help. If a healthy person is bitten and is alone in the woods more than an hour from help, he or she is best off sitting quietly and sweating out the pain, say snake experts. Drinking alcoholic beverages does not help, and may, in fact, be dangerous. A snakebite kit certainly does help. Cutting incisions into the bite and trying to suck out the venom may or may not help, depending on the experience of the person performing the operation. Arteries have been cut in this way, causing a loss of blood more dangerous than the snakebite.

Coral snakes (*Micrurus* spp.), quite dangerous, are limited to the Gulf region and a small part of the extreme Southwest. They are banded red, yellow, and black. Other harmless but similar-looking snakes are banded with the same colors in different arrangements. Folklore best tells men when to beware:

> *Red next to black, friend of Jack;*
> *Red next to yellow, kill a fellow.*

Identifying our native pit vipers—rattlers, copperheads, and cottonmouths—is not easy for the neophyte. Hundreds of beneficial brown water snakes are killed in southern swamp areas every year by people who insist that the snakes are cottonmouths. Trying to identify these poisonous pit vipers by the telltale pit is not easy, either. Some beginners mistake the nostril every snake has for a pit, and kill the snake. The pit appears as a dark dot below the eye and between it and the nostril. These pits have a remarkable use as a sort of snake radar that's so sensitive they can "feel" the heat from warm-blooded prey at night. The snake sways its head back and forth in the darkness so that it can get a fix on the exact location of the source of heat and, if a foot or less away, strike out accurately to kill it.

The rattlesnake has rattles to identify it, but other harmless snakes can also coil up and quiver their tails, mimicking the rattler. In dry leaves, the sound is much like that of a rattler. Beneficial black rat snakes can put on this act expertly.

The rattlers, copperheads, and cottonmouths do have heads more pronouncedly triangular in shape, although this is not a sure identifying sign for the beginner, who has not compared snake heads very often. The copperhead has a distinctive coppery-colored head and body with hourglass-shaped crossbands at fairly regular spacings. Most other brown-and-black-splotched snakes have more irregular patterns. Again, unless one has had opportunity to compare copperheads with similar-looking snakes, identification is difficult. The cottonmouth, as the name implies, appears nearly pure white inside its jaws, but, as with looking at pits, when one is close enough to peer into the mouth of the snake, one is perhaps too close for safety. The best protection in venomous-snake country is to wear good high-top boots and to avoid reaching onto rock ledges or under logs, boards, or rocks on the ground without seeing what's there first.

Snakes are more afraid of humans than vice versa and generally do not strike unless they cannot escape or they are inadvertently stepped on. In the food web, poisonous snakes, particularly rattlesnakes, are very beneficial, eating many pest rabbits and rats.

Thanks to the movies, the Gila monster of the Southwest, like the rattlesnake, has been given an image of great danger in the popular mind. But the little reptile has no fangs and must chew pretty hard on its victims to inject any venom. Authority Natt N. Dodge says that it would be very difficult for a Gila to bite a human poisonously unless it were teased or handled or stepped upon by a barefooted person. "Please do not kill or capture them," he pleads. "These interesting lizards are a unique feature of native wildlife threatened with extinction."

Other American snakes are among the most beneficial predators in the food web, and they will bite to protect themselves only if there is no alternative. Their bites are nonpoisonous and relatively harmless, unless, of course, infection sets in, as with any bite. A nonpoisonous snakebite might leave teeth marks in a half-moon shape (if any mark at all), readily distinguished from the two-puncture wound of poisonous fangs.

The milk snake (*Lampropeltis triangulum*) is a beautiful, smooth-skinned, totally beneficial snake that is often ignorantly killed. The milk snake is often encountered by humans because it eats rats and mice that live where humans live. In fact, another name for milk snake is house snake. Because it frequents barns (another habitat of mice), folklore over the centuries included tales that the snake sucked milk from cows, which gave farmers another excuse for killing one of their best friends. The milk snake can vibrate the tip of its tail somewhat like a rattler, which doesn't help its relationship with humans, either. It varies in coloring from light brown to brown with irregular patches of light tan, with nearly white blotchings sometimes intermingled. The skin is shiny smooth, not rough like that of a garter snake. The milk snake belongs to the king snake family, a large and very beneficial family that includes species that prey on rattlesnakes and are apparently immune to rattlesnake poison.

Snakes commonly called blacksnakes are usually the black rat snake, *Elaphe obsoleta* (of which the Dumb Farmer's tree-climbing blacksnake is one). They could be blue racers (*Coluber* spp.), which are skinnier snakes than blacksnakes, and rounder. The blacksnake is a constrictor that crushes the life out of its prey, then eats it. The milk snake coils around its prey, but only to hold it. All snakes are able to swallow prey much larger than their bodies, but oddly enough, their skins will not expand as they grow, and must be periodically shed and replaced by a new skin.

Garter snakes (*Thamnophis* spp.) are very common, especially in gardens and deep grass. They vary widely in coloring, predominantly some shade of brown and yellow striping, although sometimes they sport a bit of bluish and greenish coloration. Although they eat small toads, they make up for it by eating many slugs and insects. Garter snakes should be encouraged to live in the garden. A good way to do this is by mulching parts of the garden with a light straw or hay, something the snake can crawl under for shade during the day. A few piles of fluffed-up lawn clippings on top of tall grass also make ideal

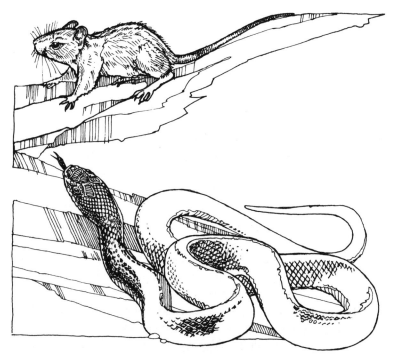

Blacksnake Stalking a Rat

shelters for them. On a good, ecologically sound farm, the Dumb Farmer will tell you, garter snakes love to crawl under hay windrows in the field during the heat of the day. So do other snakes. Sometimes they are baled up alive with the hay. The Dumb Farmer likes to tell the story about the fellows making hay in rattlesnake country and complaining about how heavy the bales were, which they had to hoist up onto the hay wagon. As he picked up one bale by the twines that bound it, the loudest complainer heard what was to him the familiar and ominous sound. He heard a rattlesnake's rattles coming from the underside of the bale, just as he was about to heave it up onto the wagon. "He gave a holler and flung the bale clean over the wagon and off the other side," says the Dumb Farmer.

Common water snakes (*Natrix* spp.) frequent streams and ponds where minnows live, often lying in wait under rocks to lash out at passing minnows. They stick their heads out of the water and flash their forked red tongues in what appears to humans as a very unfriendly manner. Actually, snakes use their tongues this way as part of their sensory system. Filaments on the tongue literally can lick odors out of the air or off dust particles in the air, and transmit them to an organ on the roof of the mouth (Jacobson's organ, its called) where identification both by taste and by smell is made. Water snakes bear their young live, as do garters. Rat snakes lay eggs.

One of the most beautiful of all snakes, the green snake (*Ophiodrys* spp.), is quite common, though seldom seen because of its coloration. Its pale green body blends so well with the tall meadow grasses it prefers that it is nearly invisible. These snakes prey on insects, chiefly butterfly and moth larvae, so a wildlife sanctuary planned to attract butterflies (see Chapter 7, A Butterfly Sanctuary) should attract green snakes also. The rough green snake particularly likes the larvae of the wax moth, a scourge of honeybee hives in which the moth likes to lay its eggs. The larvae then destroy the bee hive by eating the waxen cells. The snakes are rather docile, patient animals for handling. As a boy, Smith would try to tie their long, slender bodies into knots (not a wise thing to do if the knots are tight enough to harm the snake). No matter how complex the knot, the snake would untie itself with consummate ease.

The most interesting common snake to observe is the hognose snake (*Heterodon* spp.), which lives primarily on toads. Disturbed by a human, the snake hisses in a most ugly manner and rears and flattens its head precisely like a cobra, a stance that is supposed to strike terror into the hearts of man and animal alike. Hognose, also called a puff adder, is a great faker. If its cobra act does not vanquish danger, it goes into its opossum act and plays dead.

The brown snake (*Storeria* spp.), often called city snake because it frequents urban areas, and the worm snake (*Carphophis* spp.) eat slugs and earthworms.

Bats

To humans, the bat is an ugly creature. Cornered, the mouselike animal with the humanoid face bares its little teeth hideously, and all the cultural biases of literature and folklore reinforce our repugnance at the sight. Yet bats are entirely beneficial little animals as extremely effective controllers of many pest bugs. It is possible, but rare, for a bat to carry rabies. Other than this slight blemish on its character, bats in the United States are not harmful. Species in other countries can transmit a disease to cattle by biting them in the neck and withdrawing blood, which is probably the source of the amazing, ludicrous folklore about vampires, but none such live in the United States. Bats do not attack humans, nor will they become tangled in long hair.

Bats know exactly where they are going, even in total darkness. As they fly, they emit a high-frequency sound inaudible to the human ear. Echoes of their cries bounce off walls, trees, and flying objects, relaying information to the bat that enables it to avoid collision and to chase after insects. This amazing bit of biological technology is called echolocation. If you want to test it, locate a bat flying around above you at twilight, then toss a small object into the air in its general vicinity. Even in complete darkness, the bat will react immediately and dive for the object accurately due to its acute hearing.

Not all bats roost by day in dark caves, attics, or barns. Red bats (*Lasiurus borealis*) hang with wings folded from dark, shady limbs of trees, looking so much like dead leaves that they are rarely noticed. Some bats migrate like birds: the red bat, the silver-haired bat (*Lasionycteris noctivagans*), and the hoary bat (*Lasiurus cinereus*). Other common bats that might frequent a backyard are the big brown bat (*Eptisicus fuscus*), the small brown bat (*Myotis lucifugus*), Keen's bat (*M. keenii*), the least brown bat (*M. subulatus*), and the Seminole bat (*Lasiurus seminolus*). Bats are not faring well in the struggle with humans for space. Some species are endangered, like the Indiana bat (*Myotis sodalis*). Encourage bats. Help children see their beauty. Can all that Halloween goblin and bat garbage.

Owls

One of the less brilliant statements the supposedly wise Pliny wrote centuries ago was this little diatribe against one of civilization's best friends:

> *The screech owl always betokens some heavy news and is most execrable and accursed. In the summer he is the very monster of the night, neither singing nor crying out clear, but uttering a certain heavy groan of doleful mourning, and therefore if it be seen to fly abroad in any place (in daylight) it foretells some fearful misfortune.*

The flight of the screech owl does foretell fearful misfortune, but only for cutworms, grasshoppers, locusts, moths, mice, rats, and other prey of the little robin-size owl. The famous ornithologist Edward Howe Forbush said the screech owl seemed to have "a marked predilection for destructive insects." This owl, whose ear tufts stick up like little horns to help identify it, can be either gray or red in color. The colorations have no connection to age, season, or sex.

The screech owl lives close to humans and often can become one of the regular inhabitants of your backyard. It prefers a hollow tree for a home but will readily take to a nesting box. Formerly, many nested in old hollow apple trees in orchards and preyed on pine voles, which orchardists now try to control with expensive and dangerous poisons.

The screech owl's regular night song is a hauntingly beautiful, high, tremulous wail — Pliny was tone deaf. The sound is best described by the southern name for the bird, "shivering owl." The song also will send a shiver down the spine of those unfamiliar with owl sounds. When one hoots in your yard at night, react positively, not fearfully, teaching children the beauty inherent in the song.

The screech owl is not particularly fearful of humans, especially at nesting time, and will dive at and even attack a person who approaches its young. It gives warning first, however, snapping its beak loudly. There is an ornithological report of a screech owl that flew down a chimney and snatched a canary right out of its cage, so the Beekeeper says. Another supposedly nested in one compartment of a martin house. And, says the Beekeeper, the screech owl has a unique way of disguising itself. If humans approach its roosting place on a limb, it will elongate its body until it looks more like a dead branch-stub than a bird.

Another owl that does not mind humans nearby is the barn owl. It will readily make its home in a barn, as its name indicates, but just as often in church belfries and other city buildings. The barn owl may be the best rodent control available to man, but its ghostly appearance more often than not makes humans fearful. The black coloring around the eyes, surrounded by its bone-white face, set off sharply from the rest of the head by a thin brownish border, gives the impression of a skull with large, luminous eyes. Like the screech owl, the barn owl's supposed foreboding of death pertains only to rodents. Ornithologists have found as many as 189 dead mice next to a barn owl nest. Barn owl parents have brought as many as 16 mice, 3 gophers, a rat, and a squirrel to the nest in a half hour.

Somewhat surprisingly, the great horned owl and the barred owl can become fixtures of suburban backyards if there are patches of forest nearby. Both these owls will persist in staying in a woodland they like, even when housing developments move in. Smith's neighborhood has a couple of horned owls because of the Friends' cemetery nearby. The cemetery was established in the 1600s, and for going on three centuries, the trees have been virtually unmolested unless they fell down naturally. Although the good Quakers may not know it, they support this great and majestic bird by keeping the large old oaks alive. The great horned owls return the favor by preying heavily on rabbits, rats, and occasionally on skunks. The Dumb Farmer is not altogether pleased with this last development, but he endures it because of another marvelous characteristic of the owls. They prey on stray cats. Since feral cats, a by-product of human habitation, are presently the greatest danger to all songbirds, the Dumb Farmer says he would breed

Great Horned Owl

horned owls if he could, raise them on cat meat, and turn them loose. Perhaps they'd develop a taste for stray dogs, too, he says, hopefully.

Great horned owls do not always fare well in more rural areas. Since the big owl has been known to kill chickens and will take a game bird or songbird occasionally, that is all the excuse the gun-happy shooters need to kill them, which is illegal. Smith kept track of the prey a great horned owl brought to its nest in the cemetery one spring. The take was almost entirely rats. Of the few birds, most were blue jays (a nest robber), starlings (a pest), and one cardinal.

One can expect to see certain other owls in the backyard only rarely. The little saw-whet owl (*Aegolius acadicus acadica*), smaller than a robin, usually frequents northern coniferous forests. The snowy owl (*Nyctea scandiaca*), a large bird of striking beauty, comes south into the United States only occasionally, during winters when mice, lemmings, and rabbits are scarce in their northern haunts. The short-eared owl (*Asio flammeus*) prefers open country and nests on the ground. The long-eared owl (*Asio otus*) could show up in a backyard (although it hunts in open fields) if the sanctuary contained some dense evergreens and there were little other cover in the surrounding agricultural lands. These owls have a habit of hunting in small flocks, sweeping by night over open fields for mice, then roosting by day in clumps of dense evergreens. In danger, the owl will expand its feathers like a strutting turkey to make itself look larger than it is.

Contrary to popular belief, owls can see in the daylight, and some, like the barred owl, can see very well. Their seeming bewilderment on being attacked by a flock of birds during the day might be more a matter of lethargy than eyesight, as many a bird has learned by getting too close to the owl it was teasing. Owls can't roll their eyes, nor do they have much peripheral vision; they must turn their heads to see to the side. But so agile are their necks that they can turn their heads completely backwards without moving the rest of their bodies.

Vultures

Humans use the word, vulture, as a synonym for wanton greed, but the common turkey vulture (*Cathartes aura*), or buzzard, as it is more often called, is a very beneficial bird, cleaning up dead carcasses.

Its southern cousin, the black vulture, is not quite as beneficial in human estimation because it preys on young herons and heron eggs. Considering the historical fate of birds in the face of increasing human populations, buzzards might long ago have been gun-blasted into scarcity because of their great size (up to 32 inches in length, with wingspreads to 72 inches), but the buzzard is one of the wariest animals in the man-dominated environment. It spends most of its time soaring high above the landscape. Its telescopic eyes can spot carrion at amazing distances, and a discovery is in some mysterious manner telegraphed to other buzzards soaring miles away. Within minutes of a buzzard beginning on a dead animal, scores of other buzzards float in to the feast, although hardly more than two or three pairs normally patrol the land per square mile.

One day, stray neighborhood dogs killed one of the Dumb Farmer's sheep, such being one of the hazards of farming in the suburbs. In older rural societies, a man would shoot his own dog unhesitatingly if it chased sheep. He supported his neighbor's right to shoot it, too. But members of today's society, separated by ease and luxury from their sources of food and clothing, lean indulgently in favor of dogs—a burden on the food supply—and any irresponsible masters who let them roam on other people's property. It is still legal to shoot a sheep-chasing dog, but, as the Dumb Farmer says, you had better be able to prove the dog was indeed killing sheep, which is not always easy to do, or you may end up being fined.

Still, it is an ill wind that blows no good. The dead sheep gave the Dumb Farmer the chance to fulfill one of Smith's never-ending requests: to view the buzzard at ground level. "You must be very sneaky," the Dumb Farmer cautioned Smith as they walked in back of the barn the next day, toward the spot in the pasture where the dead sheep lay. "We'll stay below the crest of the hill till we're up close, and then crawl forward so that just our heads peep over the hill."

Smith was not prepared for what he saw as he slid forward on his belly, binoculars ready, his memory suddenly jolted back to Korean ridges where he had slid forward in much the same way. Through the pasture grass on the crest of the hill, he trained his binoculars into the area 50 yards ahead where the Dumb Farmer was silently pointing. The sight first awed him, then almost revolted him. At least 30 big buzzards, looking even larger than life in the binoculars, were waddling around the carcass, squabbling gluttonously over it. More quarrelling than actual eating was taking place, as one, then another of the black birds pushed its way atop the already bloated sheep and fended off other diners between beaking and tearing away at the wool and flesh itself.

Even if they had been engaged in a less loathsome activity (loathsome to Smith), the big black birds with naked red heads would have appeared ugly. Though a picture of superb grace in the air, on land they were hulking, awkward creatures. The Dumb Farmer was no help. "Sometimes they gorge on carrion to such an extent that they can't get airborne again," he whispered into Smith's ear, bemused at the latter's rapt revulsion. "Then they vomit down to flying weight. Worse than a bunch of old Romans." He paused wickedly, looking for a greenish tinge to spread over Smith's face. "The old-timers say if you disturb a buzzard on her nest, she'll puke on you. And the smell is worse than skunk."

Smith pretended to ignore the Dumb Farmer, entranced by the scene before him. He raised his head ever so slightly to get a better look at the swaggering birds, their heads thrusting forward, shoulders hunched, wings half open, the lot of them looking very much like a coven of witches around a cauldron of brewing mischief. But even his slight movement was noticed, and the whole flock rose into the air, wings at first clumsily beating for altitude, then spreading gracefully, as the birds caught the air currents and soared swiftly into the sky. Within seconds the buzzards all seemed to disappear, as they wheeled higher and higher, each back to some preordained and preassigned air space, until they were mere specks in the blue or had passed entirely out of sight.

"As long as we stay out here, they won't come back," said the Dumb Farmer. "A couple of those old crones are watching us from away up there in the clouds, and there's no place we can hide and wait except back in the barn. The rest of them are watching the ones that are watching us, and when the closest ones see the coast is clear and come down, the others will follow. But we'll not be able to sneak up on them again till they're all back on the ground."

They retreated to the old deserted barn not far away, and from the loft, Smith kept his binoculars trained on the sheep carcass. Within a half hour, two buzzards materialized literally out of the blue, circling slowly lower and lower until, assured of safety, they extended their feet and dropped in for a landing, changing once more in the space of a few seconds, from birds of soaring beauty and grace to hulking, clumsy earth-swaggerers. In five days, the skeleton and a few balls of wool scattered about on the grass were all that remained of the sheep.

Hawks

Humans are not fearful of, nor revolted by, hawks; misunderstandings about them result simply from a misreading of the statistics. Since several species of hawks, notably the goshawk (*Accipiter gentilis*), Cooper's hawk (*A. cooperii*), and the peregrine falcon, or duck hawk (*Falco peregrinus*), do prey largely on game birds and songbirds (although, obviously, never to the permanent detriment of these species), hawks have been indiscriminately killed by certain strains of *Homo sapiens* who like to kill things. Their excuse is that they are protecting other birds. Since the birds most often eaten by these hawks are blue jays, blackbirds, and pigeons, not to mention an occasional squirrel—all of which, in one way or another, can be harmful to songbirds—the hawks account by far for more songbird predators than songbirds.

The rest of the hawks, largely rodent-eaters, are lumped with the bird predators. All are indiscriminately and illegally shot under the guise of protecting the poultry of America—99 percent of which are confined in buildings and not available to hawks if they did want them. The red-tailed hawk (*Buteo jamaicensis*), the red-shouldered hawk (*B. lineatus*), the broad-winged hawk (*B. platypterus*), the marsh hawk (*Circus cyaneus*), which nests on the ground in open areas, the rare merlin (*Falco columbarius*), and the sparrow hawk (*F. sparverius*), almost any of which might nest in a grove of trees, even in a backyard, are not going to seriously deplete our supply of either songbirds or poultry. The mice, jays, blackbirds, grasshoppers, house sparrows, squirrels, gophers, and rabbits they do eat will more than make up for any small preying on more beneficial animals. A large nest of sticks in a deciduous tree is usually either a hawk or a crow nest. If it's a hawk's, you will soon know from the screams of the parents or the babylike whimperings of the young.

Spiders

One item that appears every spring in newspapers and some magazines is the canned cautionary advice from the U.S. Department of Agriculture (USDA) on the dangers of black widow and brown recluse spiders. These columns are free, which is why newspapers print them. "You gets what you pays for," says the Beekeeper. The advice often appears in northern newspapers in regions where neither the black widow nor the brown recluse lives, but no matter. The publicity serves to keep the poorly informed public fearful of spiders, creatures essential to the scheme of life. Even in the South, where poisonous spiders live amid millions of people, bites are few and fatalities are nearly nonexistent. The Beekeeper says that more people have been harmed by USDA approved toxic chemicals in a year than from spiders in half a century.

Dangers from tarantulas found in the United States are largely mythical. Their bite is no more deadly than a bee sting, but tarantulas have better dispositions than bees. Spider-lovers make pets of them. Only a few South American tarantulas are dangerously venomous, but none in this country, 10,000 western movies to the contrary. Tarantulas are large, hairy insects with a leg spread the size of a human palm, which makes them scary to behold. They eat insects, lizards, and even mice.

The brown recluse spider is often called the violin spider. On the orange section directly in back of its head (its cephalothorax), markings form a tiny but distinct violin. The female black widow has its characteristic red hourglass shape on its black abdomen. Do not reach into dark, moist places in cellars, coal bins, woodboxes, under porches, and the like, without looking first. The spiders would rather run than bite, and they use their venom only as a last resort. Bites become swollen and painful. The brown recluse's bite crusts over heavily. The crust loosens and falls away, but an open wound, craterlike in appearance, may remain for a month or more.

Spiders are extremely interesting wildlife and are easily accessible for observation. Some common ones are vividly beautiful. The common black-and-yellow argiope (*Argiope aurantia*) likes to spin its ornate circular orb web among the vegetables in late summer. Though it appears ferocious, it harms only bugs. Smith finds the shamrock spider (*Araneus trifolium*) on his raspberry bushes, although it seems to prefer to stretch horizontal webs in the grass. Its thick, white-and-black legs and white speckled body make it easily identifiable. The marbled orb weaver (*A. marmoreus*) and the arrow-shaped micrathena (*Micrathena sagittata*) appear to belong to the lush and colorful tropics but are common in American meadows. The Mabel orchard spider (*Leucauge mabelae*) found on woodland edges, shrubby meadows, and orchards not sprayed heavily with toxic materials is gorgeous with its

A Garden Spider

eight evenly spaced silver stripes and three pinkish orange spots. It hangs upside down underneath its web.

Crab spiders (family Thomisidae), with translucent legs, hide in blossoms and catch insects drawn by the flowers. The lovely green lynx spider (*Peucetia viridans*) and other hunting spiders do not build webs, either, but rely on their speed to catch their prey. The trapdoor spider (*Bothriocyrtum californicum*), which lives in California, closes its hole in the ground with a door, behind which it hides. When it hears an insect outside, it flings open the door, rushes out, and grabs the surprised bug. Though rare, some spiders spit a sticky substance on insects to capture them. One kind of spider, *Hyptiotes* spp., builds a triangular web and holds onto an end of one of the strands, pulling it taut. When a bug hits the web, the spider lets go, snapping the web around the hapless insect. Fearsome-looking wolf spiders (*Lycosa* spp.) are night hunters. To spot one, shine a flashlight over the ground. Their eyes will reflect the light. Bluish green flashes of light along the road at night are usually reflections of your headlights in wolf spider eyes.

Wasps

Wasps are feared with even less justification than spiders, except, of course, by those severely allergic to stings. Wasps will sting if they are tormented, threatened, or if their nests are attacked. But if treated with calm respect, they are amazingly cool and tolerant. Paper wasps built a nest above the screen door of Smith's deck despite the fact that humans were constantly going in and out of the door just inches below them. They never once attacked. Bald-faced hornets calmly built a large nest on his porch, evidently becoming accustomed to humans passing nearby as they worked. Smith could approach the nest, his face hardly a foot away, and the hornets would pay no attention to him as they busily turned wood pulp into the papery layers of their nest and stuffed the chambers with insect food for their larvae. Smith credits them with causing the scarcity of flies around the house. As winter approached, the hornets all died, as is their lot in life, except for a few queens who evacuated the nest to live through the winter underground and emerge in spring to start other colonies elsewhere. Smith hung the old nest they left in his study.

Mud dauber wasps are so busy building their mud nests and filling them with spiders for their larvae that they seem not to have time to sting anyone. Even if you knock down their nests, they seldom become angry, but fly away for more mud to build anew.

The cicada-killer wasp is a large, yellow-striped, fearsome-looking creature that preys on cicadas. The cicada is usually too heavy for the wasp to carry off into the air, so the wasp climbs a tree with its burden and, with enough altitude, wings away on a long, gentle dive back to its underground burrow.

The potter wasp builds little clay pots, about ½ inch in diameter or smaller, in each of which it lays an egg. Then it fills the pot with caterpillars and sawfly larvae as food for its own hatching young. The little pots are usually set in a row on a branch and sealed with a daub of mud when filled. The larva remains safe and sound until it cuts its way out as an adult.

Yellow jackets have the nastiest tempers of all wasps and are more apt to attack and sting than the others. But it is hardly true that they will attack "at the least provocation," as some books say. When they are eating fruit in the fall, for which they can become quite pestiferous, they are in good humor. Then they will buzz around without showing any indication of wanting to sting, unless a person accidentally steps on one or pinches one inside a half-eaten grape or apple. But a person who steps or falls directly on an opening to their underground nest, or who runs over it with a lawn mower, is lucky to get away with only a few stings. The Dumb Farmer claims that a nest of angry yellow jackets can kill a horse, and that when he was a kid he once saved his little brother's life, after the little boy had blundered into a yellow jacket nest, by throwing him in the horse trough and jumping in after him. Smith does not believe him, since he once stepped directly on a yellow jacket nest and received only two stings for his mistake. The Dumb Farmer's wandering skunks eventually dug up Smith's nest and ate all the yellow jackets.

Another way to get rid of a nest easily is to set a bucket or large bowl firmly upside down over the nest-hole at night. The wasps will not dig another hole out and will starve to death.

Wasps do not kill their prey by stinging—they merely paralyze it so that the bugs will keep nice and fresh until the larvae are ready to eat them. How they have learned precisely where, in the nerve center of the prey, to insert their stinger to paralyze and not kill is a mystery.

The female giant ichneumon wasp (*Megarhyssa* spp.) is equipped with a long ovipositor that looks like a very wicked stinger. She uses it, not to sting, but to bore holes in tree bark *exactly* where the larva of a pigeon horntail or some other borer is hidden. She then places an egg in the larva. How the wasp knows exactly where the horntail larvae are located under the bark is not known for sure, but she never misses her target. It is thought that she can feel vibrations from the borer through the bark.

The pelecinid wasp is also fearsome to humans because of the female's extremely long (2 inches), slender abdomen, which appears to be a giant stinger. But she does not sting. She eats only nectar and water. She uses her long abdomen to thrust into the earth where she somehow knows the larvae of May beetles are located, and she lays an egg in each one. Her larvae then parasitize this pestiferous beetle.

Leeches

In the creek behind the subdivision, in the garden pool in Smith's backyard wildlife area, and in almost every permanent body of warm water in the United States swims a tiny wormlike animal, 2 inches long at best, that for at least 23 centuries has had its destiny linked to humans. The leech, wriggling along in undulating, snakelike rhythms, evokes better than any other creature the ambivalent sensibilities of humans for nature. The pale, tan parasite with dark spots and stripes, sucks blood. It latches onto unwary swimmers and waders, makes an opening in the flesh with its razor-sharp jaw plates, floods the opening with an anticoagulant, hirudin, and proceeds to bloat up to 5 times its normal size on blood. What could be more loathsome to modern mankind, separated so far, culturally, from the realities of nature? The mere idea of a leech, let alone a dozen of them clinging to human flesh, fills the weekend nature-lover with such revulsion as to send him scooting back to his midtown apartment. There he prays his friends will not remember that it was he who quoted with such grandiose feeling that famous line of Aldo Leopold, "In wilderness is the salvation of mankind." Unfortunately, such nature-lovers, having arrived at the beginning of truth, have not had the stomach to proceed to a deeper understanding of that quotation. They continue to pay their dues to the Audubon Society, but they keep their distance.

Hardly a century ago, every enlightened person wealthy enough to afford them kept leeches, often in precious pottery jars. Letting leeches suck blood from one's body possessed status on the level with today's penchant for running, aerobic dancing, and hot-tubbing. So popular were leeches in France that laws had to be passed regulating the number that peasants could gather and sell. Doctors became known by the name of their principal stock in trade—"leeches"—not with the disdain that term suggests today, but with respect.

Moreover, leeches are still being used in advanced and innovative plastic surgery, and to draw off excess blood that collects when the delicate veins of severed fingers are joined back together again. As Ted Williams, in a most absorbing article in *Audubon* (March, 1982) entitled "Leeches in My Breeches," puts it: "*Leechcraft works.*" But its applications change with each generation of doctors.

Although there are leeches in warmer parts of the world that are dangerous to man, terrestrial as well as aquatic species, those in the United States are hardly a threat, even though the report of one can empty a farm pond of 30 swimmers in ten seconds flat. Most of our common leeches do not need mammalian blood at all; the American medical leech (*Macrobdella decora*) feeds mainly on frog and turtle blood and the eggs of aquatic animals. North American horse leeches (*Haemopis* spp.) look somewhat like their vicious and dangerous relatives in India and Ceylon, but feed mostly on aquatic worms and insect larvae. Duck leeches (*Theromyzon* spp.) infest waterfowl, sometimes fatally (though rarely), by blocking nasal or throat passages and causing suffocation.

To loosen a leech, sprinkle salt on its skin. The salt burns, and the leech withdraws its head. Then pull or scrape the posterior suckers loose and dispose of the creature. Don't panic if the wound bleeds profusely for a bit—that's the leech's hirudin at work. You'll live. According to some theories of medicine, you might even feel better.

The leech offers another valuable lesson, refuting rather effectively the romantic notions that "nature always knows best" and that "Mother Nature" is a synonym for wisdom and ecological efficiency. Leeches have both male and female sexual organs. Some species (not the medical leeches) fertilize each other in a most bizarre and, by any standard, frightening way, called hypodermic impregnation. The leeches deposit capsules of sperm cells rather haphazardly over each other's bodies. These capsules exude an enzyme that literally eats holes through the flesh of the leech so that the sperm cells can enter the body and get into the bloodstream, to then move on to the ovaries. The sperm cells are attacked and destroyed on the way by antibody cells, but a few reach the eggs and fertilize them. It takes the leech three days or more to heal the holes in its flesh. The fact that not all leeches reproduce in this manner might suggest that even leeches know there has to be a better way.

Chapter 8

Human Use of Nature's Food Web

White was shocked at the news. Or pretended to be, at least. He tucked his newspaper under his arm and walked over to tell Smith the reason for his dismay. Smith was trying to train a chipmunk to take a peanut from his hand, the way the Widow Lady's chipmunks do from hers. He did not particularly appreciate the interruption, which sent the chipmunk scurrying for its home in the rock retaining wall beside the house. Now it would be days before the little chippy would again stand and watch in the presence of a human.

"I told you it was a bad idea to let all those refugees into our country," White scolded, as if Smith were responsible. "Just look at this. They're killing cats and dogs off the streets of San Francisco and *eating* them, for God's sake."

If he expected sympathy from Smith, he was disappointed. The latter only shrugged. "Sounds like an excellent way to get rid of all those stray animals, if you ask me," he replied.

"You've got a sick mind, Smith. Eating *pets?* Why, that's almost cannibalism."

"Foo, foo. I notice you didn't have any trouble eating steaks from the Dumb Farmer's pet steer."

"That's different."

"The steer wouldn't have thought so. And what about the dear, old, kindly Widow Lady. She traps and eats rabbits and squirrels. I suppose you think that's grotesque, too."

White muttered something under his breath about living in a primitive society right here in high-tech U.S.A. and stalked off to see what the Beekeeper had to say on the subject of eating dogs.

"Never ate one myself," the Beekeeper remarked, matter-of-factly. "But I've read that some tribes of Indians considered dog meat a delicacy. When I was growing up, we ate a lot of things, but we needed the dogs to catch them. Groundhogs, possums, coons—stuff like that—if we ran out of pork."

"Coons?" White quavered.

"Yeah, roast coon is delicious," chimed in the Dumb Farmer, who happened to be visiting the Beekeeper when White arrived. He grinned wickedly. "By golly, I know a Vietnamese family. Think I'll get the recipe for Brunswick dog stew from them. I think we've just stumbled upon the answer to a cheap source of protein for this country."

White decided not to pursue that line of logic any further. He changed the subject slightly. "Did you know that the Widow Lady is so poor she's been eating squirrels and rabbits?"

The Beekeeper looked swiftly at the Dumb Farmer. If White had been a close observer of human expression, he might have divined that they were both trying very hard not to laugh. "She could buy and sell any one of us," the Beekeeper finally said, with a sigh.

Unlike the rest of the food web, humans are creatures of culture as well as evolution. They can choose deliberately not to eat perfectly edible and nutritious foods (like cute little rabbits), or choose to eat things harmful to themselves (like tobacco juice), all for reasons that have little to do with biology. A gourmet might order horse-meat steak in a fine French restaurant and consider it a delicacy—much to the loathing of a typical suburban American teenager. The teenager's greasy hamburger and carbonated sugar water might in turn equally offend the gourmet eating a horse steak.

Among Mexican farmers, the armadillo is a delicacy. But it would hardly occur to a suburbanite in Louisiana or Texas to eat these rather ugly little creatures, even if their numbers are now reaching the nuisance level in some areas of the Gulf states. Like the badger moving eastward across the northern states, the armadillo is also on the move in the South, spreading up from Mexico into territory it has not frequented for 15,000 years, where its traditional predators, wolves and bobcats, are not around in sufficient numbers to discourage it.

The advance of the armadillo has not been viewed with alarm, and indeed it should not be, since the animal is quite beneficial to man.

It eats mostly ants, especially fire ants, which are becoming a serious problem in parts of the South. English gardeners build burrows for their wild hedgehogs to lure them to their gardens because the hedgehog eats many harmful insects. Americans have not yet developed such a crafty sense of ecology and tend to curse the little armadillo for digging holes in its search for insects. Yet, cattlemen beseech the Environmental Protection Agency (EPA) to allow them to aerial spray thousands of acres with potent poisons harmful to a wide range of life in an effort to stop fire ants from building their tall anthills on pastureland, thus ruining it for cattle. Since beef producers have had few profitable years in the last decade anyhow, one might wonder why they do not focus some creative thinking on the problem: Let the armadillos pasture the anthills and let the humans eat the armadillos.

Culturally and traditionally, such a suggestion sounds totally absurd. But another culture following this kind of biological logic *could* arise, since humans have proven time and again that they are the most adaptive of all animals. Unfortunately, such adaptation usually comes only under duress, forced on an old culture by a young one more in tune with biological reality, or by nature itself. Much of what is called "high" technology is an effort to prop up "high" cultures trying to exist separate from, and therefore in conflict with, nature.

The Beekeeper, who always knows something no one else knows about nearly everything, uses the armadillo as an example of

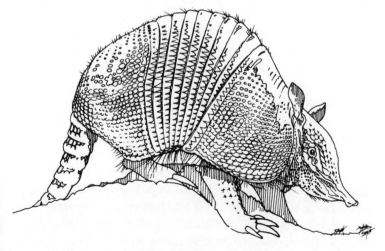

An Armadillo Eating Fire Ants

why no endangered species should ever be considered so unimportant as to allow it to become extinct. Since the armadillo is far from endangered, one must listen closely (and usually at some length), while he makes his point.

"Well, you see, it's thisaway," he begins in his high, querulous voice. "Suppose this were just 1970, and there were two armadillos left in the world, and they lived in the valley where the government was putting up the Tellico Dam. As in the case of the snail darter, the armadillo would have lost that fight because the big, short-term money would be able, in 1970, to argue that the dam was worth more to people than the armadillo. The power people could have trotted out enough evidence to convince everyone but environmentalists that nobody needs a stupid armadillo. So that would've been the end of the armadillo—no big loss, right? Well, in 1971, you know what scientists discovered about the stupid armadillo? It's susceptible to leprosy. For a century, science had been searching for just such an animal to use in experiments to cure human leprosy. And now, ten years later, we have experimental vaccines for leprosy. It's only a matter of time till we'll be able to cure this disease or prevent it, thanks to the armadillo."

The Widow Lady's Niche in Nature

The Widow Lady says she might eat an armadillo—if it didn't have leprosy. In any event, she does eat squirrels, and healthy, vigorous rabbits obviously not infected with tularemia or rabbit fever—although her diet is closer to that of a vegetarian than of a meat-eater. Talking to her about wild food one day, Smith realized with a start that while he had been busy introducing wildlife into his backyard, the Widow Lady had done him one better. She had simply allowed her 2 acres to become a wildlife sanctuary and put herself into it as unobtrusively as possible. Unlike Smith's place, where the life of the human household was distinct from the life of the backyard, with the wild not welcome in the human house and humans only visitors in the yard, the Widow Lady's round of activities, her very home, was an integral part of the natural world around her. Inside her ill-kept thickets of hedge border, one stepped into a sort of jungle. The trees looped up over her bungalow, all but hiding the roof. Bushes of all kinds crowded in around the house and over what was once a lawn. A hiker, straying onto her place, walking with head down, might almost bump into the house, so hidden it was. Bird nests and birdhouses seemed to cling to every nook and cranny. Maple seedlings grew in the eave troughs, bees nested in the south wall, mildew grew on the old shingles, chipmunks tarried in the attic, swifts nested in the chimney, and ivy climbed the north wall, testing it for cracks. A blacksnake once crawled up the ivy onto the roof to sun itself and stayed to shed its skin. The Widow Lady understands that her house is slowly sinking back into the living nature from which it sprang, but she is not too perturbed. "I am, too," she says simply.

Not only do chipmunks take peanuts from her hand, and chickadees cracked corn, but squirrels walk boldly into a wire pen where she puts nuts for them. Should she want a squirrel for dinner, she trips a string and the door falls shut. Deer, like the Widow Lady, live near and yet are invisible to the people of Gwynnedde Township. Along with the patches of thicket and woods that the subdivisions have not penetrated, they favor her bushy 2 acres. One old buck, wise in the ways of humans, hangs out there most of the time, keeping, says the Widow Lady, "just three bushes away from me."

Even what was once tame on the Widow Lady's property has gone wild. A thicket of gooseberries has spread from a single plant and conquered one end of the garden. But the thicket now produces more fruit alone than all of the raspberry bushes and strawberry patches her husband kept so meticulously before he died. Wineberries, once status symbols in fancy gardens, run wild in the north hedge. Mazzard cherries, volunteer seedlings from the rootstock of finer domestic sweet cherries that had succumbed to disease, grow where birds have dropped the seeds. Every year they provide the Widow Lady with an abundance of seedy but tasty cherries because they are not as susceptible to disease or insect and bird attack as are fancier sweet cherries.

Her chickens are half wild—banties,which would as soon roost in the trees as in the hen house. Sometimes she can't find the eggs, and then a few weeks later, a hen comes marching up the old brick sidewalk with a dozen chicks behind her.

Only the goat, Susie, is tame, and perhaps too tame at that, insisting on coming up onto the porch in the heat of the day to catch the cooling breeze there. If eating squirrels did not get her into trouble with her neighbors, keeping Susie, contrary to a township ordinance, might. But only a few know about the goat, and they would lie about it for the sake of this person they all respect. Besides, a chain-link fence completely surrounds the Widow Lady's property, the only indication of her rumored wealth. Few people get inside, and the goat never gets outside except when the Widow Lady takes her to the goat farm for breeding. Then Susie rides in the back seat of the Widow Lady's old Pontiac sedan. At home, the goat thrives by browsing on the bushes. "Without Susie, I long ago would have been overrun with puckerbrush," says the Widow Lady.

Truth be told, the old woman has achieved a high degree of self-subsistence and back-to-the-land independence right in the middle of suburban America. Like the deer, ring-necked pheasant, horned owls, big-eared bats, blacksnakes, raccoons, opossums, spotted salamanders, mink, muskrat, and Canada geese, she has found suburbia a suitable habitat, in many ways superior to the country or wilderness habitats that would seem to support her life-style better.

The technology of urban life around her could slow almost to a halt before she would feel the pinch. She seldom uses electricity. Periodically, she needs new strings for the violin she plays. Her chain saw might wear out before she does. She ponders having to buy fuel wood in her old age. She gets what she needs now from cutting up dead wood on her acres, the Beekeeper's land, and other places in the neighborhood. It's enough to heat one room through the winter. The Dumb Farmer gives her a load of his wood every year for Christmas to keep her well supplied. She knows that someday she won't be cutting her own wood, but she prefers not to think about it now.

Most of what she needs, especially in the way of food, she harvests from her suburban homestead. Even without the banties and the goat, she could survive if the supermarkets closed. All of nature is her supermarket.

In March, her food harvest begins with maple syrup. She boils off a gallon and would do more, but the Beekeeper insists on giving her honey. She gathers witch-hazel twigs at about the same time, steeps them in boiling water, and makes a soothing lotion for sore muscles, which the Beekeeper gets in return for the honey. Up on the wooded ridge on the Dumb Farmer's place, she finds winterberries or, as she calls them, teaberries, that survive the winter. They make a good spring tonic, she says, either eaten fresh or brewed into a tea. She makes a tea from spicebush sprigs, too, and uses the berries later on (if the thrushes haven't gotten them already) to flavor bland fruit pies and applesauce. The latter she makes from good parts of the wormy apples on the wild apple trees that grow in an undeveloped lot nearby. The sound apples she stores in the cellar for fresh eating all winter.

By late spring, a meal at the Widow Lady's place can be an adventure in gourmet eating. Salad might be a mix of fresh violets, blossoms included, sliced day-lily shoots, wild onion chopped in, a bit of sour grass for lemony taste, the whole sprinkled over with crumbed black walnut meats and maybe a touch of wild ginger powder for added zest. Cream of nettle soup follows. The vegetable of the day might be creamed wild asparagus with morel mushrooms in it and a side dish of wilted dandelions, vinegar, and sliced boiled eggs. The main dish could be fried rabbit, squirrel, or smoked young goat meat, shredded and creamed, or squabs from the wild pigeon nests in the top of her rickety little barn. She serves wild strawberries for dessert, soaked in rich goat's milk, and honey if you wish.

The list of wild foods she has taught Smith to appreciate seems endless. Milkweed is a favorite, as it is with so many insects. When the weed first comes up, the new shoots can be prepared like asparagus. The flower heads, before the blossoms open, she fixes like broccoli. The seed pods, when very young and just formed, can be simmered in a bit of water, buttered, and seasoned to taste.

Other potherb or salad material she gathers includes the leaves of basswood, or linden (*Tilia* spp.) in spring, the young leaves of lamb's-quarters (*Chenopodium* spp.) and redroot (*Amaranthus* spp.), and the stems of bull thistle (*Cirsium vulgare*), peeled, sliced like carrots, and boiled. The stem of burdock (*Arctium lappa*) can be prepared the same way. She gathers and cooks winter cress (*Barbarea vulgaris* or *B. verna*) even in December and, in mild winters, in February and March. She throws away the first water the herbs are boiled in to avoid bitterness, although, as she says, much of the vitamin C goes out with that water.

The Widow Lady isn't worried about losing a bit of vitamin C in this manner because so many other wild foods she eats are loaded with it. For example, she drinks strawberry leaf tea and raspberry leaf tea, both excellent sources of the vitamin. The Beekeeper accuses her of making tea out of anything and everything "except white oak stumps." But, other than those already mentioned, she makes only a few regularly: sassafras in spring, mint and clover leaf in summer, and sometimes goldenrod.

Wild Plant Remedies

Tea, says Smith, is not his cup of tea, and he doesn't much care for the substitute coffee she makes from dried chickory roots either. But he is enchanted by her knowledge of wild medicines. If she brushes bare skin against nettles while gathering the leaves for soup, she grabs a handful of jewelweed and rubs the juicy stems vigorously over the affected skin to soothe the burning. The Beekeeper says the effectiveness of this remedy is all in her head. She applies the white juice of milkweed to warts. Surprisingly, the Beekeeper gives his imprimatur to this practice. Once it worked for Smith. Once it didn't. But his son patiently pressed out a tiny vial of the liquid, took it to school, and became known as the "wart-healer." Doctors, who burn out warts, and not always successfully, say milkweed cures are only folklore.

The Widow Lady's favorite wild plant is pokeweed (*Phytolacca americana*), which she gathers when the new shoots first appear in spring for an asparaguslike vegetable. She even cans some for winter use. The leaves and the berry juice can be applied externally to skin cancers with good effect, she says, as well as the roots. Pioneers learned that from Indians, her grandfather told her. The berries make decent wine and jam, and the juice an excellent dye or ink. Smith, brandishing a book in alarm, points out that the deeply purple-colored mature plants

Pokeweed

and the berry seeds are poisonous. The Widow Lady smiles benignly and informs him that rhubarb leaves can be poisonous, too, not to mention green potato skins. There is, in fact, something poisonous about at least a hundred common wild and cultivated plants, and those who would have the best nutrition by eating fresh foods must learn to distinguish what is harmful under what conditions. May-apple (*Podophyllum peltatum*) is invariably listed as "poisonous" though the fruits make a delicious pie. The fruit has a piquant, pineapplelike taste, and it is not harmful if eaten in moderation. The Beekeeper remembers that the roots of may-apple, dried and powdered, were once a fairly common drug used for liver ailments. He also informs Smith that the Widow Lady's regard for poke has some support from science. The berries contain a substance that in some mysterious way inhibits the division of cells, a characteristic that might be harnessed for cancer control eventually, since cancerous cells are characterized by uncontrolled cell division.

Mushrooms and Other Fungi

The poison factor hangs even more threateningly over the fungi that Smith finds in the wilds of his backyard. Unlike wild animals, man's path to knowledge is rational rather than instinctive, and he has no built-in sense of what is poisonous and what is not. Also, humans have such complicated nervous systems that some plants and fungi make some people sick but not others, a situation rarely true in the wild kingdom. So Smith is very cautious. He can identify morels (*Morchella* spp.) because he has hunted them all his life. When he found them under a dead elm tree in his wild domain, he considered the event a major triumph of his efforts. Science can't grow the delicious morel in artificial environments: the fungus cannot be tamed and commercialized. The New York Botanical Garden tried for 40 years. Morels remain creatures of the wild, and they grow where they will grow, no human rhyme nor reason to it. Looking like a sponge in texture, they're usually shaped like a miniature Christmas tree about 2 to 3 inches tall. Morels often grow under pin oaks and white ash trees, where they are grayish in color; under dead and dying elms and around red oaks, where they are yellow; under red cedars and walnut stumps, where they are rusty yellow; or in old apple orchards, where they are tan. The various species do not follow these rules closely, nor can one always expect to find small grays under ash trees and large yellows under elms. Just depends. Once, a morel grew in a foundation crack in the Dumb Farmer's basement, a feat no mycologist could explain. And morels like to grow quite frequently in the cinders along railroad tracks. Morels grow where you find them. When morels are sliced and fried in butter, Smith claims, they are better than truffles. But he is bluffing a bit, never having eaten a truffle.

It was fungi that had brought him into contact with the Widow Lady in the first place. Before he adapted his backyard favorably for beneficial wildlife, he had spotted her, a strange old lady, he had thought then, as she walked slowly across the upper end of his long yard, picking up what he considered to be merely toadstools. He hurried up to her, curious about what value she saw in them. At first she had been evasive and embarrassed, fearing that he objected to her trespassing. Reassured, she lost her shyness and explained that she was gathering the common fall meadow mushroom (*Agaricus campestris*), which was almost exactly like the domesticated mushroom in the stores. She intended to separate caps from stems, rub butter on them, broil all for a few minutes, then turn over the caps, fill them with butter and lemon juice, and broil again until the butter melted. Smith's mouth watered. He wanted to know how to tell good mushrooms from poisonous ones, exhilarated with the idea that right here in his lawn grew the same delicacy that came only at a high price from the food market. The Widow Lady shrugged. "I guess you just have to follow a mushroom hunter around and eat what he eats. If he's been doing it for 40 years, he probably knows the difference."

So Smith followed the Widow Lady around when she hunted mushrooms. He learned from her to identify shaggy manes (*Coprinus comatus*), which in the fall grow in new lawns and other places where dirt has been recently disturbed, and puffballs (*Calvatia gigantea*) in addition to morels and meadow mushrooms. He hasn't eaten the shaggy manes yet, although the Widow Lady assured him they are tasty if gathered before the caps spread open. He found puffballs so good when sliced and fried in butter that he ate too much of the rich fare the first time he prepared them and had no inclination for mushrooms of any kind for over a year. He also learned that putting the dried powder of an old puffball on a wound is an effective way to stop it from bleeding.

Many more kinds of fungi grow on Smith's land, but unless the Widow Lady is right there to make positive identification (and *she*

Parasol Mushrooms

doesn't always know), Smith wisely doesn't trust his own judgment. He is reasonably sure of the parasol mushroom (*Leucoagaricus procerus*), one of the best to eat and best to dry for winter use. It grows throughout the eastern half of the country. It has a long, slender stem, striped reddish brown to brown over pale tan, and it has a cap with thickish, dark brown scales that, in mature specimens, sometimes seem to cover it like a thatched roof. Mature specimens display a very noticeable cuff or collar on the stem. The parasol's size often distinguishes it from other fungi. The cap easily grows to an 8-inch diameter and often to 12 inches or more.

The Widow Lady points out that inky caps (*Coprinus micaceus*), which grow around rotting stumps, are good if picked very young, but Smith doesn't think they look appetizing. The oyster mushroom (*Pleurotus ostreatus*), which grows on dying tree trunks, is tasty and does look appetizing in its fresh white dress. But Smith holds back. He will eat them when the Widow Lady gathers young ones, before they get too tough. She soaks them a bit in salt water, dips them in egg batter, and fries them in butter. He is leery of trying it alone, and his wife even more so. She has, over the years, cooked too many of Smith's romantic notions. She has fried everything from elderberry blossoms to grasshoppers in egg batter, and now responds to new wild foods with cautious circumspection that begins—and usually ends—with: "Egg batter covereth a multitude of sins."

The variety and beauty of fungi rival those of birds and flowers. There are bird nest fungi (*Crucibulum levis*) that resemble tiny baskets full of eggs, which Smith finds on old raspberry canes. Once he found a fungus clump (*Clavaria pyxidata*) that looked like an underwater growth of white seaweed, growing on a tree trunk. Colors range from the bright scarlet of the little scarlet cup fungi (*Sarcoscypha coccinea*); through purple-gilled, tawny *Cortinarius corrugatus*; to an all blue milk fungus (*Lactarius indigo*); to the red-colored *Boletus frostii*, which turns blue where cut or bruised, like so many of the Boletus mushrooms do; to the bright, orange-yellow sticky clumps of *Mycena leaiana* growing on hardwoods in late spring. Some of these fungi are edible, some not, but Smith wisely refrains from eating any of them, content to enjoy them through visual pleasure only. Many of these colorful mushrooms, he learns, make beautiful dyes for woolen fabrics in nearly every color, such as red from certain *Cortinarius* species.

Identifying mushrooms can become a hobby in itself, demanding detailed knowledge of spore form and color, in some cases. A fresh mushroom cap laid gill down on a piece of damp paper will leave a spore print after a few hours, also helpful in identification. If the mushroom is one that grows in soil, these spore-printed papers can be buried under leaf mold in the backyard wilds and sometimes "seed" a new growth of that fungus. In this way, Smith has brought to his backyard several species that did not grow there previously.

Bracket fungi growing on rotting tree trunks display many colors and designs, some gaudy or striking enough to find use as decorations. The red beefsteak fungus (*Fistulina hepatica*) grows mostly on oak wood, and unlike most bracket fungi, it is good to eat before it toughens. The artist's conk, or flat tinderfungus (*Ganoderma applanatum*), has radiating rings of various shades of brown and an outer margin of white. Artists like to sketch pictures on the off-white underside of dried specimens. Fairy stool (*Polyporus versicolor*) grows on almost any decaying hardwood, even sawed boards, forming rosettes that look almost like flowers, with radiating rings of many earthen colors. Specimens are sometimes dried, varnished, and then sold as costume jewelry.

Berries and Nuts

Collecting fungi from the wild is only an interesting hobby for Smith, at least until he learns to identify more of them accurately. But gathering berries and nuts has become a lucrative and essential part of his food-gardening effort. Wild strawberries proliferate in meadow plots if the plots are mowed only once every other year, right after harvest. Blackcap raspberries grow abundantly on the edge of woodland groves or in the sunny glades inside them. Blackberries threaten to take over the hedgerow, but they pay their rent with gallons of the glistening, black fruit. Elderberries volunteer wherever sun and rich soil combine, and Smith allows a few clumps to grow for jelly and pie, if the birds leave him any. Wild blueberries are not native to his soil, although it has the proper acidity (pH of 4.5 to 5.5). So, he has planted a few domestic bushes that do well enough for the birds, but not for him unless he puts screen boxes over them (see Chapter 2, Good Fences Make Good Wildlife). Growing far enough away from the larger forest trees so that they will not be too much shaded, wild apple, mazzard cherry, juneberry, wild plum, persimmon, mulberry, and papaw add to his family's fruit larder. Wild grapes, good enough for jelly and wine, last well into winter.

Wild grapes provide a good example of the regional diversity of wild fruits. The owner of a backyard wildlife area needs to know a little more than just "wild grapes" in order to plant wisely. The common wild grape of the North is the fox grape (*Vitis Labrusca*). The riverbank grape (*V. riparia*) and the frost grape (*V. corditolin*), also called riverbank grape, grow in some of the same territory and farther on south, but they are not as succulent as the fox grape. From the middle to the far southern states, several other wild grapes are more suitable and adapted. The muscadine (*V. rotundifolia*) is the best of the wild grapes, and thrives in midland to southern areas. The canyon grape (*V. arizonica*) grows in the Southwest, and Arkansas to Texas is the realm of the mustang grape (*V. candicans*). In addition, there is the wide-ranging summer grape, or pigeon grape (*V. aestivalis*), and the sweet winter grape (*V. cinerea*) of the South.

This diversity exists with all wild fruits, including blueberries, huckleberries, and even elderberries. The safe course to follow is to plant species found in the wild nearby, if the plants don't volunteer in your wildlife area (grapes usually do). Another point to keep in mind, especially with wild grapes, is that taste varies from vine to vine *in the same species*. Some fox grapes are not nearly as musky-tasting as others and so make better wine. Before transplanting, sample the fruit. Grapes are easily transplanted by moving a foot-long cutting of the current year's growth to the new site in the fall, pushing it into the soil so that only one bud joint remains aboveground, with one or two below.

As mentioned earlier, the best place to grow a wild grape is up a tree, if the vine is periodically cut back to the tree's lower limbs. Otherwise, the vine might eventually kill the tree. Cutting back also induces fruiting closer to the ground. Tame but environmentally tough domestic varieties, like Concord and Catawba, can be planted and maintained as wildlings with fairly good results. In fact, the grape beetle seems to prefer wild fox grapes to Concord. But the birds may eat the Concord grapes before you get your share.

In managing wild berries, remember that their health and vigor depend on their ability to move to new ground each year. If you try to keep them in strict bounds, they will become puny and diseased in a few years. This presents special problems for the backyard that is small and hemmed in by definite property-line borders. You must somehow establish fixed meadow plots, for example, and let the wild strawberries wander about within those limits. A sensitive use of the mower can forge a compromise between the stability of the plot and the mobility of the strawberries. Often, though, the compromise means having to skip a year of strawberries in favor of controlling tree seedlings sprouting up in the meadow plots. Smith has his meadow plots on various mowing schedules (as described in Chapter 4, Maintaining a Home for Wildlife: The Basic Steps), and if he has to mow off promising strawberries, he will first transplant a few healthy, well-rooted runners to another plot not scheduled for mowing that year. As with tame strawberries, it is the new runners that will fruit best the next year.

Wild cane fruits, especially raspberries and blackberries (but all bush fruits to some degree), must also be able to move into new territory to remain vigorous and fruitful. Blackcaps spread the same way garden varieties of black raspberries want to spread—by tip-rooting. The canes grow up, then bend back to the earth, where the cane tip roots, starting a new plant. Blackberries more often move from suckers coming up from underground roots spreading out from the parent plant, although they also tip-root, especially the low-spreading dewberries.

In a backyard wildlife area of limited space, it is difficult to allow for these rambling habits of growth. The heavy shade of trees will act as a control, but in full to partial sunlight, the solution lies in periodic mowing after the bearing season is past. Settle on a particular area for the berry patch, then mow over it all every other year. The year after mowing, there will be no berries because you have mowed off the canes that would have produced that year. But the next year, the plants will rebound and produce a crop which you harvest. After the harvest, you mow again. In doing this, you have prevented tree seedlings from overgrowing the berry canes. If you have two such patches on different mowing schedules, you can have berries every year.

Gooseberries, elderberries, blueberries, and huckleberries move more slowly and can be kept in stable bushes for a number of years, even without pruning out old canes. It's best to let them creep out on one side of the bush and mow off the old canes on the other side at the same slow pace as their growth rate.

Tree fruits are easier to manage than the bush types because they are not inclined to move around as much. However, many wild fruit trees do spread by suckering, particularly persimmon, papaw, mayhaw, most of the wild dogwoods, mulberry, plum, and hazel. A plum "thicket" is not a figure of speech, for example. Persimmon becomes a weed on some soils if allowed to sucker at will. A yearly mowing or pruning of suckers is usually enough to keep all under control, and the parent tree will continue to bear for many years. Hazel, however, should be allowed to move a little, like bush fruits. If it's kept pruned to a single-trunked tree, after several years, a wild hazel will lose vigor.

The other nut trees, oak, hickory, chestnut, walnut, pecan, butternut, and beech, spread mostly by seeding, and a tree should be considered a permanent fixture—in some cases for more than 100 years. The problem with nut trees is that in maturity they are usually quite large, which limits the number of them practical in a small yard. Other than that possible problem, the nuts from wild trees provide much unsaturated fat and essential proteins. They could substitute for much of the meat in human diets. The Widow Lady roasts white oak acorns, the most plentiful "nut" in the neighborhood. The roasting lessens the bitterness of the tannic acid. She eats them like chestnuts or grinds them into a flour that, mixed half with regular flour, makes a nutty, nutritious, filling bread. Acorns from the black oak family, including pin, scarlet, and red oaks, are too bitter to use, she says.

The tannic acid in acorns is another of those "poisons," if one has a cast-iron tongue and could continue eating such bitter fare in huge quantities. Grinding the nuts and leaching them in water, as Indians did for centuries, is the traditional way to get rid of the acid. With the sweeter white oak acorns, the Widow Lady believes roasting is easier. Some acorns, like those from the chinquapin oak, are sweet enough to eat out of hand.

Of the conventional wild nuts, pecans are no doubt the easiest to gather and crack out in quantity. Where it's too cold for pecans, hickory nuts are a good substitute; they are harder to crack but maybe just a little bit better tasting, if that's possible. Some hickory nuts crack more easily than others, and for starting hickories in a wildlife area, generations as yet unborn will thank the planter who goes to the trouble of procuring seeds or trees of selected strains or varieties. The Widow Lady's husband belonged to the Northern Nut Growers Association (see Appendix, Source Lists) before his untimely death, and had planted two hickories of the Wilcox variety on advice from that society. Since the nuts of this selected variety crack out into whole halves most of the time, the Widow Lady can easily crack and store away 20 pints of hickory nut meats every year the trees produce (they usually bear well only every other year). She does the work in the winter evenings in front of the glowing woodstove, when she tires of her violin and it is too dark to talk to the birds.

She gathers and cracks out another 20 pints of black walnut meats. Cracking out walnuts goes faster than hickory nuts because the meats are larger. But the walnuts have to be hulled first (hickories and pecans fall clean from their hulls). She dumps the unhulled green walnuts on her driveway after they fall from the trees, then runs back and forth over them with her old Pontiac. The tires squish off the outer hulls, rain subsequently washes the nuts fairly clean, and the sun dries them well enough for winter storage. When she's ready to use the walnuts, she cracks out the nutmeats from the shells.

Smith, the engineer, decided that cracking out that many hard-shelled hickory and walnut meats required more sophisticated technology than the Widow Lady's cement block and hammer. He ordered a heavy-duty, hand-operated cracker from C. E. Potter Company (see Appendix, Source Lists). A nut could be inserted in the cracker's cupped vise heads in precisely that position in which it would crack open best when pressure was applied. Experimentation showed that larger pieces of nut meat could be extracted from walnuts if cracking pressure was applied end to end. For hickories and pecans, pressure from side edge to side edge was best. Thicker-shelled shellbark hickories responded better to the Widow Lady's hammer and block method.

Either way, the Widow Lady says the secret is to soak the nuts beforehand, so the kernels absorb a slight bit of moisture. That makes them flexible enough that they stay in larger pieces instead of shattering with the shell. Too much moisture makes them swell and tightly grip the inner fissures of the shell, though. She soaks black walnuts for 24 hours in water at room temperature, then just for a minute or so in hot water. She allows the nuts to dry to the touch, and then cracks them immediately. The kernels have to be spread out and thoroughly dried afterward, if they are to keep well. She soaks hickory nuts for only a few minutes, then puts the wet nuts in plastic sacks overnight. The kernels do not have to be dried for storage. All wild nutmeats will last about a year in common storage before becoming rancid. If they're frozen, they will last indefinitely.

There is an added benefit to presoaking. Dried-up nuts, or those in which kernels did not develop, float to the surface and can be discarded, saving much cracking time. It is generally faster to crack a quantity of nuts at one time, then go about the job of extracting the meats from the broken shells. Go through the cracked nuts and pick out the bigger kernel pieces; don't waste too much time digging out every tiny piece with a nut pick. Some veteran nut harvesters use an electrician's nippers instead of a pick, nipping off edges of shell pieces in which nutmeats are bound, releasing them with far less waste than when using a pick. Often, the steel on the outside of the nipper jaws is ground off so that the cutting edge is brought out to a point, making a very fine cut possible.

Butternuts are handled like black walnuts, but are harder to hull. Hazelnuts crack out easily, the nut coming in one piece. Wild hazelnuts taste much better if slightly roasted or toasted in a pan in the oven. Beechnuts are best cracked between the teeth, like a sunflower seed, or picked apart with fingernails, since they are too small for the mechanical crackers. Slit chestnuts and acorns before roasting them or they may burst. The nut pines, especially *Pinus edulis* and other pinyons, are very practical wildlife and human food in the West. Even though a good crop can be expected only once in about four years, the trees yield enough then to last careful collectors until the next good harvest. The nuts will last several years if frozen.

Wildling Recipes

Smith recently invited the Whites over for dinner, hoping they'd enjoy a new gourmet dish Mrs. Smith had discovered— Hungarian French Hen, Smith said, roasted in the Normandy style. Pushing back from the table, White declared he had never tasted any meat so good.

Not even the freshest pork tenderloin, his favorite, equaled it in flavor. "But it surely doesn't look or taste like any kind of exotic fowl I've ever eaten before," he concluded. Smith smiled, and Mrs. Smith excused herself to serve dessert. "Well, White, I'm glad you liked it. I've got a bit of a confession to make. It isn't any kind of fowl."

A wary look spread on White's face. Smith was up to his tricks again. "It isn't?"

"Naw. It's, well, do you remember that big old snapping turtle we saw last spring lying in the mud in the shallow end of the Dumb Farmer's pond? I believe you said it was the ugliest creature you ever laid eyes on."

"You don't mean this . . . was that?" White gasped.

"Well, I was afraid if I told you, you wouldn't have eaten any and learned how enjoyable it can be, living in a primitive society occasionally."

Smith chuckled and continued to smile broadly through dessert. White peered closely under the pie crust. "It sure enough looks like a blackberry pie," he muttered, unable any longer to keep from grinning at his own embarrassment, "but the way this neighborhood is deteriorating, it's probably pokeberries."

The Dumb Farmer's Solution to Coons Eating Sweet Corn

The following recipes (adapted from the *Farm Journal's Country Cookbook*, 1959, 1972 by Farm Journal, Inc. with permission of the publisher) are the ones used at traditional coon suppers throughout the Midwest, where, says the Dumb Farmer, they know how to protect their corn.

Roast Raccoon

4 raccoons, 4 to 6 pounds each	3 cloves garlic, minced
¼ cup soy sauce or Worcestershire sauce	8 medium-size onions, peeled
	1 stalk celery, cut in 2-inch pieces
2 teaspoons ground pepper	1 carrot, cut in 1-inch pieces
2 cups whole wheat flour	12 small bay leaves
1 cup vegetable oil	water to cover

When skinning and butchering the raccoons, remove glands from under their forelegs and on each thigh. The glands look like small kidney beans. Cut the meat into pieces, saving the backs and legs, which carry the most meat, for roasting. Save the other pieces for broth and stuffing, if desired. Coat back and leg pieces with soy sauce or Worcestershire sauce, sprinkle with pepper, and dredge in flour. Heat oil in a large, heavy skillet. Add meat, and brown as you would chicken. Transfer pieces to roaster and add garlic, onions, celery, carrot, bay leaves, and water. Cover, and bake in oven at 350°F until tender, about 2 hours.

Serves 24

Raccoon Broth

bones of 4 raccoons   water to cover

Cook bones, seasoned to taste, in water until meat is tender, about 2 hours. Strain broth and store.

Raccoon Gravy

whole wheat flour (2 to   Raccoon Broth
   3 tablespoons per cup   Roast Raccoon drippings
   of broth)

Add flour and broth to drippings and stir over low heat until gravy thickens.

Raccoon Stuffing

3 loaves whole grain bread (day   2 tablespoons butter
   old) cut in cubes   2 teaspoons soy sauce or
1 teaspoon ground pepper   Worcestershire sauce
2½ teaspoons rubbed sage   4 eggs, beaten
4 stalks celery, chopped   4 cups Raccoon Broth
1 large onion, diced

Mix bread, pepper, and sage in a large bowl. Saute celery and onion in butter. Mix sauteed vegetables, soy sauce or Worcestershire sauce, eggs, and broth into bread mixture. Place stuffing in a large shallow pan and bake in oven at 350°F for 30 minutes.

Serves 24

A Neighborhood Solution
to an Overpopulation of Squirrels

In the South, where this traditional feast is enjoyed, the stew is served with heaping mounds of spoon bread. In the North, a large pot of a very similar stew called Hunter's Stew is prepared at family gatherings. It can contain almost any kind of wild meat, from venison to rabbit, even to young groundhog. The Widow Lady says that any tasty meat can be prepared as Hunter's Stew, including blacksnake fillets and breast of blackbird. (The following recipe also was adapted from the *Farm Journal's Country Cookbook* with the permission of the publisher).

New Brunswick Stew or "Squirrel Muddle"

About 70 squirrels
2 stewing chickens, cut up
6 gallons water
2½ pounds salt pork, chopped
2½ gallons butter beans or lima beans
3½ gallons peeled and cubed potatoes
4 gallons peeled and chopped tomatoes

1 gallon peeled and cubed carrots
2½ gallons freshly cut corn
1 gallon shredded cabbage
1 pod red pepper, chopped
¼ to ½ cup ground black pepper
1 cup soy sauce or Worcestershire sauce
2 cups honey

Clean, dress, and cut up the meat. Bring 4 gallons water to boil in a 30-gallon iron kettle. Add squirrel and chicken pieces. Cook, stirring often until meat comes off the bone. Add remaining water as needed. Fry salt pork and add pork and drippings to boiling mixture. Add beans, potatoes, tomatoes, carrots, and corn in order as each is prepared. Continue cooking and stirring until vegetables are tender. Add cabbage and seasonings and cook, stirring for 1 hour until stew is thick and flavors are well blended. Remove kettle from coals.

Yields 15 gallons

Chapter 9

Watching Wildlife

The best way to watch birds, Smith was telling White, is with your ears. White found that statement intriguing, even though he was not much interested in birdwatching. He considered birdwatchers nice enough people to have for neighbors (because they were quiet), but weird characters nonetheless.

"Well then, I suppose blind people make the best birdwatchers," he said sarcastically.

"Really, White." Smith replied. "You can almost always hear birds singing before you can see them, especially when you can't see them at all up in the tops of the trees. If you know your bird songs, you know what birds are around before you get out of bed in the morning. For example, if you hear 'teacher! teacher! teacher!' you know there's an ovenbird in the woods."

White laughed. "Maybe it's just some kid got lost on a school nature walk," he suggested.

"Well, of course, the ovenbird doesn't really say 'teacher, teacher, teacher,' but it sounds like that," Smith said, ignoring White's irreverence in the face of his hard-won knowledge. "Actually, the accent is on the second syllable, and as Roger Tory Peterson says, the song is really 'cher*TEA*, cher*Tea*, cher*Tea*.' The novice often mistakes the ovenbird for the tufted titmouse, the latter's song sounding like a repetitive 'Peter, Peter, Peter,' but not increasing in volume the way the ovenbird does."

White shook his head in amazement at Smith's sudden professorial tone of voice. "I knew a guy who had a mynah bird in a cage," he replied. "That bird could say a few things that would make your ovenbird call for the vice squad instead of a teacher."

At that moment, Smith threw up his hand, signaling for quiet. "Hear that? Hear that bird singing right now? What's that sound like?"

At first White heard nothing. Birds songs were so much a part of his suburban environment that they had passed into his subconsciousness, like the sound of cars passing on the street.

"Oh yeah, I *do* hear it," he finally said. "I suppose it's trying to tell us something, too?"

"Listen closely. Doesn't that sound like 'drink your tea'? That's a towhee."

White again shook his head sadly at his neighbor. "I think it's more than tea you've been drinking."

Sounds of the Wild

Whatever White's position on the matter, the would-be wildlife watcher will learn quickly enough that Smith is correct: The ears serve to instruct before the eyes perceive. Not only is this true of bird song, but of the many other sounds of wildlife activity. A true woodsman can sit beneath a tree with his eyes closed and reconstruct in his mind much of what is going on around him. He knows the sound of the brown thrasher scratching in the dry leaves. He knows the sound of falling nut shells, betraying the location of a hungry squirrel. He knows the sound of a kingfisher splashing on the surface of the water, rising quickly with a minnow in its mouth. He is alerted when another human enters the woods, because the blue jays scream, the squirrels scold, and the kingfisher rattles. He knows when a mourning dove passes overhead, though it does not sing; the beat of its wings against the air creates a characteristic whistling sound. He can distinguish the staccato drumming of a woodpecker drilling a hole in an oak in search of bugs from the more leisurely hammering of a sapsucker drilling into a maple for sap. In turn, he can differentiate this sound from the careful pecking of a nuthatch breaking into bite-size bits a kernel of corn it has wedged behind the bark of a shagbark hickory. If the forest is suddenly quiet, he can guess that a hawk is gliding low over the trees looking for dinner.

He recognizes a shrill short whistle as the call of a mother groundhog to her young when she senses danger, warning them back into the den hole, around which they tumble and play like kittens. In the early spring, mink bark on the mating trail. Beavers slap their tails on the water surface to sound the alarm. What seems like the drone of a far-off airplane is the hum of hummingbird wings beating as many as 70 times a second as the tiny bird hovers insectlike over a flower, sipping nectar. Frogs and toads sing as beautifully as birds, each species with its own flutelike tune. The skunk, on his hunting trail, grunts and snorts softly, as if the exercise taxes him too greatly. If he is disturbed, he thumps the ground with an outraged foot. A cottontail rabbit screams—actually sounding like a baby crying—as the talons of the hawk close over its back.

Birdwatchers not only learn to recognize birds by their songs but also use bird cries to lure them out of hiding. Tape players are now standard equipment of professional birders. The cry of a screech owl on tape stimulates the mobbing instinct in smaller birds. Sparrows, warblers, blackbirds, jays, and finches will gather around, looking for the owl that in daytime they can safely harass—if they don't get too close. (Perhaps instinct drives them to mob the owl as a way of chasing it to another, quieter territory.) Usually, they chatter excitedly above the tape player for about five minutes before realizing that no owl is to be found.

The characteristic songs of some bird species can be mimicked to lure the birds up close. A male cardinal, hearing the cardinal's cheery whistle, will come hunting the source, no doubt suspecting that another male has intruded into his territory. The alarm call of the wren will draw not only other wrens, but many other small birds, all curious as to the cause of the wren's anxiety. This sound can be imitated fairly easily. Make the sound of a mother quieting a youngster—with a 'p' on the front of it, pronounced by the lips but hardly sounded: p-shhhhhhhhhhhhhhhh. Striking the tip of one's tongue off the roof of the mouth directly in back of the front teeth produces a chipping "tsk tsk" sound similar to the alarm note of many other small birds that with practice will lure them within close range.

Tracks

Sounds are not the only help in identifying the wild residents of the backyard when they themselves cannot be seen. Wildlife leave calling cards in the form of signs and tracks. Raccoons leave behind the wreckage of a corn patch—stalks knocked over, ears stripped off, sometimes even before kernels are formed. Birds, on the other hand, eat only the kernels on the tips of the ears, shredding the husk only partially away. Rabbits chew bark, but not as thoroughly as mice. The telltale sign of rabbit damage to young trees and bushes is the presence of small branches clipped off at a neat angle, as if with a knife. Deer concentrate on leaves or whole twiggy branch-ends. They leave bushes and trees more or less intact at the main stem, but with the end twigs bitten off bluntly.

Droppings—what wildlife watchers refer to as scat—can sometimes help in identification. Rabbit manure resembles sheep manure—individual, pea-size pellets scattered over areas frequented by the animals, but sometimes in little piles. Raccoon droppings are the size and shape of dog manure but invariably are found up on a log, stump, or rock, and in summer they are solid with the seeds of whatever fruit is in season.

Footprints are another aid in identifying wildlife. Only deer (of the more common animals) are heavy enough to leave tracks in the dry dirt of summer, but in mud and snow, all the animals, even the tiniest mouse, leave a trail. One of the joys of the backyard sanctuary in winter is to find, after a soft, new snow, that much more wildlife lives there than the human caretaker realized.

Trying to judge wildlife populations from tracks can be deceiving, however. Just a couple of rabbits can almost cover a backyard with tracks in a single night, if they are hungry enough to be on the move.

Reading animal tracks accurately is a difficult skill to learn. Accuracy hinges on detailed knowledge of other signs, the habits of animals, the animals (or birds) native to an area, and other information without which the tracks alone are useless. A really well-defined track occurs only in mud of the proper consistency. In snow, especially over an inch deep, the marks of claw, toe, and foot pad blur into a blob. As a footprint in snow melts, it grows larger than it originally was. A half-grown animal will make a track smaller than the adult of the same species—the same is true, of course, of droppings. The positioning of hind and front feet change in relation to each other, depending on whether the animal is walking or running.

In snow, a squirrel track may look like a rabbit track occasionally, especially when both are walking, not running. But if the track begins at the foot of one tree trunk and quits at the foot of another, you know the trail is that of a squirrel. If a track just seems to begin out in a clearing between trees, as if by magic, you can assume that a flying squirrel has landed there. A track that looks like a skunk's in the snow, but is too blurred for the five toes and five very fine claw marks to show, is probably not a skunk, because this animal rarely moves about in winter.

To identify tracks accurately, you need to study a very detailed book on the subject (*A Field Guide To Animal Tracks*, by Olaus J. Murie is excellent). You can learn a few generalities about common backyard animal tracks quickly. Most tracks in the backyard will be dog and cat tracks. Dog and cat tracks—all members of both families, including wild species—show four toes and a foot pad or paw. Most other animals whose tracks you are likely to encounter in your backyard leave a print of five toes. The tracks of wild canines and some domestic breeds of dogs are much more apt to show claw marks than are cat tracks. In other words, cat prints show oval or roundish toes, whereas canine prints reveal more pointed toes. Of course, in deep snow, details become blurred. A cat generally leaves a trail of single tracks evenly spaced in a line. Canines bound around a lot and leave sets of four prints, each set separated by more space than the space between individual prints.

If you have determined the track to be a cat type, but much larger than a domestic cat, then you may be looking at, in order of increasing size, a bobcat, lynx, or a mountain lion, although none of these are likely to appear in the backyard. If you have determined that the track is a dog type because it is larger than a cat, but without any indication of claws, you are probably looking at mongrel domestic dog tracks, which seldom show claw marks. If the claws are very clear, you are likely looking at a wild canine, although some domestic breeds, like cocker spaniels, show claw marks in a good print. If you are sure the track is canine, and it has a brush mark along or behind each set of four prints, the track is most likely a fox, especially if the snow has any depth, since the fox drags its tail. Coyote tracks in snow are apt to show the individual toes more clearly than a fox track. A coyote often moves

mink
or weasel

coyote loping

rabbit

squirrel

tail brush mark

fox running

Telltale Patterns of Wild Animal Tracks

at a lope, in which case it will leave four footprints in a line that is straight but slanted from its forward direction. When at a slow run, a fox's set of four is more in a Y shape.

If the track shows a print of five toes, then clearly you are dealing with something from other than the cat or dog families. Rabbit tracks are rounder than squirrels and usually appear in sets of four in the same kind of Y shape as a dog's, only smaller. Squirrel tracks are narrower than rabbit tracks, and a group of four forms a more square configuration, becoming almost a set of two prints as the squirrel bounds at a faster speed (the back feet and front feet hitting the same spots in the snow), with slash marks denoting feet dragging in the deep snow, and sometimes a tail brush mark between the footprints. The most common mink track reveals a series of twin prints where the hind feet register in the front tracks, blurring detail, with about 15 inches between the twin sets. A weasel track often looks the same, except that the tracks are smaller and the twin sets closer together. A muskrat drags its tail in a telltale continuous S between the tracks. A snapping turtle drags its tail, too, but in a straighter line, with the footprints farther apart than the muskrat's. Shrews drag their tails sometimes, but their tracks are tiny and often are blurred together in snow, in a continuous "plow" pattern, as the small animal forges through the snow in a swimming motion. Most of the time, mice and shrews tunnel beneath the snow, leaving miniature molelike ridges. There is often no way to tell mouse and shrew tracks apart, especially deer mice and other long-tailed species that occasionally drag their tails.

The raccoon's track is common along streams and pools. The back paw makes a print like a baby's foot, the front more like a baby's hand, although a really good print in firm mud might show in very fine detail the claw marks above each toe. Opossum tracks, which are similar to and often found in the same places as raccoon tracks, seldom if ever show claw marks separate from the toes, as can a coon track. The other distinguishing mark of an opossum track is that the hind foot, which shows up in the track next to a front footprint, has a knobby "thumb" toe. This toe sticks off at a right angle to the other toes and shows up in the tracks as an elongated appendage of the paw pointing toward the front paw-print adjacent to it.

Deer tracks can be mistaken for pig or sheep tracks, but there is a difference. The two front tips of a deer's hoof are sharper, closer together, and pointed a little more toward each other than pig or sheep tracks.

The porcupine makes a fairly large, ovalish pad of a print. The hind foot is nearly twice the size of the front, and it looks very much like the shape of a prehistoric stone hatchet. Moles, badgers, woodchucks, and other burrowing animals are better identified by the way they move earth than by their tracks. A badger hole is elliptical, like a drainpipe slightly flattened, and large with much dirt heaved up and about. Pocket gophers, which badgers eat, make mounds of fine dirt that they remove from their tunnel. A much smaller bulb of dirt just to the side of the mound covers the hole from which the gopher pushed the larger mound of dirt. Chipmunks make small holes, 2 to 3 inches in diameter, but rarely leave telltale piles of dirt at the entrances.

Bird tracks invariably show three toes, with a fourth often present that points in the direction opposite to the other three. Waterfowl prints show the webbing between toes by a line connecting them.

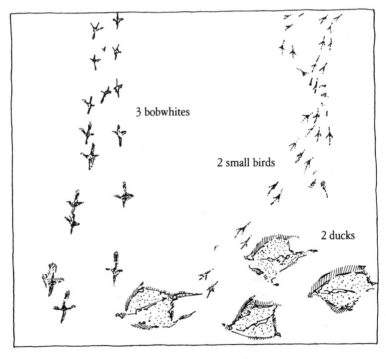

Patterns of Wild Bird Tracks

Stalking

Having learned to listen and to look for signs of wildlife, the wildlife watcher must next appreciate the art of stalking, and the art of blending into the wildlife area so as to be less noticeable or to present a less fearsome image to wildlings. When stalking, the wildlife watcher actively hunts for his quarry; when blending in, he waits passively for wildlife to come to him.

White is convinced that there are few wild animals in Smith's acreage, because he never sees any. White walks heavily through the area, tramping on twigs, swatting viciously at mosquitoes, loudly cursing the deerflies, looking more or less straight ahead, eager to break through to the other side. Even the robins flee before him.

Smith, on the other hand, has taught himself the art of stalking. He walks in his wild area slowly, pausing after nearly every other step, placing his feet down gently, heel first, then sort of rolling the rest of his foot down very gradually. Progress is slow. Sometimes he must retreat in his search for a quiet place to tread, free of dry leaves or crackling twigs. He tries to move from tree shadow to tree shadow, or to shield himself under the edge of the hedge. His ears are alert; at the least sound, he freezes. He learned to develop his peripheral vision. He sees not only in front of him, but also picks up motion on either side.

He usually makes his rounds in the morning before work or in the evening when he returns home—the two times of day when animals are most active. He claims that there is some new thing to see, or some change to observe, every day, and he never tires of his strolls. Before his walks, he avoids as much as possible anything that produces a strong odor that would tip animals to his presence (odors do not apparently alarm birds): strong soaps, skin lotions, minted candies, strong-smelling medications, aromatic foods, liquor, clothes saturated with tobacco smoke or exhaust fumes, and dry-cleaned clothes.

Above all, he refrains from any jerky, quick motions, especially of arms or hands. He has learned that staring directly at animals makes them nervous, as it does other humans. He pretends to be looking somewhere else, following the animal or bird with peripheral vision, only occasionally glancing directly at it. If he makes a noise, as stepping on a twig, he freezes. The animal, tense at the noise, often relaxes when there is no follow-up motion. In drawing near to an animal or bird, he moves when it moves, pauses when it pauses. If the quarry is involved intensely in nest-building, feeding, or mating activities, this gambit often enables him to move within the animal's "safety zone," the term naturalists have given to that distance wild animals allow humans to approach before they fly or run away. Once, Smith was able to stalk to within 15 feet of two flickers involved in their strange mating games. The female would fly from sapling to sapling, as if totally unaware of the male. The male followed like a shadow, landing on the opposite side of a skinny trunk, facing her—or, rather, both of them ludicrously facing the tree trunk. Then he would peer around at her, bobbing his head in a seemingly distraught manner, all the while burbling what must have been pompous male braggadocio, and swelling out his breast feathers to prove to her that he was the most beautiful creature on earth. The strange ritual went on for days before the female returned his devout attention and the scene dissolved into familial bliss and hectic house-hunting.

Stalking, even at its best, will not bring a human as close to wildlife as hiding and waiting for wildlife to approach. A blind to hide in and watch from need not be an elaborate affair. Smith learned quite by accident that a hammock makes a very nice blind. Lying in it, he is in a more or less prone position, which is much less fearsome to wildlings than the human standing position. The sides of the hammock lap up over him, concealing most of his body anyway. The comfort of the position allows him to remain quite motionless for relatively long periods of time.

A clump of bushes can serve as a blind, although a backrest is almost imperative if one is to remain comfortably motionless. A seat on the ground with back against the shadowy side of a tree trunk works fairly well, especially if the tree has low limbs with heavy foliage to provide a curtain of cover. Sitting or lying against a log or large rock often provides sufficient cover.

A house makes an adequate blind if birds and animals are fed right outside the window. The wildlings soon lose their fear of movement behind the window, especially if the lights are off, partially concealing that movement. Some photographers set a camera on a tripod, aimed at a feeder through a partly opened window or through the glass (glass may or may not cause distortion; it is less likely to do so if the camera lens is right up next to the glass). The camera is focused on a marked spot on the feeder. When a bird steps on that spot, the photographer trips the shutter, usually by way of a long cable release that allows him or her to be free to move about the room a little. Equipped with a motor, the camera automatically advances the film to the next frame. In this way, wildlife can be photographed while one is cooking, cleaning house, writing, talking on the phone, or doing some similar activity.

An automobile or even a lawn mower can be a sort of blind. Animals get used to these machines, and strange as it may seem, a human on a riding lawn mower can sometimes draw closer to a bird than one tiptoeing quietly across the lawn on foot.

Building a Blind for Viewing Wildlife

For the warier creatures who will not approach human habitations, at least not during the day, some sort of formal hiding place becomes necessary. A simple and effective blind can be made with a pile of brush, as famous naturalist Edwin Way Teale proved with his "branch office." Nail together a simple box frame of 2 × 4-inch boards large enough to accommodate a human or two and a comfortable seat. Set the frame on the ground at the desired location, and cover it with brush, leaving a small opening for an entrance. Of course, the brush cannot be piled on too thickly, or the blind will block its occupants' view, too. Often, small birds will alight right on this kind of blind, since to them a brush pile is a safe haven from predators.

A similar blind can be built by cutting a bunch of saplings with leaves into poles and leaning them against each other to form a teepee-shaped structure. Tie the poles together at the top, spread the butts out in a more or less circular pattern, and the job is finished. This type of blind provides the wildlife watcher better "holes" through which to aim a camera or a pair of binoculars than does the brush pile blind.

A garden toolhouse, woodshed, or gazebo easily doubles as a blind. If the latter is screened, it'll keep out mosquitoes and other biting insects. But the screen will soften the effectiveness of cameras and binoculars.

Brush pile and sapling blinds don't keep out the wind, rain or snow. A tent will, but if it is to be used as a blind, it should be set up well in advance of use so that resident wildlife become accustomed to it. Permanent weatherproof blinds are easily built by pole or stud wall construction, a simple slanted roof, and an outer covering of exterior plywood or tar paper. Slits and holes, no larger than necessary, can be cut into the walls, from which to view and photograph wildlife. If the building is painted camouflage colors, such as various shades of green, or perhaps a few leafy tree branches are cut and placed on the roof, so much the better.

Thinking about building a blind motivated Smith to embark on one of his most ambitious sanctuary projects. He decided to build a tree house for his blind. To be perfectly honest, he did not so much want a blind per se as he wanted a tree house for his children. And, to be even more perfectly honest, he did not want a tree house for his son and daughter nearly as much as he wanted it for himself. Since adults are not supposed to be tempted by the whimsies of childhood, he told his wildlife-watching friends that he was building a blind, and he told his other friends, who, like White, already questioned his normalcy, that he was building a tree house for his offspring. In either case, he believed that wildlife would approach a blind up in a tree much sooner than one on the ground. Still, if it did not prove to be true, being high up in the enchanting breezes of the treetops with a good book, hidden from even White's gimlet eyes, might be a perfect way to spend a summer Sunday afternoon anyway. The Beekeeper, upon hearing the news, nodded understandingly—another indication, he opined, that man had spent long periods of evolutionary development in trees. "It's just that this monkey instinct," he said sardonically, looking at Smith, "is stronger in some people than in others."

Although the idea of building a tree house seemed simple enough, Smith found that the actuality was another story. He studied his grove of trees for an ideal site. There was none. At one spot three trees grew close enough together so that he could have nailed 2×4-inch boards between them, connecting them with a three-sided platform and a three-sided railing above it, as hunters do to make deer stands in wooded country. But he reasoned that in windy weather, the three trees would sway in different directions, eventually tearing and racking the platform apart.

There was no need to nail the floor joists to the trees anyway, if the floor could be framed around one or more tree trunks so that it could not slide in any direction. All he needed were two trees fairly close together with limbs projecting on both sides of the two trunks at about the same height. He could lash two 4×4-inch beams on branches on either side of the two trunks so that the wind could not blow them away, and then nail boards across the beams to make a platform or floor.

Finding two trees with four limbs in the proper position was not as easy as Smith thought it would be. Luckily, he had a pair of pin oaks growing hardly 9 feet apart that proved to be adaptable. Not only were their limbs at the right height, but because the two trees were growing close together, branches between them had shaded each other out to a considerable extent, leaving a fairly open space in the foliage where the tree house could sit without the necessity of Smith removing many branches. The fine-leaved pin oaks provided good camouflage concealment from the outside, but inside the leafy bower, one could see out into the surrounding territory quite easily.

On a jutting branch above the limbs where Smith intended to lay his tree house floor, he affixed a pulley, ran a rope though it, and by this means hoisted up the four 10-foot-long, 4 × 4-inch beams upon which his tree house would rest. First he raised two beams in place on one side of the two trunks, and then the other two on the other side. On a ladder, he jostled the beams through the foliage and into place, while his wife manned the rope below. Then he nailed boards about 2 feet apart on the beams, making a platform approximately 7 by 8 feet long, with a floorboard at each end on the outside of the tree trunks, so that the trunks were completely framed in, holding the platform in place (see illustration).

Although he had originally intended to make walls and a roof for his tree house, Smith, always one to prefer an easier way, built instead a railing around the edge of the platform, nailing 3-foot uprights directly onto the outside 4 × 4 beams. He curtained the sides then with roll-up bamboo. Next he hauled up a beach umbrella that he lashed to the railing, not only as cover against sun and rain, but also to hide under from the eyes of birds passing overhead. By now Smith no longer referred to his creation as a tree house, or even a blind, but as his "Crow's Nest."

There still remained the matter of getting up and down conveniently. Originally, Smith had nurtured the romantic notion that he would climb up to his hideaway on a rope ladder like a modern day Tarzan, pulling the ladder up behind him. Swaying around on the end of a rope ladder was not, however, the snap it had been years ago in Army basic training. It was taxing enough to clamber up and down the wooden extension ladder he had used during construction. He decided to leave the ladder extended somewhat higher than the Crow's Nest platform and leaning against the trunk of one of the trees, so that he could step off the ladder onto the platform while holding firmly to a limb above, with little danger of losing his balance and falling. To make the ladder even safer, he lashed it tightly to the tree trunk at the top the way a good chimney sweep ties his ladder-top to the chimney he is working on.

As he had predicted, Smith's children immediately took over the Crow's Nest, and they derived hours of enjoyment from it. At first he made some effort to forbid them to play in the tree house when their friends were visiting, all in an effort to prevent broken bones. But regulation was in vain. One Saturday afternoon, Smith looked out to see his son and a neighbor boy not in the tree house, but higher yet, on the fragile limb of another tree, gaily swinging about in such a way as to make an adult's blood run cold. It had been the same with forbidding them to play in the garden pool when they were smaller. Pools and trees offer temptations beyond a child's strength to resist. Smith decided that a wildlife area that could not accommodate the wild yearnings of human youngsters was no sanctuary at all. He changed the regulation from barring them to requiring quiet, to preserve the tranquility necessary to watch wildlife.

The tree house came in handy in unexpected ways. Smith's wife found it the perfect place for relaxing. For Smith, it also became a sort of watchtower. From it, he could get a view of the neighborhood not as obstructed by the suburban forest in which they lived. The Crow's Nest was a good place to find out what was burning when the fire siren sounded nearby, or to find where an automobile accident had occurred. He could even tell when the Dumb Farmer had fired up his wood stove, signaling the proper beginning of autumn. He could watch for tornadoes, or at least see if a summer storm were brewing and heading his way, as had been his custom when living on the open plains of the Midwest.

Most of all, the Crow's Nest became a vantage point not only for wildlife watching, but for human watching as well. Smith found himself observing his neighbors with the same sort of curious detachment with which he watched birds. White, mowing his lawn when it did not need to be mowed, seemed to follow some as-yet-unnamed instinct as compelling as the one that drove the squirrel to bury nuts,

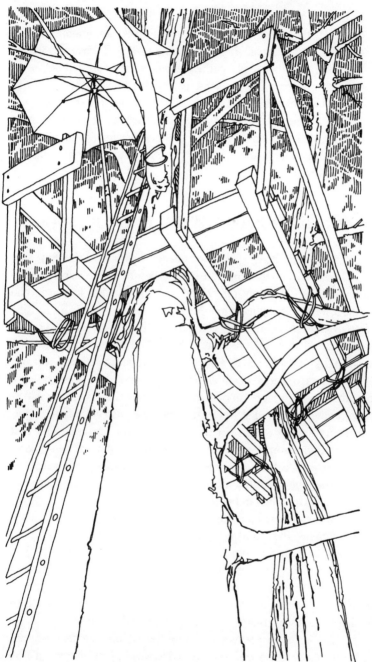

Smith's Crow's Nest

even though it would forget most of its hiding places. Were the teen-agers down the street, feverishly polishing their automobiles to the heavy beat of rock music, under the same spell that drove the ants to frantically move their eggs as the barometric pressure fell before an approaching storm? Did the same power that twisted the sunflower heads to the sun as it moved across the sky also beckon the sunbather from the house to the yard? Smith did not try to answer these questions. He preferred the sense of mystery they instilled in him. But he reached one conclusion: The backyard sanctuary has no boundaries. All life is wild.

Optical Aids For Wildlife Observation

No matter how well trained the eye, how skilled the stalker, or how cleverly hidden the blind, watching wildlife enjoyably and success-fully depends absolutely on optical aids: binoculars for birds and animals, a magnifying hand lens for insects, and a microscope for tiny microorganisms and to study cellular structure upon which accurate identification often must be based. The bird fluttering in the trees that to the naked eye seems to be a nondescript brownish yellow is revealed by binoculars to sport a breathtaking orange flame of breast feathers—a Blackburnian warbler. Binoculars not only bring far-away objects closer and put them in sharper focus, but they also amplify the light, enhancing all of nature seen through them with a luminosity that direct sunlight provides only at certain times and at certain angles. Smith, helping a naturalist catch and band warblers, was surprised to find that the beautiful warblers of his binocular world were not quite as colorful when in his hand.

Without a magnifying lens, the activity of insects is often unintelligible—the naked eye just cannot adequately see the spider pulling silken thread from itself and weaving a web with it. It just cannot adequately see an ant carrying aphids from below-ground storage to apple-leaf "pastures." A hand-held lens enables you to immediately distinguish a moth with knobbed antennae from one with feathery antennae—that is, to distinguish female from male.

A microscope seems a luxury for the wildlife watcher only until he has a chance to use one. A drop of pond water seems like only a drop of water until examined under a microscope. Then it turns into a wildlife area of its own, full of tiny plants and animals, without which larger wildlife areas could not exist.

Since hand lenses are relatively inexpensive, the well-equipped wildlife watcher should consider carrying two kinds. The first, and most important, is the small but more powerful lens of 10 power, capable of showing the detailed facets of an insect's eye or the texture of pollen grains on a flower. The diameter of this kind of hand lens is usually less than an inch, and it can easily be worn on a chain around the neck or like a pocket watch. In addition, the larger magnifying glass, from 2 to 4 inches in diameter with a handle on it, comes in handy. Although usually only about 3 power, not strong enough to give necessary detail in most instances, the magnifying glass is better for watching insects in action over a wider range of vision—for instance, watching a spider rush out upon a bug caught in its web. You can make a little leather carrying case for the magnifying glass and wear it on your belt like a hunting knife.

Many models of binoculars are available in a wide price range. Many wildlife watchers go through the same three stages of binocular use that Smith did. First, he bought cheapies—$49.95—because he didn't think backyard watching required anything grander than that. Within three years, moisture and dirt had gotten inside the binoculars. When he banged them against a doorway, the jolt knocked the prisms out of whack ever so slightly, so that peering through them made him dizzy. So he bought a $100 pair, which produced a clear enough image, but after five years, also went on the blink. He bought a third pair, spending around $200 this time, and he has used them comfortably and enjoyably ever since. Had he bought the $200 model in the first place, he would have saved money. But with a little luck, he also could have gotten by well enough with the $50 pair.

One can spend a great deal more than that on binoculars, up to around $400 for the top-line models from Bushnell, Nikon, Bausch and Lomb, or another reputable company. Professional naturalists (and hobbyists who don't mind spending the money) can buy the very best from German firms like Ernst Leitz, Inc., or Carl Zeiss, Inc., for over $1,000. The money spent on quality like this is usually a good investment. Leitz and Zeiss binoculars carry lifetime guarantees and can be used continuously for hours without eyestrain. Thousand-dollar binoculars today will no doubt cost $2,000 in a few years, while a $50 pair will be worth zero. Of course, most of us have $50 to spend on binoculars before we have $1,000.

For the backyard wildlife watcher, the most popular sizes in binoculars are 8 × 40 and 7 × 35. The first number indicates the magnifying power and the second number the diameter of the objective lens (the front lens) in millimeters (mm). Six-power binoculars are also quite suitable (6 × 30), especially for those who may be hiking and prefer a smaller, lighter pair. Ten-power binoculars are difficult for some people to hand-hold because the extra magnification emphasizes the tremors of the hand holding the binoculars, resulting in a shaky image.

Two types of binoculars are on the market: the older type equipped with Porro prisms (named after the man who invented them), and the newer type equipped with roof prisms. Porro prisms give better stereoscopic vision, but the arrangement of prisms requires a larger binocular barrel than one equipped with roof prisms. Wildlife watchers generally prefer the latter because they are lighter and can be incorporated into very compact models with little sacrifice of power.

For those who want to concentrate on owls, bats, and other nocturnal animals, or for people who view their wildlife mostly in the morning before work, and in the evening after dinner—in other words, when the light is diminishing—there are special binoculars for low-light conditions. These models have large objective (front) lens relative to the magnifying power, which produces a high exit pupil measurement. Exit pupil is a term used to denote the amount of light transmitted through the binocular to the eye. The exit pupil measurement of a particular binocular is determined by dividing the power of the lens into the diameter of the objective lens. Thus, in a conventional 8 × 40 pair, or a 7 × 35 pair, the ray of light coming through to the eye, or exit pupil, is 5 mm in diameter, which corresponds roughly to the size of the pupil of the human eye in normal light. But the human pupil contracts or expands, depending on available light, from about 3 mm to 7 mm in low-light conditions. Therefore, low-light binoculars usually have 8 × 50 or even 8 × 56 power, providing an exit pupil quotient of 6 to 7 mm to match the expanded eye pupil. Such binoculars allow sighting of owls even in semidarkness.

In buying binoculars, especially in the lower price ranges, the prospective buyer can use certain criteria to evaluate models and brands. First of all, the images seen through the binoculars should appear more brilliant than if seen with the naked eye—that is, more luminous and full-colored. This luminous brilliance is achieved in modern binoculars by lens coatings, usually magnesium fluoride. With uncoated lenses, about half the available light is lost as the image is reflected from prism to prism inside the binocular barrels. Coating the lenses—and in good binoculars *all* the optical surfaces are coated, not just the first and last—increases the efficiency of the light transmission up to nearly 80 percent. Coated lenses look purplish when held at an angle to the light.

Next, look carefully through the binoculars and check the sharpness of focus, which is called resolution. Along the edges of the field of vision, do objects appear in clear focus? If blurring occurs at the edges, the optical system in the binoculars is of low quality. Then, focus on an object that has much intricate line detail. A brick wall is perfect. Any really noticeable distortions of line means poor-quality lenses. The cheapest prisms, or prisms not properly aligned, may form a rainbow halo on the edges of images on which you are trying to focus. Poor lenses go out of focus at the slightest turn of the focusing knob. Good ones move in and out of focus slowly as you turn the knob.

Test the two binocular barrels for alignment problems. Both sets of prisms have to be perfectly parallel to each other in their respective barrels if the two images are to meld perfectly into one. If the two images do not merge perfectly, the human eyes will compensate to some degree for the resulting blurring, causing eyestrain. Focus the binoculars on a barbed wire fence, telephone line, or electric line from a distance of several hundred feet. Move the binoculars away from your eyes until you can see the small image of the wire in each eyepiece. If the line is higher in one than in the other, the binoculars are probably misaligned. If this happens to a pair of binoculars you already own, probably from dropping them, you can usually get them realigned at a good optical repair shop.

If you wear glasses, it pays to buy binoculars with retractable rubber eye cups. These eye cups allow you to reduce the distance from retina to eyepiece to compensate for the glasses. They also keep glasses from getting scratched on metal eyepieces.

Good binoculars are hermetically sealed against dirt and moisture. But there is no way to tell how well sealed a new pair in the store is; you have to trust the good reputation of proven manufacturers and reputable dealers—even if you have to pay more than for those "bargains" you hear others bragging about.

For purposes of the backyard wildlife viewer, a modestly priced microscope (around $150) is adequate. Very powerful microscopes are not necessary and can be a drawback, since more often the viewer will want to watch fairly large microorganisms moving about in, say, a drop of water. A good choice is a microscope with three or four barrels and a zoom lens that slides smoothly from 50 to 1,200 power. Some models now come with adapters that allow you to mount a camera and take pictures through the microscope. Microscopes sold more or less as toys often have poor lenses that distort the image or ring it with a rainbow halo. Avoid them—even for toys. Children intelligent enough to become interested in microorganic life deserve something better. Large horticultural tool and supply catalogs carry microscopes suitable for the backyard naturalist.

Photography

Inevitably, the wildlife watcher yearns for a way to enshrine the beauty and variety he finds in his backyard in some sort of collection. Some are content just creating lists of the species they observe. The artistically gifted may turn to sketching, painting, or carving likenesses of what they find. Others preserve actual specimens when practical: insects, dried plants, eggs, feathers, cell tissue on glass microscope slides, perhaps even stuffed animals. Such collections have their disadvantages. Taxidermy may be a wonderful way to preserve an animal or bird that has died or been killed anyway, but no stuffed animal in a room can ever equal its live counterpart in the backyard, and given the latter, what purpose has the former? The same with insects. As mentioned before, collecting butterflies does no harm to the ecosystem, but a display of butterflies nailed to the wall all in a row is a pale substitute for the live ones fluttering in the garden. Since, in a properly managed ecosystem, the live ones will flutter in the yard each year as sure as the sun rises, why collect them? Taking one bird egg of each species from the nests once in a lifetime may not endanger bird populations, and in a specific instance might even make life easier for the other nestlings when they hatch. But if *every* wildlife lover pilfered a bluebird egg—or an egg of any species having a hard time surviving in a human-dominated world—it just might make a difference, for the worse.

There is a much better way to collect wildlife: with a camera. Wildlife photography combines the pleasures of collecting, hunting, and artistic expression, and provides a permanent, handy record that will not rot, disintegrate, be eaten by mice, or require mothball storage. With modern advances in photographic technology, amateurs can train themselves to catch on film almost any of the myriad natural phenomena occurring in their backyards. There are opportunities to exhibit and publish hitherto unphotographed wildlife activities, not to mention species that have not been classified as yet. Smith one day spied a purple grackle on his lawn, half the length of whose tail was *white*. He did not have a camera. No one in his neighborhood believed he saw it. Although albinism in grackles has often been verified in the scientific community, Smith and his neighbors didn't know this. If he had taken a photograph of the bird, perhaps he could have convinced his doubting friends.

The type of camera a backyard photographer chooses is largely a matter of preference—and pocketbook. If you have several thousand dollars to spend, a Hasselblad 500 EL/M may be the ultimate camera. Its 2¼-inch negative is large enough to avoid problems of graininess and detail that might show up in enlarging the more popular 35 mm film of a single-lens reflex camera. Take off the Hasselblad's waist-level viewing hood, slide on the eye-level prism-finder with through-the-lens metering system, and the camera becomes almost as handy as a conventional single-lens reflex camera. On a tripod with waist-level viewing hood back in place, the Hasselblad can be used for composing pictures of plants almost as finely detailed and luminous as the masterpieces Eliot Porter creates with large and cumbersome cameras that use 4 × 5-inch negatives. With an electric motor to advance the film and cock the shutter, the Hasselblad comes close to matching the quickness of a similarly equipped single-lens reflex camera for sighting a moving animal, focusing with one hand, and tripping the shutter with the other. Or the camera can be set up at a nest or den of a wildling and operated by remote control from a distance. But few backyarders can afford such elaborate equipment.

The professionals will argue forever about the advantages and disadvantages of different types of cameras, and most of them own one of each to use in various situations. The backyarder usually must be content with a modestly priced 35 mm, single-lens reflex camera. With such a camera, equipped with a zoom telephoto lens and a close-up lens, he can more than adequately handle almost any situation in photographing backyard wildlife. For still pictures, the novice might indeed prefer a Polaroid camera that will give him a finished color print for his records in a few seconds. If one photographs a rare fungus with a conventional camera, it may be days before he receives his developed prints or slides. If the pictures are not satisfactory, it probably will be too late to take more photos because the mushroom likely will have deteriorated. With a Polaroid, the novice, as yet unsure of himself, avoids this risk.

The 35 mm, single-lens reflex camera can be mounted on a gun stock and made even handier and quicker for shooting action shots of wildlife. The photographer sights the camera almost as if it were a rifle, operating the zoom lens with the left hand and tripping the shutter with the right, while the electric motor automatically advances the film and cocks the shutter.

A zoom telephoto lens is almost a must for wildlife photography. But understand the limitations of the one you are using. Telephoto lenses of 100 to 200 mm focal length will not take adequate pictures of a bird even 300 feet away. On 35 mm film, the bird at that distance will still be just a dot and will not enlarge to an adequate size in a print. But at a distance of 10 feet, this size lens brings even small birds close enough to fill the entire frame, so that it can be enlarged or projected on a screen adequately. From 50 to 100 feet away, a small creature like a bird requires a more powerful telephoto lens—500 mm at least. Most professional bird photographers use an 800 mm. These lenses are quite expensive. A cheaper alternative is to purchase a couple of simple magnifying lenses, called extenders or doublers, that can be inserted between the barrel of a telephoto lens and the camera. A double magnifier will increase the power of a 200 mm telephoto to 400 mm. The magnifiers decrease the amount of light getting through to the film, however, and require fast films and large lens openings to capture fast-moving wildlife. This always means a decrease in the depth of field. Your photographs will be less sharp if you use a magnifier.

A close-up lens is necessary for good pictures of plants and insects. Using one, the amateur photographer soon learns not to photograph outdoors on windy days. The slight swaying of the plants in the wind translates in the close-up lens to rather violent movement.

Another problem is that depth of field decreases dramatically as the lens comes closer and closer to the object being photographed. To keep both the front end and rear end of an insect in sharp focus at close range, it becomes imperative to use a small lens opening—at least F 16, and preferably F 22. Since there is rarely enough available light to allow the use of such a small aperture on your camera in the weeds or in the woods where you are working, close-up nature photography requires additional light—a mini-strobe light, mounted on the camera or hand held, powered by four small, dry-cell batteries. Strobe lights are simple to use. Talk to your local camera shop manager.

Another trick in shooting with a close-up lens, especially subjects such as insects that are prone to fly away just as you get ready to take the picture, is to prefocus the camera at the distance you deem best for the picture—usually at the closest limit the lens will allow. Instead of trying to get a sharp picture by adjusting the lens in and out, simply aim the camera, then lean forward until you achieve perfect focus. Quickly trip the shutter before the insect flies away.

Since a zoom telephoto lens and a close-up lens are both more important in wildlife photography than the conventional lens on the camera, and a motor-driven film advancer is very handy in many situations, be sure to figure in these costs when budgeting for your camera. Most backyarders will settle for a modestly priced, single-lens reflex camera. In this case, the two additional lenses you need can cost as much as the camera.

Although it is more expensive, collecting wildlife with the camera ought to be done in color, for the sake of beauty as well as accuracy. The goal of the photographer, then, must be to expose his film correctly, so that the colors are true to nature. This requires the amateur photographer to become keenly aware of the power and magic of sunlight. Taking a really great photo as compared to just a so-so one depends more than anything else on the angle at which the light is striking the object being photographed. A dogwood tree in red fall foliage looks merely like a dogwood tree in red fall foliage when the sun is not shining, (or when it's shining more or less directly down on the tree). But the slanting rays of morning or evening sun will transform that tree into a glittering scarlet fire.

Only a few years ago, the amateur could get better color in slides than in prints, at a much cheaper price. But slides involve a screen, a projector, and a good filing system. Looking at pictures on slides becomes an unhandy and time-consuming operation. Today, the technology of mass-developing color prints has improved greatly, and though it's still more expensive, the pictures can be filed with the index card on each plant or animal, or mounted in scrapbooks and easily referred to for purposes of study or to show to others. But with color prints, it becomes extremely important, especially on 35 mm film, to *fill* the frame with the object being photographed so that, in the print, that object is large enough to be seen in detail. If the picture is exceptional, then 8 × 10-inch enlargements can be made without problems.

Making movies of wildlife is even more exciting than still shooting, and technology has brought this skill within easy reach of the amateur. In terms of potential value, films of little-known wildlife activities will rank far ahead of still shots as the demand grows for video cassettes viewed through home television.

Smith keeps thinking to himself: Probably no one has ever watched a movie of a leaf-eating *Hydrocampa propiralis* building a leaf-boat and setting sail across a pond in search of water plants to eat.

Chapter 10

When Wildlife Overpopulates

In terms of wildlife, the loveliest years of Gywnedde Township occurred after the cultivated and closely grazed fields of commercial farming had all but disappeared (except for the Dumb Farmer's place), but before the proliferation of abandoned fields, brushy streambanks, unmowed roadsides, ungrazed tree groves, protected old trees, varied ornamental landscaping, backyard gardens and No Hunting signs turned the township into a wildlife mecca. In that lull between the two environments, wildlife numbers were relatively low compared to what they would become but higher than when the iron hand of commercial farming held sway over all. Smith, the Beekeeper, the Widow Lady, and even the Dumb Farmer had no trouble welcoming all wildlife with open arms during that time. Although the Dumb Farmer kept telling the others they'd end up being very sorry for opposing hunting, all of them accused him of ecological insensitivity and opposed his notion that some wild creatures sometimes needed to be "harvested" just like nearly everyone understood that rats should be "harvested." The Dumb Farmer loved to use that word "harvested" with heavy irony in his voice, implying that nice suburbanites found the word "kill" too harsh except, he pointed out acidly, in reference to Iraqis threatening our oil supply.

Smith became active in the movement to outlaw all hunting in the township. The Dumb Farmer shook his head. "Yes, you say it's all right to kill rats, but when groundhogs, raccoons, squirrels and rabbits increase in population to where their main source of food is your gardens, they'll begin to look a whole lot like rats to you."

Smith demurred. The Dumb Farmer came from another, more barbaric time, he told himself. In the modern era, what wildlife remained should be considered a treasure and a blessing. He stood by his philosophy for several years. With remarkable patience he suffered bats in the attics, raccoons in the garbage can, skunks under the porch, bees in the walls, chipmunks in the insulation around the foundation, snakes in the basement, woodpeckers drumming holes into the wood siding, cardinals and robins bouncing against the window in their dreary fight with their reflections, opossums in the henhouse, groundhogs under the garage, moles turning the lawn into an off-road obstacle course for mowers, mourning doves fluttering in the chimney. "Hey, I can handle all that," he said with a generous wave of his hand. "Makes life interesting." He even remained magnanimous when the coons and groundhogs and rabbits first started "sharing" his garden and ornamentals.

The Dumb Farmer smiled and waited.

In the most patient of men, there is always a limit. Smith would share his plants, yes, but when the coons and groundhogs and rabbits started taking EVERYTHING, he drew the line. He drew it in front of his sweet corn patch.

Smith Learns How Smart "Dumb Animals" Can Be

The Dumb Farmer, who had been through all this before, told Smith that only an electric fence would make an effective Maginot Line. Smith did not like the sound of that. Electric fence smacked of the technological world from which his garden was his retreat. Electric fencing would also be a lot of botheration, and what if one of the kids got caught in it? Being an engineer with doctor of philosophy letters behind his name, Smith figured he might avoid the cost and fuss of fencing simply by outwitting wildlife, a pronouncement that sent the Dumb Farmer into a fit of almost hysterical laughter. "If a rabbit gets hungry enough and the reward of victory is food, it will beat you in a game of chess," he said, doing a little caper to show how much fun he was going to have watching Smith brought down by "dumb animals."

Smith first chose the raccoon to outwit. Such a shy little animal with such a small brain would certainly be easy to scare away with the superior inventiveness of *homo sapiens.* "By all means," the Dumb Farmer said, doing his little jig of delight again. "By all means."

Smith ignored him. A farmer simply couldn't appreciate what years of schooling taught a man. First, you had to do your research. Smith diligently went to work on the body of literature about raccoon control, and found it to be quite extensive. Didn't the Dumb Farmer know? Even discounting some of it as only quaint folklore, Smith felt sure that among the remainder he had but to express the right formula and press the right buttons, so to speak, and presto! no more coons in the corn. Among the solutions he selected for further experimentation were to

1. Hang lighted lanterns in corn patch.
2. Spread mothballs in corn patch.
3. Surround corn patch with pumpkins.
4. Surround corn patch with band of newspaper with mothballs on it.
5. Surround corn patch with strip of black plastic.
6. Spread blood meal on ground around corn patch.
7. Spread lion or tiger manure from zoo around corn patch.
8. Play hard-rock music in corn patch.
9. String creosoted twine through the corn stalks.
10. Hang kerosene-soaked rags around corn patch.
11. Spread red pepper on ears of corn.
12. Tie dog on leash at edge of corn patch.
13. Urinate as often as possible around edges of the corn patch.

Smith discarded Solution Number 12 because he didn't own a dog and, in fact, despised dogs. Dogs yelped in the night except when thieves were about, chased away desirable wildlife, ate far more than they were worth, got loose and dug holes in the garden, usually someone else's. Unfortunately for Smith, Solution Number 12 was the only one of the above that works, and then not always, as he discovered (see Chapter 12). He decided to dispense with Number 13, too, because it seemed a little crude, although the Widow Lady said she had found it partially effective. The Widow Lady could say that, Smith sniffed. Her place was so overgrown with brush that her privacy was guaranteed at all times. "Well," she huffed modestly. "You can urinate into a receptacle in your bathroom and then pour the stuff around the garden, you know." Smith said nothing, not wishing to admit that he hadn't even thought of that.

Smith bought a coal-oil lantern and hung it in the corn patch. He thought it looked quite romantic. So did the coons. They ate corn in the dim gloaming of the lantern's luminescence like kids eating marshmallows around a campfire. Smith ran an extension cord to the garden with an electric bulb at the end of it, installing in the light socket a little gadget engineers know about that makes the light blink on and off. All night the bulb winked. The coons winked right back and continued their corn feast.

Smith's scientific composure was strained to the breaking point. He bought mothballs. Fortunately for him, he bought naphthalene mothballs, not paradichlorobenzene, the latter being a chlorinated hydrocarbon. He spread the mothball crystals around the outer perimenter of the patch. To make sure, he laid down newspapers on one side and black plastic on the other, spreading the mothballs on top. The first night, the coons stayed away, probably suffering stomach aches from previous gluttony. Smith beamed a very scientifically pompous beam. But the second night the coons were back, leaving another path of half-eaten cobs in their wake. With cusswords that scientific engineers seldom find it necessary to use, Smith flung more mothballs into his corn patch, heedless of where they landed. Some landed in the leaf whorls of the few remaining good ears of corn attached to the cornstalks. The coons did not bother these ears. Smith found out why. Even shucked and roasted, they tasted like mothballs. The Dumb Farmer tallied up the score for the summer: Raccoons 135 ears, Smith 24 (only 12 edible).

Smith was getting smarter, but he didn't know it just yet. The next year he wired his corn patch into a Rube Goldberg fantasy of lights and noise. The garden looked like the Midway at the county fair, the Dumb Farmer observed. Lights of many colors blinked from several cords. A doorbell attached to an electric timer tinkled merrily at regular intervals through the night. White, irked by the gaudy, clattering display, suggested that Smith leave up his creations until Christmas and maybe get his money's worth out of them as holiday decoration.

To leave nothing to chance, Smith spread bloodmeal and tiger manure (the latter a difficult commodity to come by, he learned, even with a zoo only three major traffic jams away in south Philly) and hung kerosene-soaked rags on a creosote-soaked string stretched around the corn patch.

The masked bandits stayed away three nights. The next planting of corn was not quite ready yet and they knew it. When it was, Armegeddon. The Dumb Farmer slapped his leg and howled in laughter.

A Shocking Solution to Raccoon Raids

Smith made two adjustments in his doctor of philosophizing. He agreed with the Dumb Farmer that coonhunting ought to be reinstated into the tradition of Gwynedde Township, and he discovered that until such time, electric fencing was the only effective way to control coons, even if it cost as much as the damned corn.

Finding an electric fence that really fit into his gardening system was at first difficult, since the garden suppliers, who rarely gardened themselves, were only slowly learning the extent of the problem. But Smith, the engineer, rigged up a system, using posts, wire, and insulators that the Dumb Farmer loaned him, and buying a regular farm fence charger plugged into a 110-volt outlet in the garage. It worked well enough if he was very careful to keep grass and weeds from growing up and shorting out the wire in rainy weather. He found that one wire about 6 inches above the ground kept groundhogs and raccoons at bay, but two worked better, the second 12 inches off the ground, above the first. Once the wild animals learned about charged wire, they avoided it as a matter of course. At least for several days. Needless to say, monkeying around with electric fence nearly doubled the time Smith spent gardening.

In a few more years, farm supply businesses became aware of the onslaught of wildlife in gardens (for some strange reason, garden

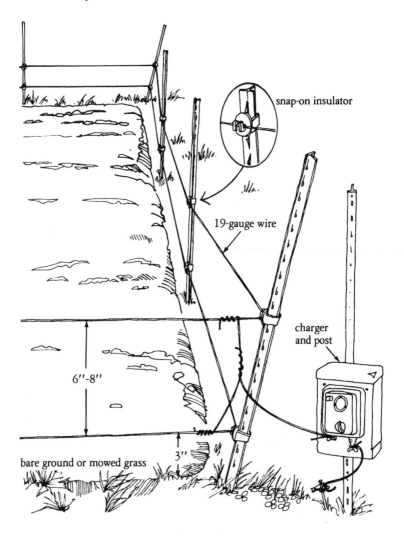

snap-on insulator

19-gauge wire

charger
and post

6''-8''

bare ground or mowed grass

3''

An Electric Fence

catalogs did not) and came out with electric fences of single wire
and mesh screens that were easy to install and less prone to short out
from a stray blade of wet grass or weed stem. The new voltage systems did not deliver enough shock to hurt children or animals. A
fence could be effectively electrified with low-voltage battery sys-

tems—in fact, some were even powered by the sun, so they could be used far from electrical outlets. The Dumb Farmer told him about the Nasco Farm and Ranch catalog from 901 Janesville Avenue, Fort Atkinson, Wisconsin 53538, which carried more kinds of fencing and fencing tools and books on how to install various fences than Smith ever dreamed existed. Another source he often turned to for the latest in all kinds of electric fencing was Premier, 2031 300th, Washington, Iowa 52353.

Smith could not electrify his trees against birds (although he was tempted to try it), and so he struggled through the whole anti-coon rigamarole, trying to keep robins out of cherry trees: fake snakes, fake owls, real cats tied beneath the trees, shining objects whirling in the wind, hard-rock music (which brought a formal complaint from White to the township commissioners) and firecrackers. He even tried tin cans hung in the trees on wires in such a way that the wires scraped on the inside of the cans when the wind blew, making noises even more unearthly than AC/DC's "Thunderstruck," if not as loud as a concert rendition.

Results? Zero. So Smith tried the aerial version of fencing, that is, screening. Trying to stretch netting over even a small tree was a trial, and birds learned how to snatch fruit through the netting or to find a way underneath. But screening worked fairly well on bushes and strawberry beds and saved some of the crop on smaller trees.

For rabbits, he now knew better than go through the coon maneuver again. A simple chicken-wire fence 18 or 24 inches high worked quite well attached to a post every 5 feet or so, no electricity necessary. Rabbits seldom seemed to learn that they could jump over such a fence or squeeze under it. "That's because they aren't hungry enough yet," the Dumb Farmer said.

To protect his peas, Smith installed two lines of 24-inch chicken fencing just a foot apart and as long as the row he desired. Then he planted the peas, not in rows, but broadcast over the entire little corridor between the two lines of fence. The fence kept the rabbits away when the pea plants were small and then provided a trellis for the peas to climb on. The rabbits did not much bother the plants after they were up and growing fast. With this kind of trellis-fence, he could also drape cheesecloth over the whole affair and keep out English sparrows, which for some perverse reason known only to English sparrows, liked to eat pea vines, too.

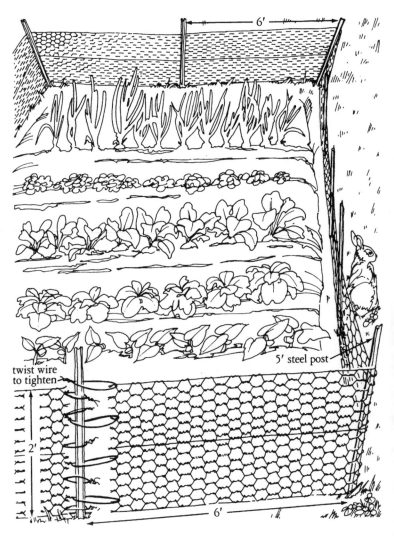

A Chicken-Wire Fence

"Why don't *you* have to protect your garden?" Smith asked the Dumb Farmer peevishly, visiting him one day and noticing the unfenced sweetcorn, which the Dumb Farmer was not only eating but selling.

"Because I KILL coons," the Dumb Farmer said grimly. "See

that cage trap? Coons will fight for the right to be the first one inside if you bait it with corn or fruit. If I catch a pet cat, or an opossum (which I consider a beneficial animal), or a chicken or a bird, I can let it out, no harm done. When I catch a coon or a wild house cat, absolutely the most harmful predator of songbirds, I set the trap with the animal inside in my pond and drown it. Killed a dozen coons this spring, and you can be glad I did, or you wouldn't have *any* corn to eat. And you wouldn't have all those bluebirds fluttering around your place either. Coons are hell on bluebird nests."

A year ago, Smith would have walked away in disgust. Now, his belief in man's superior wit over hungry animals in tatters, he just stared at the Dumb Farmer, who stared right back. "I sold the coon pelts," the latter continued, "gave two carcasses to the chickens for protein supplement, gave two to the Widow Lady, who likes an occasional coon dinner, and gave the rest to the Coonhunter's Club for their annual supper." The look on his face dared Smith to object. "Coonhunters used to hunt my land and keep the coon population in check until folks like you got that no-hunting rule into effect."

"But you don't even seem to have much rabbit damage," Smith said.

"That's because I have a very smart dog," the Dumb Farmer replied. "She's death on rabbits, night or day. Keeps the coons guessing, too. Besides, rabbits have the run of that 10 acres of clover out there in the field. You suburbanites want to kill all the clover in your lawns. Rabbits like clover and when they have plenty of it, they won't get as hungry for peas." He paused. "But that won't do it alone. Ten acres of clover without plenty of predation by owls, foxes, hawks, dogs, and humans would just mean ten thousand more rabbits, more or less."

The Great Neighborhood Deer Controversy

Smith's struggles with wildlife and with his conscience did not seem so amusing to the Dumb Farmer when the new era of exploding wildlife populations really hit in 1993. That's when the whitetail deer changed almost overnight from being Gwynedde Township's most sacred cow to its most divisive issue. Not even the Dumb Farmer had a solution to the problem of what to do with the growing herd of deer running loose in the township. And to tell the truth he liked having deer around, too, though he tried hard not to let what he referred to as "the fuzzy-brained environmentalists" know it.

"I looked out the window one morning and there were 22 deer—I counted 'em, *twenty-two* deer—in my corn field chomping away like a herd of cows," he said to Smith, who could not keep from smiling. He could smile because that was before the deer massacred his tomatoes.

White announced that the "deer problem" was only a sign of the myopic vision of hunters and farmers. At the first township meeting held to talk about the issue, he defended his point of view so well that most of the people, many of whom had never seen a deer, rose in holy wrath to defend "the loveliest creature in our woods" as White summed up in his argument.

About a month later, White noticed that his wife's hostas had disappeared. Then all the English ivy leaves vanished from the side of his house to a height of 5 feet. Next spring, the tulips also disappeared overnight, just when they were ready to bloom. Hmmmm. One day he looked out his front window and saw the reason for his puzzlement. He phoned the Dumb Farmer in panic.

"There's three of your calves in my yard eating my flowers and by heaven you're going to have to pay for the damage," he shouted.

The Dumb Farmer, who always said he could do without White anyway, chuckled.

"Those are deer, my dear," he said, enjoying himself immensely, "and I hope they eat every plant in your yard and then jump through your picture window and wreck your house like one did in Rary Township." He hung up and immediately called the township commissioners to schedule another meeting on the deer problem.

By the time another gathering of the community took place, a case of Lyme's disease, known to be carried by deer ticks, occurred in the township. The pendulum of public sentiment began to swing the other way. White, who had wanted to protect every deer, now wanted to kill them all. But a proposal to allow controlled "harvesting" by professional hunters was clearly not popular. When this step was ordered by the commissioners anyway, the opposition got an injunction to stop the "harvest." Compromise. "Excess" deer would be tranquillized and transported to less populated regions.

"Oh sure," the Dumb Farmer thundered at the next meeting. "Use tons of tax money to escort our unwanted deer elsewhere to become someone else's problem and starve to death someplace else." And he rattled off statistics about the millions of dollars lost in deer/car accidents. "Deer," he roared, "are statistically the most dangerous wild animal to man in America."

This assertion rankled the Widow Lady. "The real problem," she said, standing up in the front row and talking in a tone of voice that seemed much too powerful to come from such a tiny grandmotherly body, "is TOO MANY PEOPLE AND THE DEER ARE JUST TRYING TO DO SOMETHING ABOUT IT!" She sat down to a shocked silence. No one on either side of the debate could think of an appropriate answer.

The Widow Lady appeared to be the only person who had a solution to the deer problem. Without another word she stalked out of the meeting, went home, and began building a stone wall around that part of her property she wanted to keep deer out of.

"Isn't that kind of expensive?" Smith said, visiting one day. "Wouldn't a tall wire fence be cheaper?"

"Oh I don't know," she said. "My cousin hauls stone from the quarry for me for a homemade pie a load. I do all the work. The stone itself doesn't cost much. Deer won't jump what they can't see over, you know."

Smith said he did not know that, and wondered again where the Widow Lady got all her knowledge.

"I've always wanted a garden wall anyway," she said. "I'd like a little total outdoor privacy. I like to sunbathe, and I don't want anybody watching."

Smith could hardly suppress a smile. "But with your place so overgrown, you don't have to worry about privacy, do you?"

"You're discounting the wildest of all wildlife," she replied. "Small boys."

The Deer Problem Solved, Sort Of

The Dumb Farmer was in a real mental fix. Before deer became a "problem," he had achieved a unique and ingenious farm economy. Kept from increasing his acreage, as other farmers did, by the advance of suburbs around him, he adapted to the situation as cannily as wildlife did. Noting field after field of what had once been farms growing up in grass and brush, either owned by rich estates or bought by land investors to be sold later for housing, he approached the owners and asked them humbly and he hoped a little dumbly (as in *without cleverness*) if they would like him to take over the mowing chores on these fields since he had the farm equipment to do it fast. "If you don't mow, it'll all grow up in brush," he told them, which was true. He would be able to charge very economical rates, he pointed out. Most often he got the nod. On some of the land, he also inquired, again humbly if not dumbly, about whether the owners cared if he "kept the brush down" by actually farming the acreage to corn, perhaps to get a good seedbed for sowing a nice following crop of grass. And the corn would make excellent wildlife food and cover, he reminded them, drawing deer to their back yards, where they could enjoy watching and even feeding them in winter time. Often he got the go-ahead for this, too. As a result, he found himself eventually farming a considerable acreage in the developing township—land that not only cost him nothing in rent but which he was actually paid to farm. The corn he fed to his cattle and chickens or sold on the farm market, or as often to suburbanites for squirrel and deer food at a price at least double the farm market. He baled the wild grasses of the fields he mowed and sold the hay to the suburbanites for feeding deer in their backyards and as garden mulch, again for a price per bale that was twice the going farm rate. Everybody was happy, especially the deer. The Dumb Farmer was not really farming anymore, but serving the more lucrative recreational market. To round out the picture, he shot a deer or two for his own meat supply every year, using his grain harvester, which the deer were used to seeing in the fields, as a blind. He usually hunted with bow and arrow, his favorite and very quiet weapon. Out at the feed mill, in the company of other farmers and far from the ears of his suburban neighbors, he could brag that he sold crops for a high price from land he was paid to farm and hustled the crops at a far higher price than the farm market would bear to people who fed it to the deer which became part of his meat supply. That beat raising livestock, he cackled, no doubt about it.

One opportunity led to another. In an absolute reversal of all logic applied to the usual scenario of farmers being ousted by suburban development, wealthy homeowners in a nearby exclusive development approached him with a business proposition. With the ban on hunting in effect, and faced with the real probability of losing valuable landscaping to deer, they offered to pay him, secretly of course, two hundred dollars for every deer he killed using his trusty (and quiet) bow so that neighbors opposed to killing deer would not know.

The Dumb Farmer was sorely tempted, because here was a farmer's dream: a public actually paying him to "harvest" livestock they raised with food they bought from him. He began to muse how much money he might earn if he made jerky out of the venison at a price that would net him $400 per deer. $400 plus $200 for the killing, plus all the money he made from selling corn and hay that he got paid for growing . . . why, he gasped, he had stumbled upon the first foolproof way to make money at farming.

The Dumb Farmer nevertheless turned down the offer, even though by his calculations, it meant a profit of something like 3000% above costs. He was just not a man to take risks. In the quiet of a suburban enclave, even the twang of a bowstring could be heard at some distance. Nor would it be easy to lug home deer carcasses unseen, even under the cover of the heavy shrubbery around the half-million-dollar homes.

A more pressing problem caused him to stare longingly at his bow. A certain amount of corn, clover, and garden crops going to the deer was all right with him. But on one 5-acre plot of his farm, he had started a new forest of native hardwood trees: black walnut, wild cherry, and white oak, which he planned to harvest when he was 100 years old for a small fortune. A veneer quality, medium-sized log of these species might be worth $2000 or more, and at 80 trees per acre that was a possibility of something approaching a million dollars on the 5-acre tract. Though the Dumb Farmer was smart enough to know such pie-in-the-sky numbers never panned out, he would settle for $50,000.

Protecting Young Trees

But the deer were attacking his new grove in winter, eating the buds, nipping the branches, rubbing their antlers on them, either destroying the little trees outright or making the branches grow sprouty, weak, and misshapen. In spring the deer were also decimating the rarer wildflowers he had laboriously planted in the new grove. The mice and rabbits got their licks in, too, gnawing the roots and lower trunks. Tree guards wrapped around the little trunks helped some against rabbits and other rodents (although the latter could still get to the roots) but of course not the deer. With all the fierce tenacity and experience of the veteran farmer, the Dumb Farmer tried to protect his grove with fencing. A standard livestock fence was totally ineffective because deer could easily sail eight feet into the air practically from a standstill. The experts said to use a single electric wire about four feet above ground and to hang metal strips smeared with peanut butter from the electrified wire. Theoretically, deer would lick the peanut butter and forever after stay away.

No go. Deer, running in terror from dogs, cars, or people, plowed right through the electric fence or over it, peanut butter be damned. Other experts said 2 electric fences, about 10 feet apart, each consisting of 3 strands of wire, the top one 5 feet off the ground and electrified, would hold deer at bay. But that was too much money for the Dumb Farmer, even if it did work, which he doubted. So too the idea of erecting any kind of wall or wood barricade around that much land, since the fence would need to be 9 feet tall. Hanging three sets of stiff hog-wire panels, one above the other, on tall posts, made an effective 9-foot fence for small gardens, but it was too costly for a 5-acre tree grove.

He hung out several hundred bars of soap on the trees, which a university said was effective. The waste of all that soap nearly caused him to weep. He wondered if the soap company had funded the university study. The deer still nibbled, possibly at a slower rate but not slower enough. He filled little nylon bags (made out of old panty hose) with clips of human hair and tied them on the trees, as another "expert" swore by. The deer still nibbled away. He bought expensive, highly touted repellents like the ones that the Forest Service used on seedling conifer trees. The repellants smelled terrible, since the active ingredient was rotten eggs. He even found a recipe for making one's own: three eggs in a quart of water, whipped in a blender, then allowed to rot until the smell became unbearable. Add three more quarts of water and spray. (This solution should not be used on plants that are to be eaten of course.)

The new grove smelled so badly for several days that he could not go near it, and a neighbor across the road complained. Then rain washed the repellent off. In fact he found that every repellent "recommended" had serious shortcomings, especially the fact that new growth was not protected by spray put on just a couple of days previously. "What am I supposed to do, stand out there and spray every day?" he growled at the garden store salesperson. It slowly dawned on him that information suggesting the use of repellants was always written in the subjunctive mood by people who fervently wanted the repellants to work because they were opposed to killing deer. In that noble cause, it was okay to lie a little.

When in doubt the Dumb Farmer always consulted the Beekeeper, and so now. He did so hesitantly, however, because the Beekeeper was on the outs with him over deer. The Beekeeper aligned himself with the Widow Lady. The real problem was too many people, he said upon every occasion he was asked, and even on many occasions when he was not asked.

"As a matter of fact I do know something that kind of works," the Beekeeper said when the Dumb Farmer explained his dilemma.

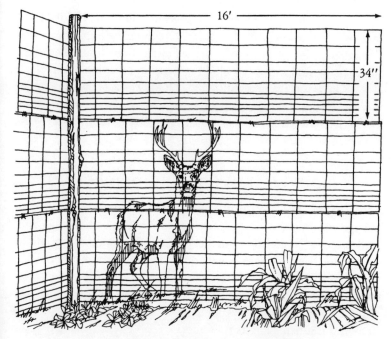

Hog Panels Stacked Three-High to Bar Deer

"Don't give me no 'kind ofs'," he growled. " 'Kind of' has darn near broke me."

The Beekeeper ambled back behind his apiary shed. What he pointed at evoked deep and focused study from the Dumb Farmer. Standing upright, 5 feet tall, were clear plastic tubes of about 4-inch diameter. Out of each was growing the stem and crown of a slender tree sapling.

"You mean to tell me a tree will grow inside a tube like that?" the Dumb Farmer asked in disbelief.

"You bet, and two or three times faster while they are in the tube. It's a greenhouse, see? Don't always grow as they should. Get some dieback. But beats the deer," the Beekeeper said. "Five feet is best against deer. Never had a 5-footer chomped by deer. I prefer 4 feet, however. The deer will usually leave them alone at 4 feet, and the tree is less likely to overgrow its root system, which means it is less likely to die back in a cold winter."

"I see there's screening over the top of the tubes around the tree trunk," the Dumb Farmer said. He was thinking about the labor and expense of tubing 2,000 trees.

The Beekeeper nodded. "Strange, but bluebirds will fly down into those tubes and can't fly out. So you gotta keep 'em out. Sometimes mice still get in from underneath, and sometimes they chew their way in, and *they* usually kill the trees. So t'ain't foolproof."

But it was the best solution the Dumb Farmer could find other than a long deer-hunting season. The best tree guards are from Tubex Treeshelters, 800 248 8239 (Treessentials, 2371 Waters Drive, Mendota Heights, MN 55120).

Plants Deer Won't Eat, Sometimes

Meanwhile, Smith was working his way through his own strange encounters of the whitetail kind. He dreaded putting up a garden fence tall and stout enough to keep deer out and was afraid even in the backyard that might require special permission from the township zoning board. For reasons only 20th-century human society could explain, maybe, fencing in suburbs was definitely not *de rigueur*. The Dumb Farmer said urban society was leery of fences because it was ashamed of its rural roots.

Smith still put great faith in research, so to his books he went once more. Aha. There were plants that deer didn't like, he discovered. He would landscape with them. But experience taught a lesson he might have deduced just studying the titles of two booklets that his research had turned up. An early one flat out promised a list of "Deer Resistant Plants for Ornamental Use" from the University of California. But it contained plants that Smith had seen deer eat. The more tentative title of the second one came closer to the truth: "Plants Deer Eat Less Often," from the Ohio Landscapers Association. This pamphlet admitted that if deer got hungry enough they would eat anything that had chlorophyll in it. "A heavy deer population also increases competition for food, with the result that plants relatively unpalatable in an area where deer are not numerous, will be readily browsed in an area where deer abound." Everyone who has kept cows knows this, the Dumb Farmer told him with an air of superiority. "Before it will starve, a cow will even eat yew and pawpaw and persimmon and poison itself to death."

Nevertheless, using the booklets and neighborhood experience, Smith came up with a list of plants that deer usually avoided, so long as there were other plants around to eat.

1. Cactus and holly. No kidding, the Dumb Farmer hooted.
2. Aloe and wild cucumber. Imagine landscaping with those.
3. Spice bush (*Calycanthus occidentalis*).
4. Clematis, daphne, datura, and delphinium.
5. Foxglove, daffodil, and oleander.
6. Persimmon, pawpaw, ironwood, wax myrtle, and red elderberry.
7. Pride of Madeira, whatever that was (*Echium fastuosum*).
8. Carolina jessamine.
9. Hellbore, jasmine, red-hot poker.
10. Most plants in the Oxalis family.

Unfortunately, the only plant of the edible garden that deer avoided was rhubarb.

Smith wandered back through the brush behind his place

again to see how the Widow Lady was progressing on her stone wall. He whistled loudly in case she was in one of her "sunbathing" moods.

"How did you learn how to build a wall like that?" he said with amazement, finding the Widow Lady nearly finished enclosing a 50 feet by 50 feet square and 5 feet high with flattish limestone rocks.

"The first 50 feet were kind of difficult," she said, "but then you get the hang of it. There's a stone for every place and for every stone a place, as Grandpappy used to say. I first dug out a trench about a foot deep and started building up from there, heaping the dirt from the trench along the foot of the wall to encourage water to run away from it rather than into it. Then you just make sure a stone always bridges the crack of the two stones below it. Helps to use a level to keep the wall vertically straight if you don't have a good eye. You just make two courses and keep the rocks tilted a little inwards against each other as you go along. You've got to bridge the two courses with

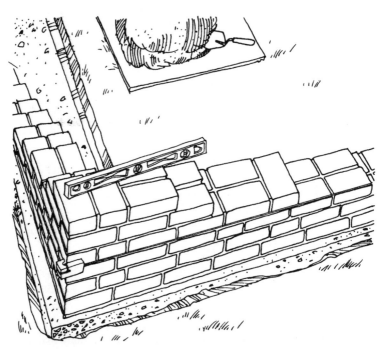

Laying a Masonry Wall—Alternate joints for a more solid wall. Plumb your corners and check them frequently with a level.

a rock every so often and you can fill the space between the two courses otherwise with rubble and little rocks you can't use elsewhere. With flattish rocks, the wall will hold together pretty well without mortar. There's a hundred books shows you how. Hardest part is lifting the rocks as the wall nears 5 feet tall. I leveled the top of the wall with masonry cement to kind of hold it together and keep water from sifting down through. Then you can gain another 8 inches or so by setting a row of flat rocks on edge on top of the wall. Pretty, isn't it?"

Good Fences Make Good Wildlife

It was beautiful, Smith exclaimed, but he calculated it would take him two years of spare time to build one. He settled on another solution. He found nice white plastic picket fence in 6-foot sections that looked like wood. The fencing was 6 feet tall, too, and by hanging the sections on sturdy posts a foot off the ground he gained another foot at the bottom that he could mow underneath. If he wanted to rabbit-proof the fence, he could run chicken wire fence around the bottom. Would deer jump his 7-foot fence? So far, no, probably because the enclosed garden is fairly close to the house and more or less out in the open. Or maybe all those white pickets scare them. Or maybe the "controlled hunting" that finally came into practice, after the township learned that tranquilization and transportation elsewhere was too expensive, lowered the pressure on the available food supply. At any rate, Smith quit complaining so much. The Dumb Farmer's disposition actually improved, and he became known for the jolly way in which he passed out his "beef" jerky to visitors who stopped by for a glass of his homemade beer.

To close out dogs, coyotes, and wolves, chain-link fence is ideal, but too expensive for most people to use for large plots or fields. A much more economical solution is the wire cattle-panel gate, which is made of stiff, pencil-thick wire in sections 16 feet long by 47 inches high, in a mesh small enough at the bottom to keep out even little pigs and lambs (and dogs). It costs about a dollar a foot, not counting the posts you'd need, and it is fairly fast and easy to put up and take down. Panel fencing's fault is that it is not very attractive.

Woven-wire fencing is the most cost-efficient (not counting labor) good permanent fence, but it requires some skill and knowledge to erect. A 20-rod roll of quality woven wire, at the standard

47-inch height, costs over $150 now, expensive enough when you add on the cost of posts, but cheaper than the alternatives. To stop dogs, the woven wire must be of the standard livestock weave, with the horizontal wires closer together at the bottom than the tops and the vertical wires no more than 6 inches apart, like the wire panels mentioned above. This is referred to as 6-inch stay, all-purpose livestock fence. A coyote might climb such a fence but rarely, and definitely will not if a strand of barbed wire is strung above it. Any canine might dig under the fence if no humans are around for days on end. Where humans are nearby on a regular basis, wolves and coyotes seldom tarry long enough to figure out a way under a woven-wire fence. Woven wire buried in the ground a few inches, with a barbed wire buried right under it, will keep even pigs from rooting under, and so surely a coyote. But sinking a fence below soil level is an arduous job and probably not worth the effort.

Of course, gates into fields have to be as dog-proof as the woven wire. The sides of the gates must hang close enough to the posts that a canine can't squeeze through. There are many dog-proof gates on the market, or you can make a standard wooden gate and then staple a piece of the woven wire to it. Here is a good place to use the wire-panel fencing mentioned above.

The top and bottom horizontal wires of woven-wire fencing should be of 9 gauge and the middle wires—both vertical and horizontal—no smaller than 11 gauge for the fence to last. (There are lighter, cheaper versions.) An all 9-gauge fence is best and will last 30 years or more. At farm sales, you can often buy rolls of used woven wire that still has a few years of service. The Dumb Farmer always shows up when fencing along superhighways is being replaced. Even after 20 years of use, highway fencing (and the steel posts) is much better quality than anything offered for sale at farm stores. Sometimes he can talk the highway foreman into giving him some of the old fence and posts. Other times he has to pay a nominal sum. The used fencing and posts reduce the cost of a good woven-wire fence by about 80%.

Putting up a woven-wire fence requires some skill and experience and lots of time. Even farmers don't always know how to do it right anymore, the Dumb Farmer says. There are books available, the best from the Farm and Ranch Nasco catalog, mentioned earlier, which also sells and pictures all the fencing tools required.

First you need a set of fence-stretching tools, which can cost over $300, unless you can pick up a used set at a farm sale or can borrow one from a farmer. (Trying to stretch a fence with a tractor is dangerous.) The set should include two stretchers—ratchet affairs with long handles, a stretcher bar to attach to the fencing to provide a solid place to pull from, two short chains, and two longer chains. Hawknosed fence pliers and a post-hole digger are musts.

Terrific tension is put on the fence to stretch it properly, and therefore endposts or cornerposts must be set solidly in the soil and solidly braced. Different farmers in different areas have their favorite designs but the Dumb Farmer insists his way is best. The endpost (or cornerpost, as the case may be) ought to be at least 8 inches in diameter and 8 feet long. He cuts up sections of replaced utility poles, which he gets free from the local utility companies. The end or corner post is set at least 3 1/2 feet deep in the ground. 4 feet is better. You need hand or tractor operated post-hole diggers for this job. About 7 feet away from the endpost, in line with the fence to be stretched, set the brace post, which can be of a little lesser diameter, 2 1/2 feet (minimum) in the soil. Between the brace post and endpost, place a horizontal, 4-inch diameter brace about a foot down from the top of both posts and notched into each of them. To be perfectly correct, says the Dumb Farmer, this horizontal brace should angle ever so slightly *downward* from the brace post back to the corner post. Otherwise when the fence is stretched tight, the brace can slowly push the endpost up a foot or more over the years, causing the post to slant forward and the fence to sag. Then wrap a double strand of 9-gauge wire around the bottom of the endpost and the top of the brace post. Place a short stout stick between the double strand of wire in the middle and twist until the wire becomes very tight, squeezing the brace solidly into the notches of the two posts. The stick used to twist the wire needs to be long enough to catch on the horizontal brace to keep it from untwisting.

Next, set all the line posts about 15 feet apart. If you're using wood posts, they should go into the ground at least 2 1/2 feet. Steel posts go in about 2 feet, and are easier to install with a regular steel post-hole driver rather than trying to use a sledge. Before setting each post, walk back and eye up its position from behind one endpost to the other. It is easy to get a post out of line if you don't pay close attention all the time.

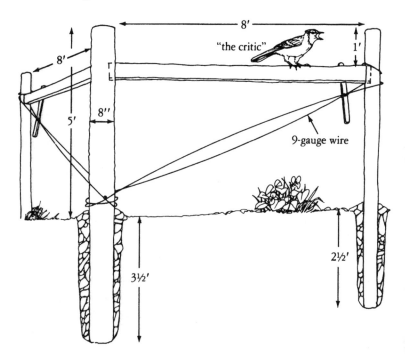

End Post and Bracing for Woven-Wire Fence

With all the posts in place, unroll the fence next to the posts, having first attached the end of the roll to the endpost. In unrolling, be sure that the bottom of the fence—where the horizontal wires are close together—is next to the post. When one roll does not reach the other endpost or cornerpost, you have to splice on another roll. Wrap the ends of the horizontal wires on one roll around the corresponding ends on the other roll or make loops as in the drawing. You can buy a little splicer tool to make bending the wires around each other much easier. Some new woven-wire fencing is made to be easily spliced, and directions come with the wire. In fact the Red Top company uses that as a selling point for its wire. With pliers, the job of splicing is more difficult but doable.

When you reach the next endpost, cut the wire from the roll with your fence pliers, being sure to leave enough to wrap around the endpost after the fence is stretched tight.

Next, set another post about 7 feet behind the endpost—in

line with the fence—and insert a horizontal brace between it and the endpost, as you did the brace post on the other side. (You could have done this earlier, when you set the other posts.) A foot or so in the ground is enough to set this post since it is only temporary. This will be the post you attach the stretchers to.

Now lay out your stretching tools. Wrap the two short chains around the stretching post, one about 1 1/2 feet from the top, the other a similar distance from the bottom. Attach the two stretchers to these chains. Next attach the two longer pulling chains to the stretcher bar at one end. The other end fits into the ratchet teeth of the stretcher. Work the handles of each stretcher back and forth until the chain comes tight. Two "dogs" on each side of each rachet push against the rachets in turn as you move the handle back and forth. When the chains are sagging loose at first, operating the stretchers is somewhat difficult but when they draw up tight and begin to pull the fence toward the stretching post, the job becomes easier.

Before beginning to tighten the fence, walk back along its length and at about every third post, lift the top of the fence up to nearly vertical position and wire it very loosely to the posts. If you try to raise the fence from its horizontal position lying on the ground up to vertical entirely with the stretchers, enormous tension is required and something might break.

Now go back and start drawing up the fence. Tighten a little on one stretcher, then on the other, so that the bottom and top of the fence come along evenly. After every several inches of stretching, walk

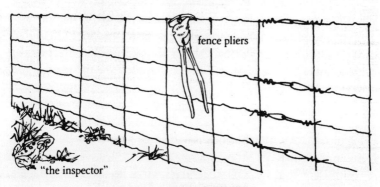

fence pliers

"the inspector"

Splicing a Woven-Wire Fence

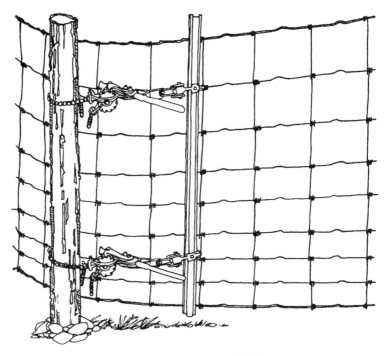

Stretching Rachets at Work

back along the line to make sure the fence or the wires holding it upright aren't catching on the posts anywhere.

Experience is important in knowing how tight to stretch a fence. The little crooks in the horizontal wires should straighten out about halfway, but that's not the whole story. If the fence traverses uneven ground, you should not tighten it as much as on level ground, because when you pull the fence down or up to attach to the posts in a dip or a rise of ground level, you will complete the tightening. You can't stretch a fence over a pronounced rise or draw. You must stretch to the top of the hill and then to the next hill bottom. Nor can you stretch a fence well around a curve. All must be done from point to point in relatively straight lines. Good fence builders stretch in perfectly straight lines.

As a fence reaches its stretching limit, it becomes quite rigid, a rigidity that experienced fence builders use as the true gauge of how tight to stretch. The Dumb Farmer says he can tell when a fence is tight enough by the tone of the hum it makes when a strong wind passes through it. Smith says that's just the Dumb Farmer's way of putting on airs. At the last tug or so on the stretchers, the endposts may pull forward an inch or so at ground level. That's okay. The Dumb Farmer says that is why a good fencebuilder sets his endposts slanted slightly backward. Then when the tightening fence pulls it forward, the post comes up vertically straight.

When the fence is tight, staple every horizontal strand to the endpost and brace post. On the line posts, staple top, bottom and at least two middle horizontal strands. Always staple horizontal strands, not vertical stays. In driving staples, cock the staple sideways a little so that the two prongs bite into different grains of the wood. Then it won't pull out. If your line posts are steel, use the wire fasteners made for this purpose to attach the fence.

With the fence securely attached to all the posts, loosen the stretchers, working them backward. Pull on the handle a little as if to tighten, which frees one of the dogs. Lift that dog out of the tooth it is in, and let the handle ease it back into the tooth it previously occupied. And so forth. Loosen a little on one stretcher and then on the other, reversing the tightening process until the chains come slack. Remove chains and stretcher bar. Wrap the tail end of the fence around the endpost, cutting it to fit if necessary. Take out the stretching post. Stand back and admire your work. Train children and visitors not to climb woven-wire fences but to enter and exit at entrance gates. If you must climb the fence, do so only right next to a post.

Your first fence may sag a little after a year or two, but once you get the hang of the job, your fences will remain reasonably tight for 20 or 30 years. As the Dumb Farmer says, "Lazy farmers make the best fence builders. They do it right the first time because they don't want to have to do it again."

Chapter 11
Other Wildlife Restraints

Some wild pests can't be fenced out adequately, especially tunneling animals like rats, mice, and gophers. Some birds, like house sparrows, are year-round pests that can't be screened away from places you don't want them, such as your purple martin house. In these situations, there's an arsenal of homemade and manufactured remedies available: traps, shields, repellents, and scare devices as new as electronics and as old as scarecrows. Some of these remedies are too effective for the backyard sanctuary and some are not effective enough.

Rat Controls

The only totally "bad" animal pest lurking on the edges of your garden sanctuary is the Norway, or brown rat (even *it* is beneficial as food for owls and hawks). It makes a good study-model from which to survey the advantages and disadvantages of all the pest-control devices available. You can buy rat poisons, rat traps, rat scare devices, rat proofing, rat terriers, and in some cultures, even magic spells and formulae to chase rats away. The fact that the rat is still with us in force points up the essential ineffectiveness of all wildlife control methods. But some are more ineffective than others.

The decision to use poison is, in a sense, an admission of ecological defeat, but in the case of the brown rat, it's certainly a justifiable consideration. Scientists believe that rat-borne diseases have killed more people than all the wars in history. The rat carries 35 diseases of man and animals, including typhus, bubonic plague, jaundice, tularemia, rabies, and trichinosis. Its bite can produce a serious illness called rat-bite fever.

Rats ruin countless thousands of dollars' worth of food each year. For every $1 worth a rat eats, say United States Department of Agriculture (USDA) Extension specialists at North Carolina State University, it damages another $2 worth and contaminates another $3 worth. A hundred rats on a farm cost the farmer an estimated $1,200 (mid-1970 dollars). Experts estimate the rat population on United States farms alone at 100 million. Add to that number all the city rats, and their population probably equals our own.

Poisoning rats doesn't work very well as the sole means of control, nor do traps. One reason is the rat's fantastic ability to increase and multiply. It breeds at three to four months of age. Gestation lasts about 22 days, and females are ready to mate again a couple of days after giving birth. Litter size averages 8, though it can be as high as 22. The number of litters per year ranges from three to seven. It's no trick for a pair of rats to produce 50 offspring a year, of which many will reproduce during that same year.

Not only can the rat reproduce in remarkable numbers when conditions are favorable, but it can survive amazingly, even when conditions are adverse. It limits its own population explosion lest the number of rats exceed the food supply. Weak rats in a crowded colony are run out or killed by stronger brethren. A healthy rat is a super-rat. It can fall 50 feet without serious injury (that's equivalent to a man falling 300 feet, the length of a football field). It can swim up sewer lines against swift currents. It can dive through a plumbing trap, or gnaw through adobe brick, cinder block, oak planks, and occasionally even metal conduit.

Another reason rats are hard to control is that they are smart— they learn fast. The cleverest traps will fool them only for a while. They even seem to learn the danger in anticoagulant poisons—the safer kind that are harmless to pets, but which may take more than one dose to kill the rat. Rats that sicken but do not die from a poison sometimes seem to learn not to try it again, however tempting the bait. That's why in new rat poisons, emphasis is toward odorless poison ingredients and an efficiency that kills after only a nibble.

Oddly enough, while the rat is the hardest pest to control by poisons, traps, and other devices, it *can* be eliminated if man has the will and discipline to do so. More than any other wild mammal (with the possible exception of the gray house mouse), rats thrive where man thrives. We provide the rat with its advantageous ecological niche. The rat lives off our food wastes, and the more food we allow the rat to get, the more it thrives. As New York exterminators found out during an intense campaign to get rid of rats in the 1960s, poisons and traps are ineffective if rats can get to food. And the food they want is the same food we want.

In short, the first and absolutely essential "device" in rat control is to quit feeding and sheltering them. Around your house and on your homestead, you must seal off from rats the food you store for yourself, your pets, and your farm animals. That does not necessarily mean rat-proofing a whole house or barn. Older homes, especially, are very difficult to rat-proof, and barns are impossible. Good solid cement foundations with deep footers, metal flashings on door and window frames, and self-closing devices on doors all help, but are not fail-safe. What you have to do is rat-proof specific containers, rooms, or bins where food is kept.

Your own canned and frozen food is safe. But dried and bagged food of all kinds should be placed at least in tight cupboards, and preferably in glass bottles or tin containers like old breadboxes. Allowing the kids to eat cookies in their bedrooms or snack on popcorn in front of the TV in the living room, failing to sweep the kitchen after every meal—all of these habits mean food on the floor to lure rats and mice. Table scraps not fed to animals must be carefully composted with scrupulous sanitation. Rat-proof composting bins (made of metal or mortar and stone) are highly desirable, even though proper composting will not draw rats.

Food that needs to be dried or cured over a long period of time, like popcorn, sweet corn for parching, seeds, smoked hams, and the rest, can be hung in attics, garages, or storerooms in ways that prevent rodent infestation. The first way is to hang the foodstuffs from a wire strung from one wall to another. Since rats, and especially mice, can walk a wire like circus acrobats, you should slip metal disks 4 to 5 inches in diameter over the wire at each end about a foot out from the wall. The rodents can't get around the disks. Large tin can lids work fine. With a hammer and nail, punch a hole in the center of each lid. Make it just large enough so the wire fits through it tightly.

You can hang food out of rats' reach in another, better way if you have a beam flush up against the ceiling of any building. Cover both ends of the beam with tin from the wall out to about 2 feet. Tap a row of nails along the rest of the beam's length, leaving the nails projecting out far enough to act as hangers. There is no way a rat can reach foodstuffs hung from the nails because it can't maintain a footing on the vertical metal sheathing on the beam ends. The only way it could get to the food would be to walk upside down across the ceiling, and even a rat can't do that.

Don't let surplus garden crops, especially corn, stand for extended periods or overwinter in the garden. Shred, plow under, or otherwise dispose of anything rats would enjoy. Store straw bales in your barn or in your shed at your own risk. The straw often contains wheat that was not threshed out properly at harvest. Rats and mice will burrow into the bales to go after the grain, and they'll make their homes there, too. Use up your bales as soon as you can. Be sure not to store them for more than one winter. On small suburban homesteads where not much straw is used, it's better to buy a few bales as you need them.

On the small homestead with a few pets or farm animals, the most important rule is to keep all livestock and pet feed in metal containers. Fifty-five-gallon steel drums are ideal, and sometimes they're available for little or for free. Be sure there are no residues in the barrels that can contaminate the feed, or keep the feed in sacks inside the barrels. A suitable piece of tin makes a good cover when weighted down with a brick. Set the barrels on wood pallets rather than on the ground so that they don't rust out. The Beekeeper says that a barrel also makes the best rat and mouse trap. He keeps one barrel open with a half-bushel of corn in it. Rodents jump in after the corn and can't get out, he claims.

Farms need larger grain storage facilities, of course. There are all kinds of metal bins and cribs on the market. Old wooden cribs can be partially rat-proofed with hardware cloth or pieces of roofing tin, but only temporarily. Rats will almost always find a new place to gnaw through. Better to build the entire crib, or whatever other buildings, up on posts. Sheathe the posts with tin or affix a wide tin plate between the top of the posts and the building. Some old buildings were set on pillars

metal sheathing

2'

1'

4"–5"

4"–5"

Barriers to Keep Rats from Food

199

made by pouring cement into glazed tiles. The smooth tile surface is as effective as tin in keeping the rats from climbing.

Also, with the building up off the ground, there is no floor for the rats to hide under. If they do try burrowing in the ground under a raised building, dogs and cats have easy access to them. A solid cement floor on the ground is not rat-proof unless it has footings down at least 2½ feet, and rats will sometimes dig even that deep. A cement floor not so bolstered makes an impregnably safe fortress for rats. They dig under it and live there. Better a chicken coop with no floor than such a floor.

For the same reason, keep all piles of wood and lumber off the ground on racks. That's better for the lumber anyway. Get rid of piles of rocks, old boards, and junk as soon as possible.

In feeding farm animals or pets, put out only enough for the animals to clean up in a couple of hours. Leaving grain in the trough or pet food in the dog's dish merely invites rats to a feast.

Rats will kill and eat baby chicks, so the latter especially need a rat-proof shelter at night. The Dumb Farmer says his cat always has kittens about the time he brings his chicks home from the hatchery. He raises the chicks and kittens together. "Mother cat keeps the rats away, and the kittens grow up from the very start accustomed to chicks around and don't attack them when they grow larger," he explains.

While trapping rats is the least effective way to deal with them, it may be of some use in catching stragglers, or the occasional new rat that comes sniffing around a clean, rat-proof environment. Leg-hold traps work if set with care (and, if possible, out of the way of other wildlings and pets). The trap should be placed in a hollow in the ground so that the pan is just even with the soil surface. Sprinkle some fine dirt over the trap spring, pan, and jaws so that the trap is nearly invisible. If you set the traps in plain view, the rats will learn to go around them. If you use leg-hold traps, tend them frequently to keep the rats from suffering unduly.

One problem with leg-hold traps is that often you will catch pets and other animals before you catch the rats. It's better to use a cage, or box, trap like a Havahart. Then if you catch a pet, you can turn it loose unharmed. For best results in catching rats, bait the cage trap with a piece of bacon. If that's too expensive for your blood, bread, grain, or peanut butter is nearly as tempting. Rats will not go into a cage trap right away. They are suspicious of any new object in their environment. Expect results, if ever, the fourth or fifth night.

Having a rat in a cage is a problem in itself. You still have to get rid of the pest. The quickest, most "humane" way is to drop the trap, rat and all, into a barrel of water. The rat drowns quickly. When you lower the cage trap end first into the water, the brace that holds the upper door closed may fall loose and the rat can escape. So wire the door or hold it closed manually as you dunk the box.

The Conibear trap, widely used for trapping fur-bearing animals, can be used for rats. Since it's a killing trap, it is not deemed to be as cruel as the leg-hold trap, so it is not as widely condemned by the animal rights movement. But it has no place in the backyard because it might catch and kill a pet or some wild animal you might like to keep around.

Controls for Other Wild Animals

Poisons are widely used to control field mice, gophers, and especially pine voles. Zinc phosphide, often called simply ZP, is a favorite. This poison is nonspecific, however, and risky to use in the backyard environment. Not only will it kill desirable animals, but a mouse poisoned by it could poison the dog or cat that eats it. Less risk is involved in poisoning gophers or other tunneling animals, since the poison is placed down in the tunnel, out of reach of other animals or children. Commercial orchardists use what they call a "gopher control machine" or a "mouse trail builder" to place poison more or less safely below ground where mice and gophers will find it. These machines, pulled by a tractor, make a tunnel through the ground that transects the animal runs. As the machine's blade burrows along, poison bait drops from a hopper into the tunnel.

Such measures are hardly appropriate in the backyard sanctuary. In fact, it is questionable whether it is ever necessary to poison field mice. In a properly balanced ecosystem, so many animals prey on mice that they are seldom a problem. Mice forage on a wide variety of plants and insect larvae, and there is some evidence that they severely harm apple tree roots only when they can't get a proper balance of other foods. Backyard fruit-growers can further discourage gnawing mice by pulling some dirt away from the crown of the tree and filling in with round, smooth pebbles, through which mice can't tunnel to get to the roots. Also, just keeping snow and mulch pulled back from the trees or tramped down in winter provides some degree of control.

Gophers are difficult to control by any method. Easterners can thank their lucky stars that the pocket gopher resides only in the West and the South. But at least the old adage about woodchucks, "Kill one, get two more," does not apply to pocket gophers. Except during mating season, a pocket gopher lives alone and won't tolerate gopher guests. A resident will fight a newcomer to the death. So, it is likely that in your garden you will have only one gopher at a time. A good cure for gophers is a badger. The latter may dig holes in your garden, but it is after meat and insects, not vegetables. A number of snakes of the *Pituophis* genus—bull snakes, gopher snakes, and pine snakes—relish gophers, although they also like bird eggs.

In a small garden, trapping can be an effective way to control gophers. Dig open a gopher run and set a leg-hold trap in it, flush with the surface of the underground trail, with the trap chain staked up out of the way aboveground. Then lay a board over the exposed runway and cover it with dirt. It is essential that no light at all pierce the tunnel where the trap is set. Check the trap by lifting the board. Don't expect to catch two in the same hole, unless a new gopher moves in later.

Ground squirrels are more easily caught in cage traps, but they are not as pestiferous as pocket gophers. Chipmunks can take a liking to almost any garden food, including sweet potatoes, gooseberries, and strawberries, but are so cute that most gardeners tolerate their forays. Chipmunks run almost eagerly into Havahart traps baited with peanuts, so their populations can be controlled in that way.

Unfortunately, most homeowners consider the mole just as harmful as the gopher and fair game to poison. They accuse it of tunneling under vegetables and flowers and eating roots and bulbs. Of several species of moles, western types may eat bulbs on rare occasions but the more common eastern moles feed almost exclusively on insects, insect larvae, slugs, and similar fare, not on plants. Mice following mole runs will eat your tulip bulbs, but moles will not. Moles are not particularly destructive when they tunnel through your garden either. Seldom does the tunneling, which loosens dirt below or beside plants, harm them unless the soil is very dry. If the soil is very dry, the moles will seldom tunnel through it because their main food, earthworms, will be lower in the soil. Moles tunnel alongside your carrots, not to eat them but to eat carrot worm larvae. If the carrots are beyond finger size, they will not be harmed by the tunnel passing by. Even if the carrots are smaller, only a few are lost due to their roots being disturbed. Tunnels through your strawberry patch will cause little damage, and the moles should be welcomed there. They are eating any white grubs, not to mention slugs, they find. But if you wish, you can rather easily discourage moles from sojourns into the annual garden by cultivation.

Most gardeners know all of this from experience. The real reason moles are in such disfavor is that they make lawns a bit unsightly with their network of little ridged tunnels. Since the lawn-as-carpet has become a dominant symbol of success and righteousness in American culture, ipso facto, the mole becomes a threat to human well-being, even though its digging actually benefits the lawn by aerating it. Because of these facts, Smith used to fly into a rage when neighbor White put poison peanuts in mole tunnels, and for several years the mole, albeit unwittingly, put a great strain on their friendship.

"Go ahead. Kill the moles," Smith would remark peevishly. "But don't come crying to me when slugs eat all your tomatoes."

"Those little gray buggers are ruining my lawn, Smith," White would reply, affecting great patience in the face of radical environmentalism. "And if you would cooperate and poison them too, our problem would be over."

"Problem?" Smith would look around in seemingly great agitation, appealing to some large invisible audience in this hour of injustice. "*Problem?* I don't see any problem. Look at my lawn. It's greener than yours. Have moles ruined it?"

How can you tell," White would answer dryly. "The grass is so tall it could hide a beaver den."

"Precisely. And if you would quit trying to turn your lawn into a living room carpet, you wouldn't know you had moles, either."

Eventually, though, the debate settled itself. White saturated his grass with so many magic potions from the lawn supply industry in his effort to get a perfect lawn that the soil under it could scarcely harbor an earthworm. Without worms, the soil offered no allurements to the moles. They stayed in Smith's tangled grass jungle or burrowed through his garden. Smith, watching from his hammock, was delighted one day to see an earthworm pop up out of the ground just ahead of a mole pushing along underground after it. Across the hedge, he noted White fussing and fuming over his nearly perfect lawn. Everybody was happy, except the earthworm, perhaps.

Another disadvantage of poisoning moles is the chance of

poisoning shrews in the process. Shrews don't make a habit of traveling in mole runs, but occasionally they might. To poison one is to poison one of the gardener's best friends among wild animals.

Shrews, of which there are at least seven species in the United States, are inconspicuous little animals that look like mice at a casual glance. They are confused sometimes with moles. The shorttail shrew is the most common species. Its stubby tail is the characteristic that best distinguishes it from mice. Shrews eat insects and insect larvae. Because of very high metabolism rate, they eat more or less continuously, scarcely sleeping more than a half hour at a time. A shorttail shrew will eat its own weight every day, and the tinier masked shrew has been known to eat 3 times its weight. They do not hibernate, but keep on eating insects and larvae hiding in the ground or under leaves all through the winter. Since they eat all kinds of insects, those harmful as well as beneficial to man, the shrew's value for insect pest control is difficult to gauge, but as naturalist David Rains Wallace wrote in his recent book, *Idle Weeds,* ". . . their disappearance from this insect-ridden planet would have important consequences."

The shrew is a most unusual animal. It is one of the smallest and, on the evolutionary scale of time, oldest of North American mammals. Although of such a high metabolic rate, heart beat, and nervous temperament that it literally can be scared to death, the shrew is amazingly courageous for its size. Smith raked one up from under a pile of leaves he was laboring over one afternoon. Instead of fleeing, the wee creature stood up on its back legs like a miniature grizzly bear and charged him.

Shorttail Shrew

Few animals will eat a shrew because of the musky odor it emits. An owl, perhaps a hawk, and a very hungry fox are about its only enemies. In addition, the shrew is venomous, exuding a poison from its salivary glands potent enough to cause convulsions in a mouse— although it is harmless to man. Shrews have killed birds and snakes in this manner.

Yet, the shrew is the gardener's friend. In the backyard, hardly any nonspecific poison for mice, gophers, or moles seems justifiable if such poisoning would endanger the shrew. Occasionally, the shrew will chew holes in muskmelons, says Smith (although a mouse or chipmunk is more often the culprit). In any event, the melons can be effectively guarded by placing each in one-half of a plastic gallon jug cut vertically in two, with a hole in the tray for rainwater to drain out.

Traps

As already mentioned, traps are nonspecific, like the leg-hold trap, which catches anything that steps in it, especially pets, and the Conibear, which usually kills whatever gets caught in it. The old-fashioned snare kills indiscriminately, too. The backyarder seeking to control but not necessarily kill wildlife, therefore, finds the box trap, in any of several designs, much more suitable to his purpose.

The metal box trap, Havahart, is familiar to nearly all gardeners and is readily available at garden supply centers and hardware stores and through catalogs and magazines. It, and other makes like it, comes in several sizes to accommodate everything from mice to raccoons. The animal is lured into the cage from either end with a bait placed on a pan trigger in the center of the cage. Connected to the pan is a rod, L-shaped at the end outside the cage, which when positioned against another L-shaped rod that is connected to the doors, sets the trap. The slightest touch on the pan causes the two L-shaped triggers, held against each other by the pressure of the hanging doors, to part company. The doors then slam down, enclosing the animal securely. Squirrels are so fast that they can set off smaller models from inside and exit before the doors fall shut.

There are many homemade variations of box traps that you can build inexpensively out of wood. The box should accommodate the animal easily—about 25 inches from front to back for raccoons or groundhogs, and less for smaller animals. A door that falls vertically in slots prepared for it is easier to make than a door that swings shut from overhead. Homemade versions usually have only one entrance, with the bait suspended at the far end from a line that runs back to a trigger stick that holds up the trap door (see illustration).

Trigger mechanisms vary in design, but they all work on the same principle. The weight of the door provides the tension by which what boys used to call the trigger stick is held against it. The slightest tug on the bait causes the trigger stick to slip out, and the door falls closed.

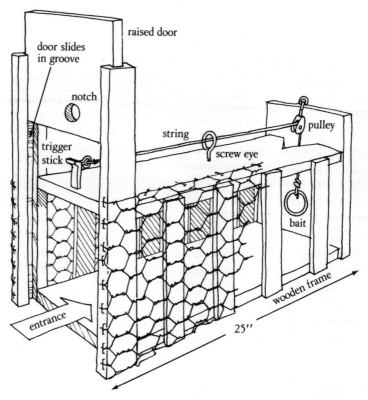

A Homemade Trap for Catching Live Animals—The trigger stick is set just under the notch cut into the door so that the slightest tug on the baited string will pull it away, allowing the door to fall.

Another variation of the box trap is a barrel with a tilting board over it. Bait is placed out at the end of the board. As the animal walks out to get it, its weight causes the board to tilt (or fall), and the luckless animal ends up in the bottom of the barrel. When used for rats, the barrel is half filled with water. Another traditional variation used on farms calls for stretching a piece of paper with a small slit in the center tightly over the top of the barrel. Bait is hung from a string over the slit. The idea is that a rat will venture out onto the paper if it's solid enough to hold it at the edges. One step too far, the paper rips, and the rat falls through.

In setting any kind of box trap, the trapper needs to know something about the habits of the animal he is after. Set the trap on or near the path the animal frequents, but in some sheltered part of the path, not out in the open. Conceal your trap with leaves or grass so that it looks somewhat like a natural object. Try to avoid leaving too much of your own scent around the area. Good trappers often boil their traps in water with walnut husks or other ingredients that deaden odors that seem suspicious to animals. Handle traps and bait with gloves that perferably have been hanging outdoors, not inside a human habitation. Don't expect results the first night.

Once you have caught a wild animal, you have to dispose of it in some way. Typically, the backyard gardener wants to turn the animal loose in what he thinks of as the wide open spaces. Smith once did this. The wide open spaces belonged to the Dumb Farmer, who did not appreciate Smith unloading a groundhog on him. "If you don't want that damn whistle-pig," he roared, "why do you think I do? I got all I can handle. That's why groundhogs are coming into your suburb. There ain't *room* for any more out here. Either shoot 'em or live with 'em." Then he went off in a huff, mumbling obscenities about city people who were dumber than dumb farmers, and who quailed about killing a varmint even though every day they stuffed themselves with meat somebody else killed for them. Almost to his house, he wheeled around and yelled once more at the visibly shaken Smith. "If you were smart, you'd eat 'em, not turn 'em loose. Young groundhog is *good*, as all you city people are going to find out one of these days when we farmers go broke producing meat we can't get a good price for."

Guards, Shields, and Barriers

Protective shields and barriers are much preferable for controlling wildlings than poisons and traps. And they're usually just as effective. Placing a metal shield 18 inches wide around a tree trunk will keep squirrels and racoons out of the tree much more effectively and far, far more safely than the most potent poison. All you need to ensure is that the squirrel can't climb up another tree and jump over into the tree you want to protect.

Small orchard trees can be wrapped with suitable material to keep rabbits from gnawing the bark, but rabbits may still be able to reach the lower limbs. If so, encircle the trees with fencing 2 feet from the trunks. If you want to save money, you can use screening from old window and door screens. This type of metal screening bends easily around small tree trunks, it bends or folds handily over itself to hold it securely in place, and it allows for some air and light to circulate around the trunk.

Wrapping tree trunks will not necessarily protect them from hungry mice. Denied access to the trunk itself, mice will chew on the roots and crown of the tree just below the soil surface. One traditional way of stopping them is with a barrier of gravel, as mentioned earlier.

Often mice are active around fruit trees after heavy snows have covered the ground, when they can tunnel through the snow safely out of view of their enemies. Tramp down the snow around your trees. You should anyway. Snow higher than the lower limbs of a tree will, upon melting, pull those limbs down and strip them off the tree, believe it or not. Besides, if a crust forms on the snow, rabbits will be able to reach up and gnaw on scaffold branches.

Tanglefoot and other sticky preparations smeared on tree trunks will keep ants and other insect pests from climbing up to the fruiting limbs.

Plant covers and row covers, used primarily to protect plants from frost or to provide small greenhouselike enclosures in which plants can get an early spring start in life, also double as protective shields against wildlings. A plastic milk jug with its bottom cut out can be set over a cabbage plant with a little dirt piled around the base to secure it, and rabbits will not be able to get at the plant. A corrugated, translucent, fiberglass roofing panel can be bent into a U shape, tied with wire and twine to hold the shape, and set over rows of new plants. Stake the panels to keep them from blowing away and cover the open ends with boards. Not only will the peas grow faster, but the sparrows won't eat them as they germinate. The same is true of the birds and your early sweet corn. A bed of lettuce grown early in a cold frame will not tempt groundhogs when the glass lid is closed.

Repellents and Scare Devices

As mentioned earlier, efforts to scare animals away from gardens have not been entirely successful, to say the least. Yet, certain kinds of gadgets have persisted in the marketplace for so long that they must be used with some success, though not much, perhaps. Despite all of the fun poked at it, even the traditional homemade scarecrow will work a little, if made and used properly. The arms of the scarecrow should swing a bit in the wind, which is easy enough to accomplish. A spare steel fence post can act as the frame of the scarecrow. Thrust a stick through the sleeves of an old shirt and hang it from the top of post with twine, so that breezes will move the stick. Attach pants to the shirt with safety pins, and tie the waist loosely to the post. Set an old hat atop the post so that it hides the twine from which the arms of the scarecrow swing. Pin a shiny aluminum pie plate to the hat as a face—it will scare a bird more than trying to make a facsimile of a human countenance. Dangle pieces of aluminum foil from each sleeve for hands, and your scarecrow is complete. You should move it about the garden every other day. Having the whole thing affixed to a single fence post makes moving and resetting fairly simple.

The Weyerhauser Corporation has developed a spray-on scent that is supposed to repel deer effectively. It is called BGR (big game repellent). By the time you read this, it will be available commercially, at least east of the Mississippi, probably under a variety of names. Mike Ondick (Pennsylvania Wildlife Research Unit, the Pennsylvania State University) says that of the 20 or so traditional and hearsay repellents he has tried, BGR was about the only one that worked effectively. Ondick also says that human hair has proven to be quite effective if replaced every four days or so. A little twist of hair in a nylon stocking hung on stakes about 4 feet high and 4 feet apart does the trick, he says. The Carey Arboretum in New York claims success with this method, too.

Apparently there is even some truth in the notion that lion and tiger manure make an effective deer and rabbit repellent. *New Farm* magazine ran an article by Mark Lee, "Organic Odors Scare Off Pests" (September/October, 1981), describing the year-long success of a man who used tiger manure to keep deer and rabbits away from the sapling trees in his 80-acre nursery. Even dogs, so the story said, are repelled by the stuff.

The Beekeeper shoots starlings and crows and seems to take some relish in hanging the carcasses around his corn patch to scare away other birds. "I learned that from the Indians in the Southwest," he explains. "It works for them. Doesn't work nearly so well for me, however. I think our birds are inured to violence because of all the wild animals they see killed on the roads by cars."

White once put a kitten in a birdcage and hung the cage in his cherry tree. Birds stayed away, but the kitten wailed so that his wife made him release it.

Sometimes the best repellent is an attractant. A Juneberry tree loaded with fruit may dull the birds' appetites for cherries, which ripen a little later. Birds that gorge on mulberries in July are less apt to devastate your raspberries. Flocks of birds in the wild cherry trees or elderberry bushes mean fewer birds in your blackberries.

Color has a repellent-attractant influence in the case of fruit. Birds prefer dark red, blue, and purplish fruits to white, yellow, and orange ones. Invariably, they will feast more avidly on black cherries than on red, and on red more than on yellow. Black raspberries disappear faster than red ones. Purple grapes go faster than green ones. The Beekeeper disputes this, however. He claims the birds simply know which fruits taste better, and points to his Amber raspberries as proof. Though pale-colored, the birds eat them before the reds because, says the Beekeeper, "any fool knows Ambers are the best-tasting raspberry there is."

Instead of a frontal assault on birds craving newly germinated corn, some growers scatter corn along the edges of their newly planted fields or gardens. The theory is that the birds will eat the corn sprouting on top of the ground and may not get around to digging the new crop until it is up and growing. Once corn is up about 3 inches, birds lose interest in digging out the new sprouts.

Another method that seems to keep birds away from newly

sprouted corn is to plant a few oat seeds, or any other small grain, with each kernel of corn. The birds aren't much interested in the grain, but its sprouting seems to deter them from bothering the corn. The theory behind this practice, as propounded by the Dumb Farmer, is that birds *hear* seeds germinating. "Sure," he says. "If you don't believe it, watch how the birds dig up sprouting corn. They never make a mistake. They never dig a hole where there ain't no corn. They always bore right down *exactly* on the seed. They can hear it growing, I tell you. But when you have several oat seeds sprouting too, the competing sounds confuse the birds." The problem with this method is that you have to weed the oats out after the corn is growing well if they are at all numerous. The two plants do not grow well together.

Traditionally, gardeners have coated seeds with a mixture of tar and kerosene to discourage birds. The Dumb Farmer uses this method too, and says it's partially effective but practical only in small garden plantings. The tar-coated seeds get stuck in mechanical planters, so they have to be sown by hand.

New repellents with which to treat seeds come on the market from time to time, but these will not guarantee unscathed seedlings, either, since birds sometimes attack the tiny plants as they come through the soil after germination. Seed treated with fungicides and/ or insecticides will not stop birds even when the seed is made poisonous to them by the treatment. The bird simply waits until the seed sprouts and then eats out the inside of the seed, leaving the outer skin with its coating of fungicide, behind.

Sounds That Deter Wildlife

A cherished theory of wildlife control holds that animals can be repelled or attracted by sounds. The more straightforward of the gadgets built on this theory use noise directly to frighten birds and animals. Propane cannons are the best examples. Their effectiveness is limited, but the Dumb Farmer says they work adequately if backed up regularly with a shotgun. In earlier times, the "horse fiddle"—a notched, wooden wheel turned against a springy piece of metal—was used to scare away birds. Cranked vigorously, the wheel raised a clatter grating to the ears 30 acres away. But, no doubt it was the presence of the hapless farmer's son walking up and down the rows playing his horse fiddle that scared the birds as much as the clattering device. In any event, cannons and horse fiddles scarcely have a place in the backyard.

However, a modern version of the horse fiddle may be worth considering, if your neighbors' bedrooms are not too close to your garden and if it is deer you would like to scare away. A fellow by the name of Thomas Demkin, of Riverhead, New York, has invented a noisemaking device that in test trials in real garden situations seems to keep deer away. Called the Tomco clapper, the device makes a clapping or chattering noise at intervals predetermined by the set of the timer. The clapper can be powered by current from a battery or an ordinary 110-volt electric circuit. Each battery-operated clapper needs a timer, but with electric power, one timer can serve as many as 20 clappers. Howard Roller, a gardener and nurseryman in New York, says, in his report on the clapper published in *Countryside* magazine (October, 1981), that the device was 100 percent effective in his vegetable garden the two years he used it. It was also effective in keeping deer from winter browsing on his nursery stock.

Whether deer eventually learn that the noisemaker is just another ruse remains to be seen. Roller says that as time went on, the deer seemed to be less afraid of the clapper but still would not come close to it at the time of his report.

More intriguing is the attempt to influence animal behavior with recordings of the animals' own cries of distress or warning. Unfortunately, despite much work and experimentation, success has been limited. Distress calls of the red-winged blackbird, for example, seem to have little effect on a flock homing in on a cornfield. Systems are available for commercial operations, but the expense is hardly warranted for a backyard garden. With the advent of the handy home tape recorder, however, one might record the sounds an irate mother robin makes when humans approach her nest of young, then play the recording back on a varying schedule in a fruit-laden cherry tree.

Electronic vibration of sound waves is the latest idea being used in an effort to scare or confuse animals. The old idea of setting out jugs that supposedly emit noises or vibrations terrifying to rabbits when the wind blows over the mouths of the jugs, is a primitive example. The Beekeeper says that brown bottles must be used to succeed in this venture, a detail he cannot explain. White says the color of the bottles is of no importance, but that one must use a series of bottles, each with a different quantity of water in it, which varies the pitch of the sound vibrations from bottle to bottle. The Dumb Farmer says they are both crazy. He, on the other hand, puts some credence (only a little, he says) in the use of small windmill and whirligigs, which, according to their champions, send vibrations through the earth as their blades whirl, thus annoying moles.

Modern ultrasonic transmitters are based more or less upon the same theory of frightening animals. These devices transmit high-frequency sound waves, which are inaudible even to dogs and cats, but which, according to the manufacturers, drive out rodents. Cost of these devices ranges from about $150 to $300.

Smith swears that a radio hung in a cherry tree and tuned to a hard-rock music station will scare birds away, but no one believes him completely. It is well known in the neighborhood that Smith loathes hard rock and will use any occasion to ridicule it.

Chapter 12

Adventures with Wildlife in the Backyard

Humanity's enduring temptation is its fascination with distances. The human tendency is to face the immensity of the sky's space, the far horizons of the sea, or the endless roll of the prairies and perceive only vastnesses to be traversed. Such perception fosters an unremitting curiosity about what lies beyond. Having journeyed to the current limits of the "beyond" in a fruitless pursuit of the as yet unseen, humans, like the air traveler moving from airport to airport, may conclude that all places are the same, varying only in the amount of space between them. In both a shallow and a profound sense, this conclusion may be true. But nothing much except restlessness is learned from it—from being fascinated by the shoreline beyond the next river bend or by the star beyond the next surge of the imagination. The stars may indeed be more numerous than the sands of the seashore, as science now suggests. But there is every logical indication that when the final verdict is in, the conclusion of science will be: "When you've seen one galaxy, you've seen them all."

A wiser human builds a wall around his garden so that, undistracted by the allurement of distances, he may immerse himself physically and metaphysically into the meanings of existence in his own small place and thereby traverse the whole universe. With this kind of vision, garden rows stretch out to join the crop fields of the world. Groves of backyard trees become links in the earth's forest chain. Garden pools reflect the ocean's soul. The gardener, watching one drop of rain strike bare earth to send a particle of soil leaping into the air, then carry another particle with it as it slides down the side of a mud clod, understands the force of erosion better than the hill farmer who does not notice that the billions of raindrops falling on his farm are carrying away as much as 20 tons of soil per acre per year. Becoming intimate with the complex insect life of one apple tree, the backyarder may learn more about its proper control than the commercial orchardist, who sprays thousands of trees routinely, being intimate only with the labels on cans of chemicals.

Smith's perception of his place—his vision—has taught him to appreciate the philosophy of the Oriental garden. The distance between two garden rocks might be perceived as 2 feet, as a billion grains of sand, as an hour's meditation, or as an eternal marriage of matter and form. The garden and its wildlife can be viewed as a small part of the universe, or, if the mind perceives deeply enough, the embodiment of the whole universe. The same stars hover over Smith's garden as over the Himalayas. The bowels of the earth are as close under Smith's land as under a Siberian reindeer farm. Traveling to South America, he could meet the same monarch butterfly that fluttered in his oak tree a few months ago. The storm that brings him rain in Pennsylvania brought rain to Ohio yesterday, and Indiana the day before. The sulfuric acid in it bears the trademarks of Detroit and Youngstown smokestacks fired with West Virginia coal. The gulls wing in from the East Coast with news about the Jersey shore. Shad swim up the Wissahickon (when it is not too polluted) bearing tales of Delaware Bay. The great gray owl that startled Smith out of his wits one winter twilight brought him greetings from northern Canada. The Blackburnian warbler that visits his wildlife sanctuary each spring sings its same songs in the Yucatan forests. The black-throated blue warbler loses a feather in Smith's garden that it grew in the Greater Antilles. The magnolia warbler eating cankerworms off his fruit trees digests them with microorganisms that began to colonize in its digestive tract a few months earlier in Panama.

With this kind of awareness and vision, Smith has found that the backyard can become the scene of spine-tingling adventure—the kind he might earlier have associated with jungle safaris or mountain climbs. In fact, backyard adventures seem occasionally to be *more* exciting because of the element of surprise. One *expects* to be thrilled on a jungle safari. One does not foresee awakening from a snooze in the backyard to a scene of heart-pounding suspense.

Adventures with Birds

Smith did so one placid Sunday afternoon. He had fallen asleep in the Crow's Nest, victim of too many sections of the *New York Times*. He was awakened by the machine-gun thuddings of a woodpecker, only louder than any woodpecker's hammering he had ever heard before. Having taught himself to wake up without a start so as not to scare away wild animals (they often come very close to sleeping humans), Smith slowly opened his eyes and, without moving his head, examined the tree above him for the source of the sound. On a dead limb scarcely 15 feet away, Smith saw a bird at least as large as a crow, with a flaming red crest and white wing feathers flashing in stark contrast to the glistening black of its body. Though he had never seen one before, Smith knew that he was staring at a pileated woodpecker. Awestruck, he watched the great bird hammer away at the branch with its beak, bark shreddings and wood flying in a profuse shower around it. Because the pileated woodpecker is a shy bird (although no longer as rare as it once was), Smith marveled at his good fortune. Right here in his backyard he was probably as close to a live pileated woodpecker as any ornithologist had ever been in the wild!

As the big woodpecker swung its kingly head back and forth, rapidly drilling a large hole in the limb to get at the borers within, Smith was reminded of its colloquial name: "Lord-god." The man who first coined that name must have been as close to it as he was now. Smith blinked his eyes—a mistake. With a flickerlike alarm call, the magnificent bird spread its wings and swooped away, the white wing feathers flashing against the black. Yes, Smith thought, Lord-god—the perfect name for the pileated woodpecker.

Not all Smith's adventures ended so grandly. Smith won't easily forget (nor would White let him if he tried) the evening his son rushed into the house with news of two "very weird" birds high in a treetop near the garden pool. Smith grabbed his binoculars and followed his son up the path to the wildlife sanctuary. Sure enough, two very weird birds were roosting in the pin oak tree. They were chunky birds of middle size, with long yellow-green legs, distinctive red eyes, and black crowns from which hung white streamerlike head feathers. Smith paged through his bird book with trembling hands. The only bird that fit the description was the black-crowned night heron, a creature of marshes and sea shores. What were these two doing here, far from their usual haunts? Had the wind blown them off course in their migratory roamings southward? Smith, puzzling over these questions as he studied the herons through binoculars, backed out from under the tree to get a better angle at them in the waning light. He backed unerringly toward the garden pool. As he tripped over the edge and fell helplessly into the water, he whooped, his son whooped, and White, watching from his yard, whooped loudest of all. The two very weird birds flew away, no doubt to tell their relatives about a very weird human they had spotted while human watching in Pennsylvania. At least, that is how White likes to end the story.

The strangest adventure involving birds in the neighborhood happened to the Dumb Farmer while he was standing one evening beside his pasture pond watching a muskrat carry cattail roots away to its underground den. So strange was the happening that many acquaintances refused to believe it, despite eyewitness testimony and documentation that the same strange adventure had befallen a man in Ohio and another in Minnesota. As the Dumb Farmer stood motionless in the gray twilight, a great blue heron came gliding silently out of the sky toward the pond. To the Dumb Farmer's utter amazement, the great bird (4 feet tall with a wingspan approaching 6 feet) glided straight at him, folded its wings, and settled on his head! "What I remember thinking mostly about," he would say later, "is how lightly it landed, as if it weighed no more than a sparrow." Maintaining his aplomb with difficulty, the Dumb Farmer coolly inched his hand upward past his ear, made a sudden grab, as of a hen off the roost, and homeward bore his prize to show his friends before he freed it. As neighbors gathered round, Smith (who naturally was beside himself with curiosity) moved too close to the bird, and it lashed out with lightning speed, sending Smith's glasses flying into the air—in two pieces. The Beekeeper, arriving later, turned a baleful eye on Smith. "You're a lucky man," he said. "Great blue herons have been known to stab their beaks through a man's eye into his brain, killing him instantly." Smith was not sure he believed the Beekeeper, but he was not sure he didn't believe him, either.

One year, when the Colorado potato beetle was causing more damage than usual, Smith became interested in quail, having heard that the bird was especially fond of potato beetles. Next he learned that a covey of quail would come to a rather small area if it provided sufficient food and cover, and would stay there more or less permanently. That characteristic seemed to make quail an ideal animal for a backyard wildlife area, thought Smith. Managers of game farms claimed that as little as ⅛ acre planted to a seed crop that quail particularly liked, such as buckwheat or lespedeza, would feed a covey all winter. Other pluses in quails' favor included a preference for mulberries over choicer fruits, a fondness for weed seeds, and heavy predation not only of potato beetles, but of cutworms, cucumber beetles, cabbageworms, and aphids—all notorious pests in the garden.

So Smith bought two pairs from a game farm and turned them loose in his sanctuary. All summer he listened in vain for their cheery bobwhite whistle. By winter, he decided that his quail project was just another of his romantic dreams that had failed. Nevertheless, he constructed a brush and weed pile as advised by Edward Howe Forbush in the early part of the century. Alternating layers of tree branches with tall weeds gone to seed, he built a brush pile that would not only shelter quail, but would feed them, too. Crusted snow is a particular hazard for quail. In a snow storm, a covey huddles together on the ground in a clump of tall grass or under low brush. The snow often covers them completely. If freezing rain or ice turns the snow surface to a hard crust, as sometimes happens, the quail can be trapped underneath and starve. If they do escape, the crust prevents them from getting to weed seeds and fruits elsewhere, and even keeps them from the gravel they need to digest food properly. The brush piles ensured a haven from such difficulties.

Whether or not his brush pile helped the quail to survive that winter, Smith did not know. But he was delighted to hear, come spring, the piercing, two-note whistle of quail. All summer the birds called back and forth in his sanctuary. They called too from over in the Widow Lady's jungle of brush and the Beekeeper's tall grass orchard floor. He saw the birds only in their accomplishments. That year he had to pick off only three potato beetles from his plants and only one beetle egg cluster.

In the meantime, Smith had planted one of his three vegetable plots to alfalfa as a way to rest the soil for a year, break insect and disease buildups, and add nitrogen to the soil. Twice he mowed the alfalfa and let it decay back to plant food and organic matter while acting as mulch for the regrowth of the legume. Now, in August, the alfalfa was knee-high again and lush green, like a little emerald among the browns of dry, late summer. Smith delighted in gazing upon its greenness, walking through it, and picking some leaves to dry for alfalfa leaf tea. One day, as he sauntered through the patch, there was an explosion of feathers in front of him. A quail shot up as if out of his shoe. Jumping back in sudden fright, Smith waited for the rest of the covey to flush. But no. Only the one flew, and it was all turns and sommersaults in the air, as if afflicted with some dreadful muscular disorder. Must be a mother quail, feigning injury to draw him away from a brood of chicks, Smith thought. It was not unusual for quail to hatch a second brood in August. She sank out of sight up in the snatch of marsh grass near the garden pool. Smith made no move. In the silence that followed her clucking mother-calls, the alfalfa around him suddenly vibrated with a chorus of high, thin cheeps. Looking down, Smith found himself ankle deep in quail chicks. He counted 14 before the scurrying brown fluffballs made counting impossible. He scooped one up. It fit neatly into the palm of his hand and lay very still, as if dead. But then it trembled. Or was it Smith's hand?

Wildlife has provided the humans of Gwynnedde Township with two other memorable events each year. In the spring, the first flocks of Canada geese wing their way up from the South, their haunting, honking cries heralding the fresh new hope of spring. In the fall, as the geese migrate south again, these same honkings strike the human ear not with hope but as a sad and keening lament at the approach of winter. Smith wonders, as he straightens up from his garden work to listen, how the exact same sound could evoke such opposite emotions.

The Canada goose, especially the largest of the many strains, *Branta canadensis maxima,* was a rare bird in the early 1900s. Now it is common in the suburbs, which it often seems to prefer over wilder places. Wherever open water lingers through the winter in metropolitan areas, in which hunting is prohibited, the big birds are apt to congregate and thrive. Over the past 25 years, wildlife specialists have been shipping the surplus of one city to another not yet overpopulated with geese, and lately there has been talk of breaking the eggs in the nest as a way of controlling population. No one dares suggest publicly a more practical solution—eating the geese. Killing the beloved urban goose would bring a public outcry among some wildlife lovers, especially those whose yards (or golf courses) have not yet been overgrazed by the geese and left studded with excrement. The Beekeeper thinks the Canada goose might be properly employed as both lawn mower and fertilizer spreader, and then as the main guest for Christmas dinner—all at great savings in money and energy.

A flock of Canada geese live almost full-time on the lake beside one Gwynnedde Township factory. In spring they pair off and nest along Wissahickon Creek and its tributaries. Given the half-tame character of the resident flock, Smith thought it only logical that some day a pair might nest in his sanctuary near the garden pool.

One May, after he had been on a business trip and tending to other duties that kept him away from the wildlife sanctuary, he glanced up from setting out muskmelon plants to see a goose standing, sure enough, near the garden pool, hardly more than its head visible above the marsh grass. So as not to disturb the goose, Smith and his family did not approach the pool.

Through binoculars, he never saw more than the one bird, however, and decided finally that no pair nested there—just one bold old fellow, probably, trying to eat the yellow water lily he had finally established in the pool.

Smith approached slowly, not wishing to alarm the bird unduly. Instead of flying away, however, the goose waited until Smith was hardly more than 15 feet away. Then, with wings raised, and head and neck stretched out close to the ground, reminding Smith of a snake, the goose hissed and charged directly at him. Surprise froze the man in his tracks, but instinct quickly took over and with a whoop that sounded foreign to his own ears, Smith wheeled and fled. When he stopped a safe distance away and looked back, a second goose had raised its head above the grass. Mother Goose was indeed on a nest, and Father Goose was about his instinctive job of protecting her.

The Beekeeper nodded belief when he heard the story. He had seen a Canada goose attack a horse and rider when they had ventured too near a nest along the Wissahickon. Mother Goose might be depicted as a gentle old woman full of nursery rhymes, but Father Goose was her mean-tempered and courageous defender. Smith's geese, however, did not stay. Whether because of his intrusion or perhaps because of harassment from wandering dogs and cats, the geese disappeared, leaving a nest of cold eggs for Smith to contemplate.

Another of Smith's nature adventures began only as a result of the sheerest whim of the weather. A freak snowstorm fell in late March, burying blooming daffodils. Curious to see how nature reacted to such an emergency, Smith took a long walk back to the farthest fence line of the Dumb Farmer's acres, where young trees were invading the pasture from the adjacent woodland along Wissahickon Creek. As he walked among the saplings at the pasture's edge, he almost stepped on a small, chunky bird with a long beak that whirred into the air and flew swiftly but erratically away. A woodcock! Looking down into the snow at his feet, Smith was astonished to find a nest with three eggs in it, a nest that in normal weather would be almost impossible to find because the woodcock is a master at concealment. But with snow on the ground everywhere except where mother woodcock had sat, indomitable, through the storm, the nest was as visible as a senator running for reelection. Smith photographed the once-in-a-lifetime scene and hurried away so that the woodcock would return to the nest before the eggs cooled.

The incident led Smith to study up on the ways of woodcocks. Though he had found the nest accidentally, it was no accident that the nest was located where it was. Woodcocks demand an area where small saplings dot or edge clearings, as in an old pasture, and where the birds can find earthworms in low, moist or marshy sites all summer long. The nearby Wissahickon Creek provided some swampy ground next to it, and the pasture itself contained low soggy areas that held water in spring and remained damp under the trees even in August. Smith learned that the Dumb Farmer's cows helped the woodcocks, too, their hooves keeping paths bare under the trees, making it easy for woodcocks to dig out the worms that rose in the damp soil to feed on the organic matter in the cows' manure. In summer, Smith invariably could chase up a woodcock along these paths in the sapling shade.

One thing led to another. Smith next became interested in the cowbirds that flocked around the grazing cows. The birds fed on the flies that bothered the animals. They sat on the backs of the sheep, too, ferreting out ticks deep in the sheep's wool, so the Dumb Farmer said. Smith had heretofore made a practice of throwing out cowbird eggs from chipping sparrow nests, thinking he was doing a good deed for the beneficial chipping sparrows. (Cowbirds do not make nests of their own, but lay eggs in the nests of smaller birds. The cowbird chicks, being larger at hatching, invariably out-compete the other hatchlings

Woodcock

for the food the parents bring, and the smaller birds often starve.) Now he reconsidered. First of all, species like the chipping sparrow had suffered the importunities of cowbirds for centuries without diminution. And from the cows' point of view, Smith realized, the cowbird was a very nice bird indeed.

Watching cowbirds and cows, Smith learned something else that amazed him. When the cows lay down near the barn where the chickens wandered, the latter would come running and gobble up every big horsefly they could reach off the cows. "Yes, it's a remarkable symbiotic relationship," the Dumb Farmer nodded with a smile. "I don't have to spray the cows so often, and those chickens are getting an excellent protein supplement. The horseflies are not only themselves nutritious, but they are also full of blood they have sucked out of the cows."

But the woodcocks eventually provided Smith with the best part of his pasture observations. He learned that the male woodcock, early in spring, puts on a most unusual courtship display to attract females. Shortly before sunrise, or, more often, just after sunset, the male will choose a clearing, usually near or among saplings, and begin a high, thin chirping sound that humans attempt to describe as "peenting." Then he launches himself into the sky, flying in a wide spiral pattern while gradually gaining altitude, until he all but disappears in the darkening sky. Then, folding his wings, the woodcock drops back to earth, chirping a little song far different from the peenting sound that announced his flight. As he lands, he is silent.

Smith realized that a backyard in the process of becoming a wildlife area might easily attract a woodcock both for courtship flights and nesting. Each year, he watched and waited at the edge of his sanctuary. But no woodcocks. In the meantime, he hiked over to the Dumb Farmer's field on March evenings. It was several years before his patience was rewarded.

Standing at the edge of the forward advance of the ash, maple, and locust saplings, he was first aware of a sound as of a human clearing his throat. A few moments later he heard a nasal, cricketlike, buzzing sound. Could it be the peenting of a woodcock? The question had hardly risen in his mind when the sound resumed, becoming gradually more like the peenting-type noise he had listened to on recordings. Then a small, dark feathered form burst from the pasture grass with whistling, whirring wings. The bird climbed skyward in an ever smaller, spiraling circle, until Smith could not see it. Moments later it reappeared, dropping swiftly to the ground like a hawk upon a rabbit, singing as it fell. On the ground, out of sight again, the woodcock peented several more times, then took off again, repeating the whole act before Smith's amazed gaze. In the gray dusk, he had a feeling he was being transported far from civilization, far back in time. Was he an engineer who worked in an office in Philadelphia, or was he a nomad of the ancient plains?

When the performance ended, Smith hurried homeward in the dark, eager to share his experience with friends. But the closer he drew to the modern environment of humans, returning as from a long journey into the wilderness, the less appropriate his story seemed to be. The magic of those moments would diminish in the glow of street-lights. Recounting his experience in the houses of humans would not recapture the haunting spirit of the real event, any more than he could describe properly the fear and loneliness of standing watch on a ridge in Korea. He could see himself punctuating each sentence about the woodcock ritual with "you-just-had-to-be-there," and his friends would nod sympathetically and return to a discussion of the football scores.

"Where in the world have you been?" his wife asked worriedly as he kicked his boots off on the porch.

"Watching the courtship flight of a male woodcock."

She looked at him, lovingly, but with the same amazement, Smith realized, with which he had looked at the woodcock. "I bet no one else in the whole world has a husband who would use that excuse for being late for dinner," she sighed. "And he has the only wife who'd believe him."

The Caretaker Gardener

Smith thinks of himself not so much as a formal gardener, but as an informal caretaker of plants. Mostly, he makes a place for nature to grow and proliferate. He acts as a half-hearted referee in the rich and varied garden of natural plenty where carrots and onions are only a small part of the grand theater of life. On stage, beside garden vegetables, are wild animals, domestic animals, nut trees, fruit trees, pasture grass, weeds, herbs, spiders, birds, bees, berries—a horn of plenty all in the act of eating and being eaten. Smith eats his share and watches over the rest—adding here, subtracting there, aiding the less competitive, hindering the more aggressive, all in an effort to bring the greatest diversity possible into his backyard.

Sometimes this naive kind of refereeing brought predictable, if surprising, results, as when Smith induced the huge parasol mushroom to grow on his place by burying spore-impregnated paper in the leaf mulch of his grove (see Chapter 9, Human Use of Nature's Food Web). Other times there were surprises even the most knowledgeable naturalist could hardly have anticipated. One hot July day, Smith found in the shadiest part of his tree grove a most unusual plant. Standing about 8 inches tall was a scaly silver-white stem topped by a nodding white flower with just a touch of pink to it, the whole similar in shape to a tobacco pipe stuck by its mouthpiece into the ground. At first Smith thought the plant was a fungus, despite its flowerlike bloom, since there was no green chlorophyll in it. His mushroom books contained nothing like it. So he leafed excitedly through his *Field Guide to Wildflowers* (The Peterson Field Guide Series, by Roger Tory Peterson and Margaret McKenny). Sure enough, there it was, *Monotropa uniflora,* commonly called Indian-pipe, one of the few wild flowers devoid of chlorophyll. Smith preferred the Indian name for the plant: ghost flower. Certainly, no flower in the woods looked more ghostly, glowing silver-white in the dense shade, eventually turning blackish, like a fungus, before dying. The Indians believed that the plant grew on old burial sites, and the pioneers, seeing the strange plants for the first time, were slow to disagree. In a broad sense, that belief is scientifically

Indian-Pipes

true, since the ghost flower is parasitic and saprophytic, feeding on decaying organic matter for its nutrients. Indians crushed the flowers and steeped them in water to make a lotion for sore or injured eyes.

Nature is never wholly predictable. One might journey to the headwaters of the Amazon and on any given day not find a plant as rare for that area as a ghost flower is for a backyard American tree grove. But finding a ghost flower in the wild is at least subject to some kind of predictable odds, since the flower ranges over the eastern half of the United States.

The gardener in Smith thinks of rabbits as the enemy, a pest that, like rats, might be exterminated without any harm to the environment. The caretaker in him knows better. Rabbits are a staple food for many beautiful and beneficial wild animals whose absence would markedly disorganize the complex food web. Wild rabbits are by no means an insignificant food for humans, either. In New York State alone, to give an example, hunters have taken as many as 2 million rabbits and more in a season, or approximately 4 million pounds of tasty hasenpfeffer, stew, and fried rabbit. So well do rabbits thrive in our man-centered environment that such hunting does not affect their normal levels of population, and plenty of rabbits are left for their other natural predators. Given weather that is not so severe as to starve them, and given access to plenty of food and cover (both of which suburb and city backyards supply), rabbits maintain high population levels despite heavy predation.

Rabbits thrive on clover, young dandelion and plantain leaves, garden vegetables, and many other wild green plants. In winter they feast on the buds and bark of blackberry, raspberry, apple, maple, oak, sumac and many other plants. Some gardeners believe that maintaining wild cover and food on one's property encourages more rabbit damage to the garden, but this does not seem to be the case. Rabbit damage to garden plants is generally worse where there is little wild food and cover available, which forces the rabbits to live entirely in the garden. Lawns with good stands of clover and thickets ample with green bark, stems, and buds help to protect the garden.

The manner in which a mother rabbit raises her young, sometimes right under the noses of humans, is remarkable. Gestation lasts 28 days, and a female can mate again 24 hours after giving birth, averaging 4 litters of 3 to 5 young annually. Mother makes a nest, but it's far too small to fit herself into. The nest hole measures about 6 inches in diameter and 4 to 6 inches deep, often on a slant so that the hole looks like the mouth of a tiny tunnel. Mother rabbit needs only the bare essentials of camouflage to conceal this hole from prying eyes. Smith has found nests (almost always after the young have grown and left) in his potato patch, in his strawberries, and especially in a patch of pachysandra next to his house. If the mother rabbit must dig much dirt in her nest-making, she cleverly scatters it out in front of the nest and covers it with dry grass or leaves, hiding all signs of soil disturbance. Then she wads the nest hole with a loose ball of dried grass. Right before giving birth, she plucks fur from her stomach and fills the inner core of the grass ball with it. Inside this downy, insulated, moisture-repelling nest she places her bare-skinned young as they are born.

She covers the nest with leaves and twigs and other debris so that it is all but invisible. For some 16 days, she returns to the nest in early morning and late evening, removes the camouflage, lies down over the nest so that the young can nurse, washes each of them clean with her tongue after nursing, covers the nest again, and hides nearby.

Young rabbits are ready to leave the nest in less than three weeks, and though small enough to hide almost anywhere, they are more vulnerable to predation than their parents because of their inexperience with the many hazards of rabbit life. One evening, as Smith sat in the Crow's Nest watching a young rabbit hop along the grass path at the far end of the sanctuary, he noticed a hawk gliding into view. Suddenly, the large bird folded its wings and dropped like a stone, swiftly, silently, unerringly. At the last instant before its free-falling body would have hit the earth with a bone-jarring thud, the hawk spread its wings, breaking its fall, and stretched forth its talons. There was a short, piercing squeal from the rabbit, then a flap of wings as the hawk rose laboriously into the air again, bearing its prize. Smith realized his heart was pounding. Like the unwary young rabbit, he had been taken completely by surprise and had not even had the presence of mind to grab his binoculars. He was not quite sure he had seen what he had seen. He kept waiting for an instant replay.

Hunting rabbits with shotguns was still allowed in the more rural parts of Gwynnedde Township, which pleased the gardeners but upset many nongardeners. The continuous mowing of lawns, and the steady increase in the size of them at the expense of brushland, decreased the proper habitat of rabbits and therefore effectively killed more of them than hunters did. Few of the wildlife lovers in Gwynnedde Township understood that. Ecology was not yet deemed a proper branch of learning, even though without it, reading, writing, and arithmetic might lead the human race to its own destruction.

The Dumb Farmer invited his friends to a rabbit hunt every year on Thanksgiving morning, keeping alive a tradition in rural families of earlier days when the fundamentals of food web relationships were part of one's upbringing and did not have to be taught in school. Smith always went along, though he no longer enjoyed hunting as he did when he was a boy. He understood more or less that controlled hunting did not endanger wildlife populations particularly, but now he found the act of killing anything, even a rabbit, distasteful. He went hunting with the Dumb Farmer mostly because his young son begged to go along, just as Smith had begged when he was a boy. Smith found mystery in this: His son, age ten, painstakingly raised a nest of orphaned cottontails by feeding them cow's milk out of an eye dropper. Yet he traded his role as nurturer for that of hunter without a qualm. The Dumb Farmer laughed at Smith's quandary. "It's my fault," he explained. "He comes over here and helps me around the farm and learns the facts of life. You don't want him to grow up being another wienie-armed suburbanite, do you?"

The Dumb Farmer's rabbit hunts were not very violent affairs anyway. They usually began in Smith's backyard where no one would think of discharging a firearm. The Dumb Farmer's beagle snorkeled through the wildlife sanctuary, into the Widow Lady's puckerbrush jungle, and across the Beekeeper's old orchard. The Dumb Farmer and the Beekeeper vied with each other in trying to impress the younger generations with their hunting lore. If there was snow on the ground, the hunt became a tracking expedition. The Widow Lady always had to point out that when she was a girl on the farm, shooting rabbits was considered a waste of bullets. On a cold day, she would track a rabbit to a clump of dead grass in the field, sneak up; and dispatch the animal with a well-aimed blow of a club. White, who once joined the Thanksgiving hunt, found the story distasteful, even though he himself bragged about how many mice he trapped and killed in his garage.

The hunt usually proceeded from one philosophical argument to another rather than from one rabbit to another. Once across the highway, beyond the suburban developments and deep into the Dumb Farmer's fields, the hunters got down to serious business, but so did the rabbits. Invariably, they escaped to the groundhog holes under the brush piles in the woodlot, where even the beagle could not flush them out.

The Beekeeper often threatened to bring a ferret along on the hunt as "in the old days." The ferret was put down into the groundhog holes the rabbits sought for safety, and without fail, he said, two or three rabbits would come running out. Hunting with ferrets was supposed to be illegal, but the furtive little weasellike animals were often kept and raised on farms to control rats, gliding down rat holes as unhesitatingly as down groundhog holes.

By noon the hunt was usually over, the rabbits, if any, cleaned, and the mighty hunters stretched out before the warm glow of the Dumb Farmer's fireplace—mulled cider for the young ones, hot toddies for the elders. The Beekeeper and the Dumb Farmer regaled them all with tales of yesterday and observations about tomorrow. No wilderness safari could end as enjoyably.

The hunt was not officially over until the Dumb Farmer delivered his annual ritualistic advice. "Remember now," he would say, addressing the younger hunters and pointing a warning finger at the future, "if the dog had not been so proud as to stop and leave his scent on the fence post, he'd have surely caught the rabbit."

Deer Stalker

One morning while picking strawberries in his garden, Smith caught a movement out of the corner of his eye. It seemed like a gray shadow moving across the meadow plots of the sanctuary. He looked up in time to see a deer melt into the grove behind the wild bramble patch. From long experience, he knew he dare not take his eyes off the shadowy movement even to set his berry box on the ground, or he would not be able to pick out the deer-shadow in the brush again. For its size, a deer can hide itself from human eyes amazingly well. Even now Smith could not actually see the deer, but by keeping his eyes glued to the shadowy dapples of deer body behind the foliage, he could discern its movement. If the deer stood still, he knew where it was only by the cessation of movement.

He decided to stalk the animal. Very leisurely, he walked toward the shadow-minus-movement. When he advanced 6 feet, the deer-shadow moved 6 feet, as coolly and slowly as he moved, keeping just enough foliage and tree trunk between them so that, standing still, the deer was almost invisible. By slow stages, animal and man moved through the sanctuary until the deer melted through the border hedge and disappeared into the Widow Lady's thick growth of brush. Smith had an uncanny sense that the deer had stopped there, hardly 50 feet from him, hoping the man would give up his pursuit. Smith decided the same tall brush and grass that hid the deer might hide him and enable him to get very close to the deer. He hunkered down on all fours and began a slow and painstaking crawl. He eased himself through a low opening in the hedge, and like a dog stalking a groundhog, he crept by slow, almost imperceptible movements of arms and legs toward the spot he believed the deer to be standing. He had traversed scarcely 50 feet when his head poked through the dense brush into a small clearing that had been trampled flat. To his astonishment, he was staring into the eyes of a doe and a fawn so close he could discern every nervous twitch of distended nostril. Possibly because Smith was down on all fours, or possibly because the doe was possessed of a strong maternal instinct, she did not run away as the fawn did, but began to walk toward Smith with a peculiar stiff-legged stride. Smith tensed but did not move, curiosity vying with fear for dominance. Suddenly the doe reared on her hind feet, her front hooves beginning to lash out like a prizefighter testing the range of his arms.

A primitive instinct for survival took over Smith's consciousness, hastened by a memory of what he had once read—that a deer could cut an adversary to pieces with her hooves. He cried out, leaped up, and fled in panic. The doe, evidently as surprised at Smith's behavior as he was at hers, turned tail and dashed away also. But Smith didn't know that, because he was running pell-mell the other way. Well into his sanctuary, he stopped to look back. Nothing. The strange fear that had overwhelmed him subsided as quickly as it had come, leaving him wondering if he had been afraid at all. Then he looked at his arms and legs. Afraid he had been for sure. He was covered with bleeding cuts and scratches. He had run blindly right through the hedge, heedless of the thorns.

Fate of the Raccoon

Like the Canada goose, the raccoon prospers in urban areas along with humans, feeding mainly on the food the latter throw into their garbage cans. The only real threat to the urban coon is the garbage disposal under the sink. Raccoons become more than mildly curious about their human food providers, and while on their nightly raids of garbage cans and corn patches, they often take time to peer into the houses from convenient tree limbs outside windows. Most likely they hope to discover something to eat inside, if only they could get the door open. The Beekeeper declares that raccoons can learn to open doors with lift-type latches, and the Widow Lady remembers a particularly hungry character that clambered up her screen door, ripped the screen loose, mounted a kitchen countertop, opened the cabinet and helped itself to the cookies inside.

But Smith did not fully appreciate the boldness of raccoons in the face of the rising tide of human population until the night the family cat raised a great commotion on the patio. The Smiths (ironically watching an animal adventure story on TV that was hardly more exciting than the drama taking place right outside their door) rushed out to see what was happening. In the sudden illumination of the porch light, they found the cat standing stiff-legged, its body forming a perfectly inverted horseshoe, tail straight up, hair on tail straight out, as one often sees in pictures but rarely in real life. Several feet away stood a huge raccoon, eyeing the dish of half-eaten cat food. To suburban children like the Smiths', the raccoon loomed on the edge of the night as awesome as a grizzly bear, and they immediately concluded that the raccoon was after the cat's kittens in the box near the door. Smith was thrust into the role of kitten-protector, a role he was not too comfortable with, being among the most nonviolent of men. Besides, he was not sure where his allegiance lay, preferring, he suspected, the company of coons over cats. Nevertheless, he grabbed the broom by the door and made a half-hearted swipe at the raccoon, which had backed up into the corner where the two low walls of the patio met at a right angle. Rather than try to escape, the raccoon reared on its hind legs, truly like a grizzly, and grabbed a mouthful of broom. Wife and children screamed and abandoned Smith to his fate for the comparative safety of the living room, where they continued to urge him on from behind the picture window. The cat disappeared into the shrubbery, and Smith, slightly bewildered, took a few steps backward. That was all the escape route the raccoon needed. It bounded away with the peculiar shuffling, loping gait raccoons are noted for and skittered up the sassafras tree in the yard. The Smiths, reunited, gathered under the tree like a pack of hounds, making enough noise to rouse the Whites and the Browns, too. Someone fetched a flashlight. Its beam reflected back two bright, beady eyes. For an hour, the children kept vigil with the raccoon, the television inside flickering its one beady eye to an empty room.

That episode was but a mild prologue to another later that summer, an adventure that would teach the Smiths something about the savagery of wildlife, something all but lost in the modern myth of "kindly Mother Nature." Smith was having trouble with raccoons in his corn patch and had not yet learned that electric fence was the only adequate solution. He borrowed the Dumb Farmer's mongrel hound, Brownie, and tied it to a stake at one end of the corn patch. The Dumb Farmer had bragged that Brownie was among the world's most proficient coon-haters and could hear a raccoon bite into an ear of corn 10 acres away.

In the middle of the night, a terrible ruckus awakened Smith. Surely a pack of foxhounds was crossing his wildlife sanctuary. The scene that appeared in the beam of his flashlight was not easy to account for. Evidently, a raccoon had decided it would have corn for midnight lunch, dog or no dog, perhaps divining as only raccoons can that the dog was tied anyway. By the time the raccoon had ripped into its second ear of corn, Brownie had lost all sense of propriety under leash, and had lunged so hard on his chain that the stake to which it was affixed pulled out of the ground. Brownie was not much larger than the raccoon in pounds, but rangier and quicker of foot. So despite the chain and stake that slowed him down like a dragging anchor on a boat, he kept the raccoon so very nearly surrounded that it could not escape to a tree. A snarling, growling, rolling, twisting, bloody battle ensued that by degrees inched its way to the garden pool. When Smith and his son arrived, the raccoon had its back to the water. The dog, its nose mauled and bloody, seemed about to move in for the kill.

As an experienced coon hunter would have guessed, the raccoon had not entirely by chance managed to move the scene of battle close to the pool. A raccoon's first line of retreat is to the nearest tree. Blocked in that direction, its next refuge of choice is water. To Smith's horrified surprise, the reason was soon apparent.

The raccoon turned as if to jump into the water. The dog lunged at its exposed flank, a little too carelessly. The raccoon whirled in a flash, coming up under and inside the dog's jaws, the raccoon's humanlike paws grasping the dog's neck, the raccoon at the same time falling back into the water, pulling the dog after it. Both disappeared beneath the water's surface.

Over and over the animals turned and thrashed. Whenever Brownie appeared above the surface, gasping for air, he yelped in terror, obviously trying to escape. Each time, the raccoon pulled him under again. "That coon is drowning that dog," Smith heard himself utter in profound astonishment. A sharp little voice at his side cut through his numbed disbelief. "Do something, Daddy!" Yes. Do something. Even the Beekeeper wasn't going to believe this one. Smith grabbed the chain to which the dog was still tied and hauled him out of the water. The raccoon relented, swam to the other side of the pool, and scrambled out toward the waiting arms of the trees. But by now Smith had been galvanized into action. Some primitive streak of wildness he had not realized was in him welled up and took charge. Catching up with the raccoon, Smith kicked it savagely in the head, stunning it. Brownie, right at his heels, snapped powerful jaws around the now-defenseless raccoon and bit and shook the animal in fury, breaking its neck. In a few seconds, the raccoon was dead. A somber father and son stood wordless for a long time before silently going back to the house.

The Human Animal in the Wild Backyard

Smith would recall the wildness that had overtaken him that night with a little shame, not quite willing to admit that beneath the surface of his civilized manners lurked an instinct to kill. But on another day, another kind of wildness swept through him in the backyard that he would recall with keen pleasure. On a blistering hot Saturday afternoon in July, he was fiddling with a little windmill yard ornament that was supposed to scare moles away (before he'd learned they were beneficial) by setting up vibrations in the ground. The vibrations were supposed to make moles nervous enough to cause them to leave the area. The windmill had little effect on the comings and goings of Smith's moles, though, in their search for the ample earthworms under his garden mulch. With an engineer's persistence, he was trying to improve the windmill's performance, bending the axle of the whirling blades ever so slightly so that the mill wobbled a bit in its revolutions, accentuating, he hoped, the vibrations. Then he pushed the legs of the windmill deeper into the soil, hoping that the increased contact with the earth might give the windmill more vibrating action.

A roll of distant thunder played on the edges of his consciousness. So engrossed in the windmill was he that it was not until his son scampered down from the Crow's Nest with news that a "mighty black cloud" was gathering in the West that Smith took stock of the sky and the thunder. Low clouds were scudding swiftly in over the treetops, hinting of high winds on the way. Lightning began to play fitfully along the edge of the approaching storm front. "We better get the chicks in," Smith said to his son. He had only recently purchased a dozen chicks to raise for meat and eggs, and they were still young enough to get badly soaked or even drown in a heavy rain.

The chicks were old enough, however, to scurry adroitly away from the two humans trying to herd them into the old toolshed at the edge of the yard. Even after wife and daughter joined the roundup, the first drops of rain were falling before the task was complete. Before the family could return to the house, the sudden storm unleashed its power, and the four of them had little choice but to seek shelter in the toolshed coop with the chicks. Wind shook the little building, and rain pounded on the tin roof. The giddy elation that had infected the Smiths as the storm approached gave way to a tense nervousness and, finally, to outright fear. For all practical purposes, the storm had cut them neatly off from the security of civilization. The family might just as well have been adrift at sea in a small boat or isolated on a faraway island. There in the backyard, surrounded by a dense surburban population, they faced for a moment the same kind of struggle for survival that a family in the wilderness might face. The children began to whimper as the small building swayed precariously. A rifle crack of lightning struck so close that it seemed to hurl them physically against the shed wall. A limb cracked and fell nearby, the sound of it clear and distinct from the roar of the wind. Smith looked at his wife and saw in her eyes a reflection of his own thoughts—a realization of the fragility of existence. "And to think," he shouted in her ear, "that we wouldn't go on that rafting trip down the river for fear it would be too dangerous for the kids."

As quickly as it had come, the wind abated, although the rain continued to fall. Smith's wife remembered the open windows of the car in the driveway, and all four of them bolted to the rescue, glad for an excuse to leave the shed that for a few scary moments had given them a sober sense of the essence of danger.

Halfway to the house, Smith stopped, halted by some mysterious attraction to the rain. He was already wet anyway, and it wouldn't take all four of them to close the car windows. The wind and lightning had passed on, so there was little danger in staying out in the rain. *I have never stood in my garden and really experienced rain,* he realized with some surprise. Like most presumably sane humans, he usually ran with hunched shoulders to the nearest protective roof or to the closet for a raincoat and umbrella when rain started to fall. What was it like to stand in a downpour like a tree or a deer? He walked slowly to his garden, head back, letting the raindrops sting his skin, roll down his body, dribble off his chin and fingertips. He sat down on the ground, watching the droplets pummel the soil with a ferocity no book had ever led him to expect, the miniature spouts of water leaping back into the air, laden with grains of dirt. He watched the leaves of plants gather the falling rain and direct it to the whorls of their central stalks, as if drinking. He laid back on the grass and opened himself to rain. Some elemental passion stirred in him as the water welled up in the grass faster than it could run off by gravity. He had a feeling that at any moment he would begin to float away. It was as if the water was not only soothing his flesh after the hot, dry day, but was melting him, binding him, rooting him to the soil. Though he wore only a pair of shorts, his usual garb in the garden, a wild kind of ecstasy swept through him and he shucked these, too, to stand naked in the privacy of the torrential downpour. For a few brief minutes he was conscious of neither time, nor thought, nor even awareness of his own independent identity. The rain washed him into the flux and flow of existence, freed him from the heavy burden of intellect, and cradled him in the peace of nature's own Nirvana.

Then, the realities of survival reasserted themselves, and the engine of intellect throbbed back into action. The rain was diminishing, but the wind was colder now. If Smith did not seek shelter and dry off, he'd catch pneumonia.

Later, Smith stood on the porch of his house, warm now, dressed in soft, dry clothes, gazing out into the darkness where his gardens lay. He felt that he had emerged from the rain clean and glistening like a butterfly newly flown from its chrysalis. He had been refreshed, spiritually as well as physically. The night noises of cricket and tree frog sweetly blotted out the memory of thunder and wind. Where was that wild place he and his family had found themselves in during the storm? Certainly a far distance from what he now watched fading into peaceful, firefly darkness. Where had he been when he stood naked, arms outstretched in exhilaration and celebration of the falling rain? Was he perhaps as weird as White maintained he was? Or was White a sad tragedy, living only half a life, unaware of the depths and nuances of existence's dramas? He did not know. And after the day's experience, he did not even try to find out. It was enough to understand that he had been on a long journey in his backyard, a journey to the faraway corners of his mind.

Wildling of the North

Another time the weather rolled back the boundaries of Smith's backyard so that they embraced, at least in Smith's mind, uncharted wildernesses. Winter had brought a blizzard that piled snow 4 feet and more deep on the lee side of the howling wind. For Smith, like other suburbanites, the depth of the snow was a reality that had to be faced only in the driveway and on the sidewalks. Snow blowers and shovels could clear a path to the car, and a path for the car to the road. From there, snowplows cleared the way to work. The blizzard was merely inconvenient, the inconvenience measured by the distance from one's garage to the street.

The evening after the blizzard, Smith decided to hitch a ride home from the train station with a friend, rather than have his wife brave the cleared but slippery roads, for lesser winds continued to blow a steady film of snow. Smith insisted that his friend drop him off at the corner where the Friends' Meetinghouse stood, so he could walk home the last third of a mile through the cemetery, across the back of the Beekeeper's and the Widow Lady's places, through his wildlife sanctuary and to his house. He needed the exercise. The bracing wind would clear the office-fogged cells of his brain.

Through the deep snow in the cemetery he plunged, hoping perhaps to see the great horned owls he knew lived in the huge, hollow-topped white oak tree that had probably witnessed the first of the burials there, two centuries earlier. The wind was still blowing, colder than Smith had realized, and though not as strong as during the height of the blizzard the night before, he noticed, as he rested at the end of the cemetery, that his tracks were fast blowing closed.

Across the back of the Beekeeper's orchard lot, where the grass had been allowed to grow taller by far than in the cemetery, the snow deepened, making walking even more difficult. Smith realized why snowshoes were invented. In snow 3 feet deep, a man could not really walk, but had to wallow along. In the semi-darkness he could not see well enough to pick a path through shallower snow, if there was any. Forward progress became exceedingly difficult, and his breathing became labored. By the time he had fought his way across the Beekeeper's lot and skirted the edge of the Widow Lady's brushy property, he found that he was too winded to proceed. At least in the wildlife sanctuary where he now found himself, he was sheltered from the cruel wind. But the snow was, for that reason, even deeper. He sank down into it and tried to regain his breath. He could see the lights of his house scarcely 600 feet away, but for all practical purposes, the distance might have been a mile or more. *It's going to take me a half hour to get across my backyard,* he muttered to himself in disbelief. *I could freeze in that time.* He lunged on another 10 yards, the idea of frostbite in his flimsy business suit and coat, within hailing distance of his wife, suddenly presenting itself as a possibility. Just a tremor of panic stirred in him, giving him new energy. He wallowed another 50 feet, then sank again into the snow, this time too exhausted to go on. He had eaten very little lunch, which might account for what seemed to him as excessive tiredness. But this was ridiculous. No man ever froze to death in his own backyard. He could always dig a hole down in the snow and stay warm till he was rescued. Maybe. He remembered stories of people who had lost their ways in blizzards and died within a stone's throw of shelter. Smith wondered now: Did they die from being lost in the storm, or did they die simply because a man can't walk far through deep, soft snow? He could shout, but who would hear above the wind, the hum of kitchen appliances, the blare of rock music, the idle chatter of television? Certainly, no one would be outside on such a night. And his tracks were being obliterated by the drifting snow.

He crawled on through waist-deep snow, throwing his briefcase ahead of him so that he had both arms free to breast the drifts. He could see the toolshed chicken coop ahead of him now. He could make it that far. He could rest and perhaps thaw out a bit there, even if he had to hold a hen under each arm for warmth. With freezing fingers, he pulled the door open far enough to squeeze inside and sank in a heap on the straw-covered floor. If his wife had fed the chickens earlier, as was her habit, there would be some semblance of a path the rest of the way to the house, and in his condition, any semblance would help. A bit of relief stole through him, much like the day he had stood in this very same shed and realized that the summer storm was subsiding and the worst was over. He also remembered that there was a kerosene lantern in the shed and a book of matches in his briefcase. Groping in the dark, he located both lamp and matches, and soon a soft lantern glow permeated the little shed. He closed his hands around the lantern's globe, soaking up the blessed warmth. He marveled that he could have come so close to a struggle for survival right in the midst of suburbia. The hens sighed their characteristic high-pitched, querulous, drawn-out night song, sounding like the howls of far-off coyotes or wolves. An appropriate sound for the occasion, Smith thought.

He rested quietly, became drowsy, wondered whether if he fell asleep, he would awaken before frostbite. With some renewed strength, he stood up and swung the lantern around. In the open wedge of snow-blocked door where he had squeezed through, he caught a blur of movement. Focusing his eyes, he saw in the light that flooded out into the darkness a heart-stopping scene. A pure white weasel with a black-tipped tail was standing on its back feet, drawn, no doubt, by the scent of chickens, or perhaps by the mice under the toolshed, which it would prefer. An ermine creature! Smith thought, so ghostly porcelain in the light that he wondered if he were dreaming. Perhaps the cold had addled his brain. "If it's a chicken you want, you're welcome, you beauty," he muttered out loud. At the sound of his voice, the weasel whirled and vanished like a wraith.

With the lantern lighting his way and the path partially broken ahead of him, Smith plowed on to the house, invigorated by the apparition of the white weasel. His wife rushed out when he thumped across the porch. "I called everywhere. Where have you *been?*" she added anxiously.

"You're hardly going to believe me," he answered. "I've been halfway to the North Pole and almost froze to death. But I was saved by a great white weasel and a hen house."

White Weasel

Appendix:
Useful Lists

An Annotated List of Wild Mammals

Considering the United States as a whole, it is difficult to say with any degree of accuracy which wild animals you might find in your backyard occasionally, and which ones you are never likely to see. The river otter, an animal one hardly expects to see very often in the wilderness, has been spotted in Westchester County, New York, in recent years. In bear country, the black bear has few qualms about wandering down village alleys at night, tipping over garbage cans like a raccoon. The porcupine is certainly not a frequenter of backyards, yet any row of homes along a country road in Maine might suffer tree damage from this barkgnawer. And where the porcupine wanders, even an animal as rare as the fisher might also come, since the fisher is one of the few animals that can prey on porcupines without suffering unduly from the quills. The following list should be considered an addendum to the animals already discussed, with emphasis on species likely to show up at the edge of your garden.

Badgers

The badger (*Taxidea taxus*), in the past, has not been an animal that frequents yards or the close proximity of man, but now it is moving from its historical western and midwestern haunts into eastern areas of denser human population. Although it digs large holes bothersome to humans and their machinery, the badger's diet is beneficial to the gardener. Badgers eat rodents, especially gophers and ground squirrels.

Bears

Other than deer, the only large animal that may frequent back-yards is the black bear (*Ursus americanus*), as already noted. Bears in the backyard, even half-tame and friendly bears, should be dealt with cautiously. When they are with young or after food, bears can be short-tempered and dangerous.

Beavers

The beaver (*Castor canadensis*), the largest of American rodents, is hardly a backyard creature and would not be a desirable occupant of a small wildlife area. Beavers need fairly large territories replete with saplings for their food, plus low-lying creek areas they can dam for their ponds. A beaver lodge near yards sometimes means beaver damage to ornamental and fruit trees.

Cats

Except for the thousands of domestic cats that have gone wild, the backyard will seldom host members of the cat family. The bobcat (*Lynx rufus*) looks like a big house cat without a tail. It needs an extensive wild habitat. Even more so does the lynx (*Lynx canadensis*), which looks like a bobcat but with pointed ears and large feet that help it pad along on top of deep snow. The mountain lion, also called a puma or cougar (*Felis concolor*), is a rare sight even in the wilderness.

Chipmunks

The chipmunks are common backyard animals. Several species of the *Tamias* genus occur in the East, and species of the *Eutamias* genus in the West. All have similar life-styles and eat a wide variety of foods, including nuts, seeds, and berries. Where plenty of wild foods are available, chipmunks rarely become bothersome in the garden.

Coyotes

The eastern strain of the coyote (*Canis latrans*) is slightly larger than the western strain and seems to be gaining in population in the wilder parts of the Northeast. Some crossbreeding with dogs has occurred, east and west, bringing the "coydog" into prominence. Hard evidence shows that in farming regions, coyotes and so-called coydogs are often blamed for livestock predation that is really done by feral dogs and domestic dogs whose owners refuse to confine them to their own property. Exhaustive studies of coyote droppings in New York state show that the animal lives mainly on mice and rabbits and, at times, gets along fine on berries, apples, and corn. Although there have been reports of calves being preyed upon, New York wildlife agents have not been able to authenticate even one killing of a calf by coyotes. Coyotes, when they do eat deer or livestock, eat dead ones (especially dead calves thrown out of a dairy barn) or deer wounded by hunters or weakened by starvation.

Deer

Of the larger hooved animals, the white-tailed deer (*Odocoileus virginianus*) is the only one that has adapted to urban and suburban environments.

Foxes

Both the common red fox (*Vulpes fulva*) and the gray fox (*Urocyon cinereoargenteus*) are too shy to den up in a backyard environment, but in their nightly hunting, they will journey through backyards up to a mile away from their dens. Gardeners should consider foxes beneficial, since they eat rodents of all kinds. If chickens are carefully penned at night, foxes are no threat. Foxes are more prone to diseases than most wild animals—distemper in gray foxes, mange in reds. Both animals are beautiful, and their pelts are generally in demand, unfortunately.

Ground Squirrels

Ground squirrels are distinct species from the chipmunks, although they live much the same way. The golden-mantled squirrel

(*Citellus lateralis*) looks much like a chipmunk but is chunkier. Another common ground squirrel, the thirteen-lined ground squirrels (*C. tridecemlineatus*), has striking rows of spots the length of its body. Some species live in rocky, mountainous areas only, and some in deserts, but others are widely distributed in open areas and may appear in Southwestern gardens. Ground squirrels are occasionally carnivorous, eating birds and bird eggs, and so are not as desirable in the backyard as chipmunks.

Mice

Humans tend to lump all the many species of mice into one category—pest. Actually, only one mouse is a real pest—*Mus musculus*, the house mouse, an interloper from Europe. Partly because humans provide the house mouse with a perfect environment in which to live, and partly because it is an introduced species, the natural food web of this continent has not yet been able to adjust properly to control it. A few native mice can also cause problems. The pine vole (*Pitymys pinetorum*) has developed an addiction for chewing on roots of apple trees in eastern commercial orchards. The field mouse or meadow vole of the *Microtus* genus (there are many species) will also cause tree damage by chewing on root bark. Though the field mouse is the most widespread of the mouse genera, its depredations in this regard are not that severe and can be controlled in the backyard. Tramping down snow around trees helps by denying the mice a safe cover to tunnel through out of sight of predators, like owls and cats. Also, there is some evidence that groves of trees with ample ground covering of various grasses and legumes supply mice with alternate sources of food and relieves them of the need to gnaw roots.

The field mouse is white underneath, and gray-brown above, while the house mouse is uniformly gray all over. Field mice occasionally get into houses, too, usually in the fall when cold weather sets in. They leave in spring, though. Mice, like rats, live only in houses where food is available to them.

The white-footed mouse, or deer mouse, of the *Peromyscus* genus, ranges over most of the continent in many species and subspecies. It not only has whitish underparts like the field mouse, but whitish legs and feet, too. It does not make tunnels in the grass or nests of grass in the snow, however, but lives in logs and stumps, among rocks, or in holes in the ground, usually in the woods. It will venture into human houses too, if there are seeds of any kind available.

If you see a mouse that jumps 2 feet at a leap, and sometimes even 5 feet or more, most likely you have come upon a jumping mouse of the *Zapus* genus or the slightly larger *Napaeozapus* genus, which range over most of the country (the latter confined to the eastern United States and Canada). Their tails are somewhat longer than tails of field mice or deer mice. Because of their jumping prowess, some people call them kangeroo mice, but the true kangeroo mouse (*Microdipodops* spp.) resides in western deserts and has a hairy tail, not the bare tail of the jumping mice.

Mink

The mink (*Mustela vison*) follows the water, preying on muskrat, fish, and other aquatic life. If a pond or creek borders the backyard, mink will pass that way, although they are rarely seen on their nightly forays. Mink are long, slinky animals, brown to black, the size of a house cat, with a pronounced hump in the back when standing still.

Moles

There are several species besides the eastern mole (*Scalopus aquaticus*) and the California mole (*S. latimanus*). A most unusual species, rather common in the Northeast, is the starnose mole (*Condylura cristata*), whose nose has 22 tiny tentacles radiating out from it for feeling and smelling. The starnose is most often found near water where the soil is soft and moist and easy to dig. It will dive into water unhesitatingly. A small garden pool such as Smith's might easily attract this interesting creature.

Muskrat

The muskrat (*Ondatra zibethica*) might be found in a backyard, but only if a creek or pond were present there. This rodent is strictly a water animal that eats aquatic vegetation. It lives in underground burrows along banks, or inside heaps of weeds and reeds piled up like small beaver dens in swamps where no dry, high banks are available for housing. The fur is prized for coats, and the flesh is good eating. The muskrat has poor eyesight. One swam out of the water onto a bank where Smith was quietly daydreaming, walked up and sat down right next to him, and brushed its face with its paws, evidently unaware of the man's presence.

Native Rats

Not all rats are as pestiferous as the Norway rat. The native woodrat, or packrat, found throughout the western half of the country and portions of the East, occurs in a number of species of the *Neotoma* genus. While it lives in forests, deserts, or the high rocky terrain of mountains, it sometimes settles down in human abodes and might conceivably build a nest in a backyard sanctuary. It eats principally nuts, grain, and berries. The woodrat is a junk collector. Its nest is usually full of human litter, buttons, tin cans, aluminum foil, bones, an old fork left by a camper, or any object that strikes the rat's fancy. Some species build large dens of sticks, often piled against three trunks, or inside an empty cabin. Alarmed, the woodrat thumps its back feet or tail against the ground or floor, causing a drumming noise that mystifies and often scares humans the first night they spend in their vacation homes.

In the southern states, there are two other families of rats, the rice rats of the *Oryzomys* genus and the cotton rats of the *Sigmodon* genus. Neither commonly frequent backyards.

Opossums

The opossum (*Didelphis marsupialis*) is apt to show up in the backyard, but it is principally a night hunter and seldom seen. Opossums are omnivorous, eating small animals, insects, and plants, but it hardly ever will be bothersome in the garden. It will eat many more insects than the few berries it might take. It ranges over most of the country now, although originally it seems to have been a southern animal. The only marsupial in North America, the opossum carries its young for a while after birth in a pouch. Accosted by a human, it generally fakes death, then scurries up a tree if left alone. It should be kept out of the hen house, but otherwise it's an interesting and trouble-free animal to have around.

Porcupines

The porcupine (*Erethizon dorsatum*) may venture into backyards in search of trees to gnaw on. Needless to say, the quillpig, as it is sometimes called, is not a welcome guest. It ruins trees. Dogs inexperienced enough to attack the slow, lumbering beast often must be taken to a veterinarian to have the quills removed. The porcupine does not throw or shoot its sharp quills, as folklore would have us believe, although it can drive the quills on its tail deep into flesh with a whisk of that appendage. The porcupine resides mostly in the forested regions of the West and the North and in the woods of the northeastern states, as far south as West Virginia. It gnaws large bare spots on tree trunks and limbs, disfiguring trees and often killing them by girdling. Tradition in the North, however, discouraged humans from killing porcupines. The philosophy then was that since porkies were so easy to kill (humans can walk up to the unwary animal and dispatch it with a club), they should be saved for those emergencies when humans were starving to death and did not have weapons to kill other animals. Porcupine meat is quite tasty.

Rabbits

The eastern cottontail rabbit (*Sylvilagus floridanus*) is far from being the only rabbit species humans have to learn to live with. Most of the others, however, seldom venture into backyards—although they very well might. The whitetail jackrabbit (*Lepus townsendi*) is common in the Plains states, and the snowshoe hare (*L. americanus*) is quite common across the North. The latter changes color to white in winter. The blacktail jackrabbit (*L. californicus*) and the antelope jackrabbit (*L. alleni*) occur in the West. The swamp rabbit (*Sylvilagus aquaticus*) and the marsh rabbit (*S. palustris*) live in swampy areas from Virginia and Kentucky southward.

Shrews

Shrews are small, mouse-size creatures that are generally beneficial because they eat many insects. Desirable around the garden, they can't dig tunnels like moles do, although they resemble miniature moles. But they do dig smaller, flattened runs in the upper layer of organic matter and in snow. The shorttail shrew (*Blarina brevicauda*) is the most common.

Squirrels

Of the four most common kinds of tree squirrels, the red squirrel (*Tamiasciurus hudsonicus*) is the smallest, being about the size of a chipmunk. The flying squirrel (*Glaucomys* spp.) is slightly larger, gliding from tree to tree or from tree to ground by spreading the membranes that attach to its legs until the squirrel looks like a miniature flying carpet. The gray squirrel (*Sciurus carolinensis*) is next up the ladder of size, and the fox squirrel (*S. niger*) is just a little larger. Closely related species occur in the West, including perhaps the most handsome of all, the golden-colored tassel-eared squirrel (*S. aberti*) of the Southwest. The pine squirrel, or chickaree (*Tamiasciurus douglasi*), is very similar to the red squirrel but has orange underparts rather than whitish. Gray squirrels are tawny gray all over, especially the tail, while fox squirrels are more orange-brown, especially in the tail.

Red squirrels limit their range mostly to the North. They eat the cones of evergreens and the seeds of hardwoods, being fond of maple, box elder and basswood seeds. They also eat mushrooms, carrying the fungi up on limbs to dry. Red squirrels are too small to make practical meat for the hunter. They are often accused of driving larger gray and fox squirrels out of a woodlot, but observation indicates that reds and grays often live amicably in the same forest. Gray squirrels prefer large tracts of hardwoods, as along a river valley or on a mountain plateau, while fox squirrels thrive best in small woodlots in farming country. Both adapt marvelously to city life, however, and are as common in backyards as rabbits.

All the tree squirrels, including the flying squirrels, will take up residence in attics if given a chance. Olaus J. Murie, in his *A Field Guide To Animal Tracks*, reports that a red squirrel once built a nest in a box in his cellar house and a weasel built its nest on a shelf above, the two spending the winter under the same roof!

Weasels

Several rather common weasels may frequent backyards where mice and other rodents are available, though they are seldom seen because of their nocturnal habits: the longtail weasel (*Mustela frenata*), the least weasel (*M. rixosa*) and the shorttail weasel (*M. erminea*). The least weasel is smaller than a chipmunk, while the others measure from about a foot up to the nearly 2 feet in length of an old male longtail weasel found in New York. Weasels change colors from brown to pure white in winter, some with black tail tips. In the process of changing, they are a pronounced gray in color. Weasels will in desperate circumstances, such as when caught in a trap, emit a liquid similar to and as odorously offensive as that of skunks. Extremely beautiful creatures, especially in winter, weasels are considered very beneficial animals by naturalists, since they eat mainly rats, mice, and insects. They will kill chickens occasionally, but not as nearly as often as they are blamed. If a pile of dead hens is found in the coop in the morning, the owner immediately blames weasels, although more often a cat or dog has been the villain. The sign of a weasel kill, according to folklore, anyway, is a neck stripped of feathers, at which point the weasel supposedly sucks out the chicken's blood. Studies do not corroborate this belief. Of 500 Bonaparte weasels examined in one study, there was no sign of blood intake from other animals. The food of 360 such weasels was found upon examination to include about 35 percent field mice, 13 percent rabbits, 11 percent deer mice, 7 percent rats, 4 percent chipmunks, 3 percent frogs, birds, and snakes, and the rest of undetermined mammals—no chickens.

The larger members of the weasel family are fairly rare animals that keep close to deep wilderness. The fisher (*Martes pennanti*) is larger than a raccoon and is dark brown to nearly black with tawny gray-fringed hair over most of its body. It lives in forest fastnesses and eats small mammals, dead deer, birds, nuts, apples, and berries. It is one of the few animals that can kill and eat porcupines, and is being used in areas of porcupine overpopulation as a biological control. The fisher's pelt brings high prices, a factor in its demise. The marten (*M. americana*) is an even rarer weasel, living in extensive coniferous forests, totally protected by law from hunting and trapping. The black-footed ferret (*Mustela nigripes*) is so rare that it has been placed on the Endangered Species list. You wouldn't see it in your backyard anyway, unless you had a prairie dog colony there. Prairie dogs provide both food and housing for the black-footed ferret.

Woodchucks

The woodchuck, or groundhog (*Marmota monax*), a common backyard animal, has cousins one might see in western parts of the country. The yellowbelly marmot, or rockchuck (*M. flavinventris*), is common in the West, although it prefers rocky, mountainous areas rather than backyards.

Select Trees, Shrubs, and Vines for Wildlife

The following list excludes all exotics, however tempting their value for wildlife. Most garden and orchard fruits, flowers, and vegetables are also excluded, even though all are excellent wildlife foods, because they usually will not compete well in a wild environment without extra labor.

Wild Apples and Crabapples

Usually seedlings of wild apples (*Malus* spp.) volunteering at a woodland edge prosper better without spraying than domestic varieties. Deer, raccoons, opossums, and many birds will be attracted. Crabapples (also *Malus* spp.) seem to be much more tasty to birds than hawthorn fruit, and the latter, especially wild haws, can grow long and vicious thorns and spread over meadowland worse than the most pernicious weed. The Dumb Farmer once visited a famous public building in the middle of New York City. As he walked up the sidewalk, he stopped short and growled. On the grounds, in manicured and pruned glory, grew a Washington hawthorn, which looks almost exactly like its wild cousin, white thorn. He wheeled around and headed back to his car. Asked what was the matter, he replied, "I'm going after my axe. If that thing isn't cut down, it will soon spread and conquer New York."

Birch Trees

Birches (*Betula* spp.) feed wildlife in many ways. The twigs, particularly on yellow birch, are favorite winter browse for deer. Rabbits and porcupines chew the bark of yellow and black birches. Finches, siskins, crossbills, redpolls, and other winter birds feast on the buds, especially those of gray and paper birches.

Blueberries and Huckleberries

These berries (*Vaccinium* spp. and *Gaylussacia* spp.) are probably the favorite fruit of more birds than any other but will grow well only on quite acidic soils. Where soil acidity has a pH of 5.0 to 5.5 and wild blueberries do not grow already, a planting of wild or domestic blueberry bushes in a sunny spot will bring birds galore—as backyard blueberry fanciers have learned to their dismay.

Eastern Red Cedar

Juniperus virginiana is a pioneer tree in its natural range. Farmers consider it a weed in parts of the Appalachian plateau, but where it grows well, on thin, poor soils and often on steep hills, farming is a questionable practice anyway. The berries are winter food for many birds, and the dense evergreen foliage makes excellent nesting sites and winter wind protection. As a hedge, red cedar is more easily controlled and kept in bounds than other traditional hedging plants. It grows on almost any well-drained soil.

Wild Cherries

Wild black cherry (*Prunus serotina*) is probably the major fruit source for birds in late summer throughout the tree's range. Wild black cherry spreads with ease but never seems to shade out other species in the mixed deciduous forest or forest edge, the way exotics like autumn olive will. Wild pin cherry and chokecherry also make good bird food and can be used in a small place where the wild black cherry would grow too large. However, black cherry is better and can be continually cut back to keep it small. Also, grown as a forest tree, its wood is second only to black walnut in its value to furniture-makers.

Dogwoods

Consider, especially, the ornamental flowering dogwood (*Cornus florida*), cornelian cherry (*C. Mas*), gray dogwood (*C. racemosa*), and the blue dogwood (*C. alternifolia*). The first two have red berries, the third has whitish fruit, and the last has blue with a whitish tint. Some 90 species of birds eat dogwood berries, making it the equal of blueberry in drawing power. Dogwood berries are barely edible by human standards, though, with the possible exception of *C. Mas*.

Elderberries

Many birds like the clusters of small, black berries from elder-berries (*Sambucus canadensis*). The bush is a rampant grower on rich land, and hacking back the canes seems only to invigorate it. But on average soil, the bush is easy to control.

Wild Grapes

Grapes (*Vitis* spp.) are an excellent fruit source through the winter for animals and birds.

Hackberries

Although somewhat bitter to human taste, the berries of common hackberry (*Celtis occidentalis*) are loved by birds even more than the somewhat sweeter berries of the less hardy and more southerly growing sugarberry (*C. laevigata*).

Hollies

The berries from holly (*Ilex* spp.) are excellent songbird food, and the trees make good nesting sites, especially when trimmed to grow densely. But holly has a limited range. It's not too hardy in the North and prospers on a somewhat acidic soil. Where it grows well, holly is the best plant for hedges.

Bush Honeysuckles

Lonicera maacki, often called Amur honeysuckle, is a shrub that grows dense enough to make good nesting sites for hedge-loving birds like the brown thrasher and the mockingbird. Its nectar draws hummingbirds and beautiful butterflies. Its fruit is enjoyed by many birds, chipmunks, and field mice. Avoid Japanese honeysuckle if it is not yet established in your area.

Mountain-Ash

Sorbus americanas is an excellent songbird food in winter and a nice ornamental in yards.

Oak

Entomologists say that a large oak tree (*Quercus* spp.) can provide food and a home for as many as 300 species of insect. These insects draw many birds, like the scarlet tanager. The acorns provide the greatest portion of the mast (fallen acorns and nuts) that feeds deer, ducks, squirrels, flying squirrels, mice, chipmunks, and often, in history, human civilizations, such as that of the Indians of California. Acorn-eating birds include blue jays, nuthatches, woodpeckers, brown thrashers, grackles, quail, cardinals, wood ducks, flickers, grosbeaks, chickadees, titmice, towhees, and others.

Wild Raspberries and Blackberries

These berries are favorite summer fare for birds and almost all the small wild animals, including foxes.

Native Viburnums

The olive-size, blue-black fruit of black haw (*Viburnum prunifolium*) is a   preferred food of wild animals and many birds. Cranberry bush (*V. trilobum*) and arrow-wood (*V. dentatum*) are eaten by birds, but usually in late winter after more tasty fruit is gone.

Woodbine

Parthenocissus quinquefolia looks and grows like poison ivy but has five leaves. The berries are blue and are much liked by squirrels, chipmunks, and some birds, but the vines do not fruit heavily.

Food Plants for Caterpillars of Desirable Butterflies and Moths

Brush-Footed Butterfly Caterpillars

Baltimore (*Euphydryas phaeton*): turtlehead, sometimes honeysuckle.
Great Spangled Fritillary (*Speyeria cybele*): violet leaves.
Mourning Cloak (*Nymphalis antiopa*): willow, elm, and poplar.
Painted Lady (*Cynthia cardui*): thistles, burdock, sunflower, and hollyhock.
Question Mark (*Polygonia interrogationis*): nettle, elm, hops, hackberry, and basswood.
Red Admiral (*Vanessa atalanta*): nettle and hops.
Viceroy (*Limenitis archippus*): willow and poplar.

Hackberry Butterfly Caterpillars

Hackberry Butterfly (*Asterocampa celtis*): hackberry.

Milkweed Butterflies

Monarch (*Danaus plexippus*): milkweed.
Queen (*Danaus gilippus berenice*): milkweed.

Regional Butterfly Caterpillars

Bright Blue Copper (*Lycaena heteronea*): a rare, perhaps endangered butterfly of southern California; buckwheat.

Buckeye (*Precis coenia*): a southern beauty; snapdragon, monkeyflower, plantain, stonecrop.

California Dog Face (*Colias eurydice*): South, state butterfly of California; false indigo.

Great Purple Hairstreak (*Atlides halesus*): South, Southwest, and California; live oak trees.

Gulf fritillary (*Agraulis vanillae*): mostly the deep South; passionflower foliage.

Harris' Checkerspot (*Chlosyne harrisii*) and other checkerspots: Northern United States; aster family.

Phoebus (*Parnassius phoebus*): a tailless swallowtail, mostly ivorywhite with red spots, found in colder mountainous and even Arctic areas; alpine arctic stonecrops and saxifrages.

White Admiral (*Limenitis arthemis*): a northern butterfly; willow, poplar, hawthorn, birch, and basswood.

White Peacock (*Anartia jatrophae*): Florida and southern Texas; spurge and vervain.

Swallowtail Butterfly Caterpillars

Black Swallowtail (*Papilio polyxenes asterius*): carrot leaves, wild carrot leaves, celery, parsley, and wild parsley.

Giant Swallowtail (*Papilio cresphontes*): prickly ash, citrus trees, and hop-trees.

Pipevine Swallowtail (*Battus philenor*): Virginia snakeroot and Dutchman's-pipe.

Spicebush Swallowtail (*Papilio troilus*): spicebush, sassafras, sweet bay, prickly ash, and others.

Tiger Swallowtail (*Papilio glaucus, P. rutulus*): wild cherry, birch, poplar, ash, and tulip tree in the East. In the West, alder willow and occasionally hop vines.

Zebra Swallowtail (*Graphium marcellus*): papaw.

Large Moth Caterpillars

Cecropia Moth (*Hyalophora cecropia*): including wild cherry, maple, willow, and other deciduous forest trees.

Cynthia Moth (*Samia cynthia*): ailanthus.

Imperial Moth (*Eacles imperialis*): deciduous and conifer trees.

Io Moth (*Automeris io*): wild cherry and many other trees and shrubs.

Luna Moth (*Actias luna*): hickory, walnut, sweet gum, persimmon, birch, and other deciduous forest trees.

Polyphemus Moth (*Antheraea polyphemus*): maple, hickory, birch, elm, oak, and other deciduous forest trees.

Promethea Moth (*Callosamia promethea*): spicebush, sassafras, and wild cherry.

Regal Moth (*Citheronia regalis*): walnut, hickory, ash, sweet gum, persimmon, and sumac.

Sphinx Moth Caterpillars

Cerisy's Sphinx (*Smerinthus cerisyi*): willow leaves.

Hummingbird Moth (*Hemaris thysbe*): honeysuckles.

Pandora Sphinx (*Eumorpha pandorus*): Virginia creeper, grapes, and wild grapes.

White-Lined Sphinx (*Hyles lineata*): portulaca in particular, but also common weeds and orchard trees leaves.

Select Nectar Sources for Butterflies

A natural meadow, mowed once or twice a year to control tree seedlings, will ensure the growth of grasses and wild flowers to supply nectar and larval food for butterflies. Lacking that, almost any flower garden substitutes fairly well. Even blossoms of some fruits and vegetables will draw many butterflies. Obviously, a combination of these plant communities works best of all.

Wild Asters: *Aster* spp.

Butterfly-Bushes: *Buddleia* spp.; particularly orange-eye butterfly-bush (*B. davidi*).

Wild Carrot or Queen Anne's Lace (*Daucus carota*); wild yarrow (*Achillea millefolium*); meadowsweet (*Spiraea latifolia*); goldenrod (*Solidago* spp.); black-eyed Susan (*Rudbeckia hirta*); dandelion, and most flowering meadow weeds.

Various species of the *Chrysanthemum* **genus:** Daisies and, in very balmy climates, Marguerite (*Chrysanthemum frutescens*).

Orange Day-Lily: *Hemerocallis fulva.*

Clovers and Alfalfa: *Trifolium* spp. and *Medicago sativa*; especially white clover (*Trifolium repens*) and red clover (*T. pratense*).

Honeysuckle: *Lonicera* spp.; although if Japanese honeysuckle (*L. japonica*) has not already overrun your area, do not plant it. Plant, instead, one of the nonspreading bush type honey-suckles, such as trumpet honeysuckle (*L. sempervirens*).

Lilacs: Liliaceae family; domestic and wild.

Milkweeds: especially butterfly-weed (*Asclepias tuberosa*) and its showy orange clumps of blossoms along the road, and swamp milkweed (*A. incarnata*), with its dusty rose blossoms.

Fringed Orchids: *Habenaria* spp.; depend on butterflies and moths with their long proboscises to pollinate them.

Thistles: *Cirsium* spp.; but favor the bull thistle (*C. vulgare*), which is easier to control than the vicious Canada thistle (*C. arvense*).

Wild weed flowers: *Eupatorium* spp.; particularly Joe-Pye-weed (*E. maculatum*) and boneset (*E. perfoliatum*), both of which appear to have medicinal value for humans as well.

Favorite Beetles for the Backyard

Bombardier Beetles: *Brachinus* spp.; Head and legs brownish yellow, elytra metallic blue. Eat pupating insects. Emit puffs of vaporizing liquid toxic to predators. Can stain human skin, but harmless.

Dogbane Leaf Beetle: *Chrysochus auratus;* eastern half of United States. Shiny green, copper, brass, and bluish. Feeds on milkweed and dogbane.

Goldsmith Beetle: *Cotalpa lanigera;* metallic yellow to greenish. Underside covered with woolly hair, except in far West. Larvae eat poplar roots. Adults eat leaves.

Scarab Beetles: Family Scarabaeidae; come in all sizes and colors, some with beautiful metallic luster. Tumblebugs (*Canthon* spp.) are, or once were, the commonest species and are very interesting to watch. A tumblebug couple mold dung into marble-size balls and lay an egg inside each. They then roll the balls for some distance and bury them. Though mainly dull black, tumblebugs can sometimes sport the lustrous bluish, greenish, or coppery tinge of the gaudier scarabs.

Stag Beetles: especially the elephant stag beetle (*Lucanus elephus*), which grows over 2 inches long and has amazingly large, antlerlike jaws. Shiny dark brown to reddish brown, though not to be confused with the smaller reddish-brown stag beetle (*Pseudolucanus capreolus*). Eats rotting wood and makes compost.

Tiger Beetles: especially the six-spotted green tiger beetle (*Cicindela sexguttata*), entirely shiny green except for the whitish spots, and the beautiful tiger beetle (*C. formosa*), usually metallic blue, green, purple, orange, or bronze. Feed on insects and spiders.

Fireflies: the pyralis firefly (*Photinus pyralis*), yellow light, and the Pennsylvania firefly (*Photuris pennsylvanicus*), green light, both found in the eastern United States. Larvae eat slugs, snails, and insect larvae.

Fiery Searcher: *Calosoma scrutator;* ranges throughout the United States. Elytra greenish or blackish blue, edged with gold. Greenish gold on sides of blackish head. Blue metallic luster on femora. Male has reddish hair inside curved middle tibiae and hind tibiae. Eats caterpillars of all kinds, especially tent caterpillars. Highly beneficial, as are the fiery hunter (*C. calidum*) and the European caterpillar hunter (*C. sycophanta*), the former with six rows of golden dots on its elytra, the latter a dark blue thorax and bright, golden-green elytra. Look for them in lawn grass or around tent caterpillar colonies.

Characteristics of Edible Wild Mushrooms in the Yard

The following list suggests the types of mushrooms you should look for, but do not use it alone for identification. When hunting mushrooms, even with an experienced collector, use a good guide, such as Alexander Smith's *The Mushroom Hunter's Field Guide*. Some species make only some people sick. If you have no idea whether a mushroom is safe, or if you are not sure, do not test it by eating a small bit of it to see if you get sick. Even the spores of certain deadly amanitas are dangerous. A small bit of *Amanita verna* could be enough to kill a very susceptible person. On the other hand, there is much to be learned abut fungi, and some listed as poisonous are eaten with great gusto by people who cannot read. Keep a wary but open mind.

Delicious Lactarius: *Lactarius deliciosus;* mushrooms of this family have milky juice in them. *L. deliciosus'* juice is orange colored, like its cap, distinguishing it from *L. sanguifluus,* which has a blood-red cap and blood-red juice. Both are edible and choice. *L. deliciosus* grows in forests over a wide area, usually under pine trees. *L. sanguifluus* is limited more to western pine forests. *L. indigo* is easy to identify, too, because in young specimens all parts, including the juice, are blue. Bruises change to a greenish color.

Hedgehog mushrooms: *Hydnaceae* family; so called because instead of gills under the caps, the fungi have tiny toothlike or iciclelike growths. In some species, the toadstool form is abandoned entirely in favor of a mass of tubercles, but the icicle-teeth remain as an easy-to-distinguish characteristic. *Dentinum repandum,* a white to reddish tan, irregularly shaped toadstool form, is common and delicious. Flesh is white. Stalk and teeth stain yellow when bruised. *Hericium caput-ursi* forms a white cluster on tree tunks, the "teeth" giving the fungus a fernlike appearance. *H. erinaceus* is also easy to recognize, a clump of whitish "teeth" looking at first glance like combed animal fur, growing on the side of a tree.

Hen of the Woods: *Polyporus frondosus;* form large clusters of tight branches ending in caps brownish in color. Grow around the bases of old trees and stumps in late summer, especially oak trees.

Honey mushrooms: *Armillaria mellea;* honey-colored caps. Appear in heavy clusters in late summer-fall in oak-hickory forest associations. Grow on underground tree roots, but appear to be growing in soil. Stems are too tough to eat.

Shaggy Mane: *Coprinus comatus;* at first, cap remains closed around stem, in the shape of a large bullet. Gradually, cap opens umbrellalike and becomes shaggy around the outer edge. Grayish brown flecked in color. Good only when young before cap opens. Found in the fall on disturbed soil, especially new lawns and road banks.

Meadow or Field mushrooms: *Agaricus campestris;* white with pink gills when young. Gills turn dark brown with age. Closely related species, *A. rodmanii,* looks similar. Like to grow in urban areas on hard-packed ground. *A. pattersonae* has a brown streaked or flecked cap, unlike the other two. Also common on well-traveled pathways.

Morels: *Morchella esculenta* and others; look like pieces of sponges, irregularly shaped but usually of Christmas tree form. From 1 to 6 inches tall, though generally 2 to 3 inches, they grow under ash, oak, elm, cedar, apple, pear, and other trees.

Oyster mushrooms: *Pleurotus ostreatus;* grow like bracket mushrooms, but are white and soft fleshed, the caps varying in color from white to gray to tan. May have a short stalk in center of cap if growing on the top of stump or log. But on a tree trunk, the stalk, if any, is to one side of the cap or layers of caps. Common growing on dead and dying trees, such as elm, aspen, poplar, alder, maple, cottonwood, and beech. Grow through summer and fall.

Puffballs: *Calvatia gigantea;* flesh inside should be pure white or mushrooms are too old for eating.

Slippery Jack: *Suillus luteus;* has a reddish brown cap with slimy coating. Wipe off coating before cooking. Rather common in pine plantings in the North.

Squirrel Bread: *Boletus edulis;* a sticky cap, light brown to reddish brown, sometimes whitish to pale tan. Unlike many other *Boletus* species, *B. edulis* does not stain blue where cut or bruised. The stalk is bulbous at the base, becoming more slender as it disappears under the thick cap. Prefers mountainous conifer stands, especially in the West, but ranges sparsely all across the eastern states, too. In some areas, this mushroom is as popular as the morel and the field mushroom.

Sulfur Shelf: *Lateiporus sulphureus;* bright yellow to salmon in color. Rather than growing on a stalk, it grows more like bracket fungi on wood of both hardwoods and conifers. For eating, cut off only the outer ring of new growth that is still soft and tender.

Edible Wild Nuts

American Beech: *Fagus grandifolia;* eastern United States. Most trees do not bear heavily every year. Wild birds and animals eat nuts readily, often before the nuts are fully mature. Its small nuts make a better food source for wildlings than for humans. Tree is very large when mature.

Butternut: *Juglans cinerea;* tree is smaller but hardier than the black walnut and, hence, grows a little farther north. Nuts elongated, with sticky hull. Often called white walnut. Wide range, northern United States east of Great Plains. Will grow to mid-South. Maple sugar-butternut candy a New England delicacy.

American Chestnut: *Castanea dentata;* grows on acidic shale soils of mid-Appalachia. Only stunted regrowths from trees killed by chestnut blight remain in the wild. Crosses with Chinese and Japanese chestnuts (introduced species) show some promise.

Chinquapin Chestnut: *Castanea pumila, C. ozarkensis,* and others; range south of Ohio River in eastern United States and in Ozarks. A small tree or tall shrub, its nuts are small but have an excellent taste.

Filbert or Hazelnut: *Corylus americana and C. cornuta;* range throughout much of United States. Grows as bush or group of small trees.

Hickory: closely related to the pecan, classified into several species. Shagbark hickory (*Carya ovata*), shellbark hickory (*C. laciniosa*), and mockernut (*C. tomentosa*) are the three best for eating. *C. ovata* is far superior for cracking. Widely distributed in eastern United States.

White Oak: *Quercus alba* and kin, including bur oak (*Q. macrocarpa*), California white oak (*Q. lobata*), gambel oak (*Q. gambellii*), live oak (*Q. virginiana*), swamp white oak (*Q. bicolor*), swamp chestnut oak (*Q. michauxii*), chinquapin oak (*Q. muehlenbergii*), and chestnut oak (*Q. Prinus*). Acorn taste ranges from slightly bitter in the eastern white oak and bur oak (taste varies from tree to tree) to quite sweet on gambel oak, swamp chestnut oak, and chinquapin oak. All regions of the United States and Canada have at least one species of white oak that grows there.

Native Pecan: now usually classified as *Carya illinoensis;* range north to the Ohio River Valley, but will grow in protected areas even farther north, around the Great Lakes to Dubuque, Iowa along the Mississippi River. Matures to a large tree. A large wild pecan can yield 300 or more pounds of nuts in a good year, and averages 50 to 150 pounds per year. Many selected and improved commercial varieties can also be grown.

Nut Pines: *Pinus* spp., including Colorado pinyon (*Pinus edulis*), Mexican pinyon (*P. cembroides*), singleleaf pinyon (*P. monophylla*), parry pinyon (*P. quadrifolia*), and digger pine (*P. sabiniana*). Grow in mostly western regions. All pine nuts are edible, but these are large enough to be practical.

Black Walnut: *Juglans nigra;* grows throughout eastern United States.

Japanese Walnut, or Heartnut, and Carpathian Walnut, or English Walnut: *Juglans ailantifolia* var. *cordiformis,* and *J. regia;* not native wild nuts, but can be grown in a wild environment. Squirrels will eat these nuts first. Hardiness about equal to pecan, although some Carpathians will endure in more northerly ranges.

Edible Wild Fruits

Species of these fruits can be found throughout North America, and almost all of them ripen in midsummer in their region, unless otherwise noted.

Amelanchier
Saskatoon (*Amelanchier alnifolia*); berry purple with a bloom, sometimes white.

Serviceberry, Juneberry (*Amelanchier canadensis*); small, oblong-oval berries; red or purple and sweet when ripe in June and July.

Arctostaphylos
Bearberry, Kinnikinick (*Arctostaphylos Uva-ursi*); aromatic, but somewhat dry, red berries.

Asimina
Papaw (*Asimina triloba*); small tree, elongated yellow fruit, about 4 inches long, 1 or more inches in diameter.

Chiogenes
Creeping Snowberry (*Chiogenes hispidula*); white, blueberrylike, wintergreen-flavored berries ripen in August and September.

Crataegus
Cockspur Hawthorn (*Crataegus crus-galli*); white flowers, small red fruit spotted with dark dots.

Downy Hawthorn (*Crataegus mollis*); white flowers and round scarlet fruit.

Frosted Hawthorn (*Crataegus pruinosa*); white flowers and small purplish, spotted haws.

Diospyros
American persimmon (*Diospyros virginiana*); yellow, golf-ball-size fruit.

Fragaria
Common Strawberry (*Fragaria virginiana*); round red berries with embedded seeds.

Northern Wild Strawberry (*Fragaria canadensis*); very small oblong berries with embedded seeds.

Wood Strawberry (*Fragaria vesca*); slightly oblong red berries with seeds on the surface.

Gaultheria
Wintergreen, Checkerberry (*Gaultheria procumbens*); aromatic red berries that persist throughout the winter.

Gaylussacia
Blue Huckleberry, Dangleberry (*Gaylussacia frondosa*); small, greenish pink flowers and blue berries with a heavy bloom. Ripen in July and August.

Malus
American Crabapple (*Malus glaucescens*); fragrant pink flowers and fragrant, greenish-yellow, acid fruit.

Wild Apple (*Malus malus*); fruit somewhat hard and acid, green flushed with red.

Mitchella
Patridgeberry (*Mitchella repens*); the ovaries of the tubular, white, slightly fragrant flowers are united at the base, thus producing a single, aromatic red berry.

Morus

Red Mulberry (*Morus rubra*); berries composed of numerous juicy red drupelets ripen around July.

White Mulberry (*Morus alba*); flowers very similar to *Morus rubra*. Berry also similar but white or pinkish and not as juicy.

Physalis

Clammy Ground-Cherry (*Physalis heterophylla*); dull golden yellow fruit.

Smooth Ground-Cherry (*Physalis subglabrata*); dull yellow flowers and red or purple fruit.

Virginia Ground Cherry (*Physalis virginiana*); deep yellow flowers dotted with purple, and purple or reddish round berries.

Prunus

American Wild Plum (*Prunus americana*); large red or yellow fruit.

Beach Plum (*Prunus maritima*); dull purple fruit.

Canada Plum, Horse Plum (*Prunus nigra*); large fruit, yellow blotched with red.

Chickasaw Plum (*Prunus angustifloliam*); large red or yellow fruit.

Pin Cherry (*Prunus pensylvanica*); creamy white flowers and small red, acid berries

Wild Black Cherry, Rum Cherry (*Prunus serotina*); large flowers and slightly bitter, dark purple fruit.

Wild Sweet Cherry, Mazzard Cherry (*Prunus avium*); white flowers and large black, juicy fruit.

Choke Cherry (*Prunus virginiana*); small creamy white flowers and long clusters of little deep ruby red, very astringent berries.

Ribes

American Red Currant (*Ribes triste*); berries bright red, translucent, tart flavor.

Golden Currant, Buffalo Currant (*Ribes adoratum*); usually berry black, or yellow, with insipid taste.

Wild Black Currant (*Ribes americanum*); smooth, oval black fruit with a slightly musky flavor.

Northern Gooseberry (*Ribes oxyacanthoides*); smooth, greenish-to-pink fruit.

Wild Gooseberry, Prickly Gooseberry (*Ribes cynosbati*); round berries covered with weak bristle, rusty red or brownish when ripe.

Rosa

Dog Rose (*Rosa canina*); smooth, oval hips.

Pasture Rose (*Rosa carolina*); round, hairy, red hip.

Sweetbrier (*Rosa Eglanteria* or *rubiginosa*); small, slightly pear-shaped hips.

Rubus

Allegheny Blackberry, Mountain Blackberry (*Rubus allegheniensis*); snowy white flowers and conical black fruit, slightly on the dry side.

Tall Blackberry, Thimbleberry (*Rubus argutus*); sparse clusters of large white flowers and large black, juicy berries.

Cloudberry, Bake-Apple (*Rubus chamaemarus*); pleasantly flavored amber fruit of few drupelets.

Dewberry (*Rubus procumbens*); large white flowers and large juicy berries.

Black Raspberry, Black-Cap (*Rubus accidentalis*); fruit purple-black with a slight bloom.

Purple-Flowered Raspberry (*Rubus adoratus*); fruit dark red and on the dry side.

Red Raspberry (*Rubus strigosus*); thimble-shaped, dull red fruit.

Wineberry (*Rubus phoenicolasius*); the flowers are very slightly pinkish and the berries a dull, wine red with a rich, winy flavor.

Sambucus

Elderberry (*Sambucus canadensis*); clusters of small buckshot-size black berries.

Vaccinium

High-bush Blueberry (*Vaccinium corymbosum*); sweet blue or black berry with a heavy bloom. Ripe in August.

Low-bush Blueberry, Early Blueberry (*Vaccinium angustifolium*); blue or almost black with a bloom that is ripe in June and July.

American Cranberry, Large Cranberry (*Vaccinium macrocarpon*); bright red berries. Ripe from September to October.

Mountain Cranberry, Cowberry (*Vaccinium Vitis-Idaea*); pink, blueberrylike flowers and red, very acid, blueberrylike berries.

Small Cranberry (*Vaccinium Oxycoccus*); small berries with dark spots. Ripen from August to September.

Viburnum

American Wayfaring-Tree, Hobblebush, Trip-Toe (*Viburnum alnifolium*); flat, irregular clusters of tiny, fertile flowers surrounded by showy, sterile flowers, and oval purple fruits.

Cranberry Tree, High Bush Cranberry (*Viburnum Opulus*); berries bright red, translucent, and very acid.

Nannyberry, Sheepberry, Wild Raisin (*Viburnum Lentago*); small white
    flowers and blue-black berries, slightly larger than elderberries.
Black Haw, Stag bush (*Viburnum prunifolium*); little white flowers
    that open the same time as the leaves, and smooth, oval blue-
    black berries.

Vitis

Canyon Grape (*Vitis arizonica*); small blue fruit.
Frost Grape (*Vitis cordifolia*); tiny green flowers in short racemes
    and long, loose clusters of black, shiny grapes that are best after
    a frost.
Muscadine (*Vitis rotundifolia*); large dull purple fruit.
Mustang Grape (*Vitis candicans*); small blue fruit.
Northern Fox Grape (*Vitis Labrusca*); grapes few but fairly large;
    brownish purple when ripe in late August and September.
Summer Grape (*Vitis aestivalis*); many little berries that are black with
    a bloom. Ripen from September to October.
Winter Grape (*Vitis cinerca*); small blue fruit.

Index

alfalfa, as nectar source for butterflies, 255
algae, as pool plants, 69
Allegheny blackberry, as wild fruit, 263
alpine butterfly, 95. *See also* butterflies
American arborvitae, for wetlands, 73
American beech, as source for nuts, 259. *See also* nuts
American chestnut, as source for nuts, 259. *See also* nuts
American crabapple, as wild fruit, 261
American cranberry, as wild fruit, 263
American hornbeam, for wetlands, 73
American persimmon, as wild fruit, 261
American red currant, as wild fruit, 262
American wayfaring-tree, as wild fruit, 263
American wild plum, as wild fruit, 262
apple trees, for attracting wildlife, 249
armadillo, 126–28

arrowhead, growing around pools, 70
arrow-shaped micrathena, 119. *See also* spiders
artificial pools, growing plants in, 70
artist's conk, 136. *See also* mushrooms and fungi

backswimmer, 76. *See also* water beetle
badgers, 240–41
    recognizing homes of, 152
bake-apple, as wild fruit, 263
bald-faced hornet, 121. *See also* wasps
Baltimore caterpillar, food plants for, 252. *See also* butterflies; caterpillars
bark chewing, protection against, 181–82, 208
barn owl, 113. *See also* owls
basswood, leaves for salads, 131
bats, 111–12
    boxes as housing for, 58–59
beach plum, as wild fruit, 262
bearberry, as wild fruit, 260
bears, black, danger from, 251
beavers, damage from, 251
bee-balm, growing around pools, 71
bees, 22–24

bee space, in hives, 22
beetles, as beneficial insects, 99–100,
    255–56
berries, 136–39
    grapes, 137
    growing of, 138–39
    soil for, 137
berry bladderfern, for wet sites, 73
big game repellent (BGR), as wildlife
    control, 209
binoculars, for wildlife observation,
    160–64
birch trees, for attracting wildlife, 249
birdbaths, 30
bird feeders, food for, 55–56
birdhouses, 46–54
    designs for, 48–51
bird nest fungi, 136. *See also* mush-
    rooms and fungi
birds
    adventures with, 217–25
    deterring, 175
    feeders for, 55–56
    footprints of, 152
    housing for, 46–54
    identification through songs, 111
birdseed, mixtures of, 55
black alder, for wetlands, 73
black-and-yellow argiope, 119. *See
    also* spiders
blackberry, 137, 138. *See also* berries
blackcap raspberry, 137, 138. *See
    also* berries
    as wild fruit, 263
black-eyed Susan, as nectar source
    for butterflies, 255
black haw, 33
    as wild fruit, 264
black-nosed dace, 82. *See also* fish
black raspberry, as wild fruit, 263
black rat snake. *See* blacksnake
blacksnake, 80, 109. *See also* snakes
black swallowtail. *See also* butterflies;
    caterpillars
    caterpillar as garden pest, 95–96
    food plants for, 30, 93, 253
black widow, 118–19. *See also* spiders
bladderwort, as oxygenating water
    plant, 69
blind, for observing wildlife, 154–60
blowfly, 16

blueberries, 137, 139, 249. *See also*
    berries
    as food for birds, 249–50
bluebird, food web of, 12–14
blue huckleberry, as wild fruit, 261
bog turtle, 80. *See also* turtles
bombardier beetle, 255. *See also* beetles
boneset
    medicinal value of, 71, 255
    as nectar source for butterflies,
    255
box traps
    Havahart, 200, 202, 205
    homemade, 205–207
bracket fungi, 136. *See also* mush-
    rooms
bramble berries, planting location
    for, 33
bright blue copper, food plants for,
    94, 253. *See also* butterflies; cater-
    pillars
brown recluse spider, 118–19. *See
    also* spiders
brown snake, 75. *See also* snakes
brush piles, to attract wildlife, 35,
    57–58
buckeye, food plants for, 95, 253. *See
    also* butterflies; caterpillars
buffalo currant, as wild fruit, 262
bullfrog, 151. *See also* frogs
bull thistle
    as nectar source for butterflies,
    30, 255
    preparation of, 131
burdock, preparation of, 131
bush honeysuckle, for attracting wild-
    life, 251
butterflies, 90–97
    food plants for, 252–54
    nectar sources for, 254–55
butterfly bush, as nectar source for
    butterflies, 92–93, 255
butternut, as source for nuts, 259.
    See also nuts
buttonwood, for wetlands, 73
butylmercamptom, odor emitted
    from skunk, 105
buzzard. *See* vultures

caddisflies, 75
California dog face, food plants for,

94, 253. *See also* butterflies; caterpillars
Canada goose, 220–21
Canada plum, as wild fruit, 262
Canada thistle, 28–30
    as nectar source for butterflies,
    255
canyon grape, as wild fruit, 264
cardinal-flower, growing around
    pools, 70
caterpillar hunter. *See* fiery searcher
caterpillars
    of butterflies, 90–92
    food plants for, 85, 90, 91,
    252–54
    life cycles of, 85–87
cats, 251
    footprints of, 149
cattails, growing around pools, 70
cecropia moth, 86–87. *See also* caterpillars; moths
    food plants for, 254
Cerisy's sphinx, 90. *See also* caterpillars; moths
    food plants for, 254
checkerberry, as wild fruit, 261
checkered beetle, 100. *See also* beetles
checkerspot butterfly, food plants for,
95. *See also* butterflies; caterpillars
cheesecloth, sources for, 175
chickasaw plum, as wild fruit, 262
chicken wire, as rabbit fencing, 175
chinquapin chestnut, as source for
    nuts, 259. *See also* nuts
chipmunks, 251
    recognizing homes of, 152
    trapping as control for, 202
choke cherry, as wild fruit, 262
chorus frog, 79. *See also* frogs
chrysalis, of pupating butterfly, 85
chub, 82–83. *See also* fish
cicada-killer wasp, 121. *See also* wasps
clammy ground-cherry, as wild fruit,
    262
climax, of forest, 26
Clinton's fern, for wet sites, 73
cloudberry, as wild fruit, 263
clover
    as alternate food for rabbits, 177
    as nectar source for butterflies,
    255

cockspur hawthorn, as wild fruit, 261
common clearwing. *See* humming-
    bird moth
Conibear trap, as wildlife control,
    201, 205
conifers, 35–36
copperhead, 106, 107. *See also* snakes
coral snake, identification of, 106.
    See also snakes
cottonmouth, 80, 106, 107. *See also*
    snakes
cowberry, as wild fruit, 263
cowbird, diet of, 222–23
coyotes, 242
    footprints of, 149–50
crabapple trees, for attracting wild-
    life, 249
crab spider, 17, 120. *See also* spiders
cranberry tree, as wild fruit, 263
crayfish, 77–78
Crayfish Thermidor, 78
creeping snowberry, as wild fruit, 261
cricket frog, 79. *See also* frogs
Cynthia moth, food plants for, 88,
    254. *See also* caterpillars; moths

dangleberry, as wild fruit, 261
DDT, 13
decomposition, of leaves, 73
deer, 177–81, 242
    fences for, 182–84
    footprints of, 151
    plants avoided by, 185
    repellents, 182
    signs of presence, 148
    stalking of, 230–31
delicious lactarius, as edible wild
    mushroom, 257. *See also* mush-
    rooms and fungi
dewberry, as wild fruit, 263
diving water beetle, 75
dogbane leaf beetle. *See also* beetles
    as beneficial insect, 256
    characteristics of, 93
dog rose, as wild fruit, 262
dogs, footprints of, 149
dogwoods, as food for birds, 250
downy hawthorne, as wild fruit, 261
dragonflies, benefits of, 74
droppings, for identification of wild-
    life, 148

duckweed, as food for wildlife, 71
Dutchman's-pipe, as food for butterflies, 95

early blueberry, as wild fruit, 263
eastern painted turtle, 80. *See also* turtles
Eastern red cedar, for attracting birds, 250
echolocation, of bats, 112
elderberries, 137, 138, 250–51. *See also* berries
as wild fruit, 263
electric fencing, to keep out wildlife, 173–75
sources for, 175
electronic vibration of sound waves, as wildlife scare tactic, 212–13
elephant stag, 99–100. *See also* beetles
European ground beetle, 99. *See also* beetles
Everglade kite, 10

fairy stool, 136. *See also* mushrooms and fungi
fall meadow mushroom, 134. *See also* mushrooms and fungi
fanwort, as oxygenating water plant, 69
fence posts, sources for, 264. *See also* fences
fences
chicken-wire, 175–76
electric, 173–75
gates for, 187–88
picket, 187
posts for, 264
rabbit, 175
wire, 187–93
fiery searcher, as beneficial insect, 99, 256. *See also* beetles
filbert, as source for nuts, 259. *See also* nuts
fire ants, 127
firefly, 97–99, 256
fish, 81–83
flat tinderfungus. *See* artist's conk
flowers, pollination of, 90
food chain. *See* food web
food web, 67
of bluebird, 12–14

competition for survival and, 10
leaf decomposition and, 109
nature and, 10–11
ponds and, 77
snakes and, 108–109
footprints, for identification of wildlife, 148–49
foxes, 242
footprints of, 149
fox grape, 137. *See also* berries
fringed gentian, as butterfly lure, 71
fringed orchids, as nectar source for butterflies, 255
frogs, 78–79
frosted hawthorne, as wild fruit, 261
frost grape, 137. *See also* berries
as wild fruit, 264
frost line, pool construction and, 68
fruits, wild edible, 260–64
fungi. *See* mushrooms and fungi

garter snake, 80, 109. *See also* snakes
ghost flower. *See* Indian-pipe
giant swallowtail, food plants for, 253. *See also* butterflies; caterpillars
giant water bug, means of attacking prey, 76. *See also* water beetle
glowworm. *See* firefly
golden currant, as wild fruit, 262
goldenrod, as nectar source for butterflies, 255
goldsmith beetle, as beneficial insect, 256. *See also* beetles
gooseberry, 139. *See also* berries
gophers, trapping as control for, 202
grapes, wild, 137, 264. *See also* berries
great horned owl, benefits of, 114–15. *See also* owls
great purple hairstreak, food plants for, 94, 253. *See also* butterflies; caterpillars
great spangled fritillary, food plants for, 252. *See also* butterflies; caterpillars
green darner, 75. *See also* dragonflies
green frog, 79. *See also* frogs
green heroic darner, 75. *See also* dragonflies
green lynx spider, 120. *See also* spiders
green pubescent beetle, 99. *See also* beetles

green snake, 111. *See also* snakes
ground beetle, 99. *See also* beetles
ground squirrel, trapping as control
for, 202
gulf fritillary, food for, 95, 253. *See
also* butterflies; caterpillars

hackberries, as food for birds, 251
hackberry butterfly, food plants for,
94, 253. *See also* butterflies; caterpillars
half-banded toper, 75. *See also*
dragonflies
halictid bee, food plants for, 72
hand lens, for wildlife observation,
161
harlequin caterpillar, characteristics
of, 92
Harris' checkerspot, food plants for,
253. *See also* butterflies; caterpillars
harvester, 95. *See also* butterflies
Havahart trap, for wildlife control,
200, 202, 205
hawks, 118
hazelnut, as source for nuts, 259. *See
also* nuts
hedgehog, 126–28
hedgehog mushroom, as edible wild
mushroom, 257. *See also* mushrooms and fungi
hedges, 31–32, 33
hen of the woods, as edible wild
mushroom, 257–58. *See also* mushrooms and fungi
hickory, as source for nuts, 259. *See
also* nuts
high-bush blueberry, as wild fruit,
263
high-bush cranberry, as wild fruit,
263
hirudin, as leech anticoagulant, 123
hobblebush, as wild fruit, 263
hognose snake, 111. *See also* snakes
hog-wire panels, for deer fencing,
182–83
holes, as means of wildlife identification, 152
hollies, 251
honey mushroom, as edible wild
mushroom, 258. *See also* mushrooms and fungi

honeysuckle, as nectar source for butterflies, 255
hop merchant, 93. *See also* butterflies
hops, as butterfly food, 93
horse fiddle, as wildlife scare tactic,
211–12
horse plum, as wild fruit, 262
huckleberries, 139, 249–50. *See also*
berries
hummingbird moth. *See also* caterpillars; moths
characteristics of, 89–90
food plants for, 90, 254
hummingbirds, 35
hypodermic impregnation, as leech
fertilization method, 124

ichneumon wasp, 122. *See also* wasps
imperial moth. *See also* caterpillars;
moths
characteristics of, 88
food plants for, 88, 254
Indian-pipe, 225–26
inky caps, 135. *See also* mushrooms
and fungi
insects, worthwhile, 97–101
beetles, 99–100
butterflies, 90–97
fireflies, 97–99
moths, 97–99
io moth, food plants for, 254. *See also*
caterpillars; moths

jack-in-the-pulpit, growing around
pools, 71
Jacobson's organ, in snakes, 111
Japanese honeysuckle, as wildlife
cover, 32
jewelweed, 71–72, 132
Joe-Pye-weed
medicinal value of, 71, 255
as nectar source for butterflies,
255
juneberry, as wild fruit, 260

kingbird, benefits of, 25
kinnikinick, as wild fruit, 260

ladybug, 100. *See also* beetles
lady's slipper, growing in bogs, 71
lamb's quarters, leaves for salads, 131

large cranberry, as wild fruit, 263
lawn sprinkler, as birdbath, 66
leaf beetle, characteristics of, 93
leaves, decomposition of and food
   web, 73
leeches, 122–24
leopard frog, 79. *See also* frogs
lilacs, as nectar source for butterflies,
   255
locust underwing, 88–89. *See also*
   moths
logs, for birdhouses, 35
long-eared owl, 115. *See also* owls
low-bush blueberry, as wild fruit, 263
luciferin, to produce firefly light, 98
luna moth, food plants for, 87, 254.
   See also caterpillars; moths

Mabel orchard spider, 119–20. *See
   also* spiders
magnifying lens, for wildlife observation, 160
manure, as wildlife repellent, 210
maple seedlings, growing of, 33
marbled orb weaver, 119. *See also*
   spiders
marsh-marigold, growing around
   pools, 70
masonry walls, for gardens, 179,
   186–87
may-apple roots, as remedy for liver
   ailments, 169
mazzard cherry, as wild fruit, 262
meadow mushroom, as edible wild
   mushroom, 258. *See also* mushrooms and fungi
meadowsweet, as nectar source for
   butterflies, 255
melons, protection for, 205
metallic wood-boring beetle, 101. *See
   also* beetles
mice, 243–44
   controls for, 201, 243
   footprints of, 151
   signs of presence, 148
microscope, for wildlife observation,
   160–61, 164
Milbert's tortoise shell, 94. *See also*
   butterflies
milk snake, 109. *See also* snakes

milkweed, as nectar source for butterflies, 92–93, 255
milkweed butterflies, types of, 92
milkweed leaf beetle, 93. *See also*
   beetles
milkweed tortoise beetle, 92–93. *See
   also* beetles
mink, 244
   footprints of, 151
minnow, 82–83. *See also* fish
mockingbirds, sense of territory and,
   25
moles, 244
   benefits of, 202–203
   disadvantage of, 203–204
   poisoning of, 203–204
monarch, food plants for, 92, 253.
   See also butterflies; caterpillars
morel, 133–34. *See also* mushrooms
   and fungi
   as edible wild mushroom, 258
mothballs, as animal repellents,
   171–72
moths, 87–90
   food plants for, 252–54
mountain-ash, as food for birds, 251
mountain blackberry, as wild fruit,
   263
mountain cranberry, as wild fruit,
   263
mourning cloak, food plants for, 94,
   252. *See also* butterflies; caterpillars
mud dauber wasp, 121. *See also* wasps
muscadine, 137. *See also* berries
   as wild fruit, 264
mushrooms and fungi, 133–36,
   257–59
   identification of, 134, 136
muskrat, 244–45
   footprints of, 151
mustang grape, 137. *See also* berries
   as wild fruit, 264

naiads, as fish food, 73–74
nannyberry, as wild fruit, 264
narrow beech fern, for wet sites, 72–73
native pecan, as source for nuts, 260.
   See also nuts
native viburnums, as food for wildlife, 252

netting, as protection from birds, 175
nettles, as butterfly food, 93
nettle stings, jewelweed for, 72, 132
New Brunswick Stew, 145
newts, 80–81
night-flying moths, attractants for, 89
northern fox grape, 137. *See also*
  berries
  as wild fruit, 264
northern gooseberry, as wild fruit,
  262
northern wild strawberry, as wild
  fruit, 261
nut pines. *See also* nuts
  as source for nuts, 260
  as wildlife food, 141
nuts, 136, 139–41, 259–60
  types of, 140–41
nut trees, 139

oak, for attracting wildlife, 251–52
opossums, 245
  footprints of, 151
optical aids, for wildlife observation,
  160–64
  binoculars, 160–64
  hand lens, 161
  magnifying lens, 160
  microscope, 160–61, 164
orange day-lily, as nectar source for
  butterflies, 255
ostrich fern, for wet sites, 72
owls, 112–15
oyster mushroom, as edible wild
  mushroom, 258. *See also* mushrooms and fungi

painted lady, food plants for, 93,
  252. *See also* butterflies; caterpillars
pandora sphinx, food plants for, 254.
  See also caterpillars; moths
papaw, 94
  as wild fruit, 261
paper wasp, 120–21. *See also* wasps
parasite, relation to food web, 10
parasol mushroom, 135. *See also*
  mushrooms and fungi
partridgeberry, as wild fruit, 261
pasture rose, as wild fruit, 262
peanuts, as bird food, 56

pelecinid wasp, 122. *See also* wasps
pennywort, as oxygenating water
  plant, 69
phoebus, food plants for, 253. *See*
  also butterflies; caterpillars
photography of wildlife, 164–68
pickerelweed, growing in pools, 70
pigeon grape, 137. *See also* berries
pin cherry, as wild fruit, 262
pinching bugs. *See* elephant stag
pipevine swallowtail, food plants for,
  95, 253. *See also* butterflies; caterpillars
plant pollination, butterflies and
  moths for, 96
plant succession, fire as chief renewer
  for, 26–27
poison ivy, jewelweed for, 72
poisons, for wildlife control, 195–97,
  201
pokeweed, 132–33
pollination, 90, 96
polyphemus moth, food plants for,
  87, 254. *See also* caterpillars; moths
pondweeds, as oxygenating water
  plants, 69
pools
  artificial, 70
  construction of, 62–63
  permanent, 67
  plants for, 69–73
  stocking of, 77–83
porcupines, 246
  footprints of, 152
posts. *See* fences
potter wasp, 121. *See also* wasps
prickly gooseberry, as wild fruit, 262
prometha moth, food plants for, 87,
  254. *See also* caterpillars; moths
pruning, of hedges, 31, 33
puffball, 134. *See also* mushrooms
  and fungi
  as edible wild mushroom, 258
purple-flowered raspberry, as wild
  fruit, 263

queen, food plants for, 253. *See also*
  butterflies; caterpillars
Queen Anne's lace, as nectar source
  for butterflies, 255

question mark, 93–94. *See also* butterflies; caterpillars
  food plants for, 93, 252

rabbit fencing, 175
  chicken wire as, 175–76
rabbits, 246
  bark chewing, prevention of, 208
  fencing for, 175
  footprints of, 149, 151
  hunting of, 228–29
  signs of, 148
rabies
  from bats, 111
  from skunks, 105
raccoon, 231–33
  footprints of, 151
  recipes for, 142–50
  repellents for, 171–72
  signs, 148
Raccoon Broth, 143
Raccoon Gravy, 143
Raccoon Stuffing, 143
raspberry, 138. *See also* berries
rats
  controls for, 195–201
  poisons, 195–97
  rat-proofing your environment,
    97–200
  trapping of, 200–201
rattlesnake, 107, 108. *See also* snakes
recordings, animal, as wildlife scare
  tactic, 212–13
red admiral, food plants for, 93, 252.
  See also butterflies; caterpillars
red beefsteak fungus, 136. *See also*
  mushrooms and fungi
redbelly dace, for mosquito control,
  82. *See also* fish
red eft. *See* red-spotted newt
red milkweed beetle, 92. *See also*
  beetles
red mulberry, as wild fruit, 262
red raspberry, as wild fruit, 263
redroot, leaves for salads, 131
red-spotted newt, 80–81. *See also*
  newts
regal moth, food plants for, 254. *See
  also* caterpillars; moths
repellents, as wildlife control, 209–10
  attractants, 210

big game repellant (BGR), 209–10
  coating seeds, 211
  electronic, 212–13
  fungicide treated seeds, 211
  human hair, 209
  manure, 210
  ultrasonic, 213
riverbank grape, 137. *See also* berries
Roast Raccoon, 142–43
rum cherry, as wild fruit, 262

saddleback caterpillar moth, 91. *See
  also* butterflies; caterpillars
saskatoon, as wild fruit, 260
sassafras, as host plant for butterflies, 94
saw-whet-owl, 151. *See also* owls
scarab beetle, as beneficial insects,
  256. *See also* beetles
scarecrow, as wildlife scare tactic, 209
scare devices, as wildlife controls,
  209–10, 211–12
  animal recordings, 212–13
  electronic vibration of sound
    waves, 212–13
  horse fiddles, 211–12
  scarecrows, 209
  Tomco clapper, 212
  ultrasonic transmitters, 213
scarlet cup fungi, 136. *See also* mushrooms and fungi
screech owl, 113. *See also* owls
screening, as protection from birds,
  175
seedlings, 33–34
seeds, treatment of, for wildlife control, 211
sensitive fern, for wet sites, 72
serviceberry, as wild fruit, 260
shaggy mane, as edible wild mushroom, 258. *See also* mushrooms
  and fungi
shamrock spider, 119. *See also* spiders
sharp-tailed snake, 10. *See also* snakes
sheep, for wild meadow, 28
sheepberry, as wild fruit, 264
short-eared owl, 115. *See also* owls
shrews, 246
  benefits of, 204–205, 246
  footprints of, 151
silkmoth, life cycle of, 86–87

silverberry, as protection, 32
skunks, 105–107
slippery Jack, as edible wild mushroom, 258. *See also* mushrooms and fungi
small cranberry, as wild fruit, 263
smartweed, as food for wildlife, 70
smooth ground cherry, as wild fruit, 262
Smyrna fig, pollination of, 96–97
snakebite, kit for, 107
snakes, 80, 107–11
    benefits of, 108
    food web and, 108–109
    snakebite kit, 107
snapweed. *See* jewelweed
snout butterfly, food plants for, 94. *See also* butterflies
snowy owl, 115. *See also* owls
sour gum, for wetlands, 73
sparrow, controls for, 175
spicebush, for moss garden, 72
spicebush silkmoth, 87. *See also* moths
spicebush swallowtail, 92–93. *See also* butterflies; caterpillars
    food plants for, 87, 91–92, 94, 253
spiders, 118–20
spiderwort, as butterfly lure, 71
splicer, for wire fences, 190
spring azure butterfly, 93. *See also* butterflies
spring peeper, 78–79. *See also* frogs
squirrel bread, as edible wild mushroom, 258–59. *See also* mushrooms and fungi
squirrels, 242–43, 247
    footprints of, 149
    recipe for, 144
stag beetle, 35, 99–100, 256. *See also* beetles
stag bush, as wild fruit, 264
stalking, of wildlife, 153–55
strawberry, 138. *See also* berries
    as wild fruit, 261
suet, as food for birds, 55
sulfur shelf, as edible wild mushroom, 259. *See also* mushrooms and fungi
summer grape, as wild fruit, 264

sunflower seeds, as food for birds, 55
survival instinct, of wildlife, 23–24
swamp milkweed, 71, 93
    as nectar source for butterflies, 92–93, 255
sweet bay, for wetlands, 73
sweetbriar, as wild fruit, 263
sweetheart underwing, 88. *See also* moths
sweet pepperbush, moss garden and, 72

tall blackberry, as wild fruit, 263
Tanglefoot, as tree protection, 208
tarantula, 119. *See also* spiders
tawny emperor, 94. *See also* butterflies
thimbleberry, as wild fruit, 263
thistles, as food source, 93
tiger beetle, as beneficial insect, 99, 256. *See also* beetles
tiger swallowtail, 90. *See also* butterflies; caterpillars
    food plants for, 254
toads, stocking pond with, 114–15
Tomco clapper, as wildlife scare tactic, 212
tools, fencing
    pliers, 189–90
    post-hole digger, 189
    splicer, 189–90
    stretching bars, 189, 193
    stretching ratchets, 189, 191–92
tracks, wildlife, 148–52
trapdoor spider, 120. *See also* spiders
traps, 177, 200–202
    types of, 205
        Conibear, 201, 205
        Havahart, 200, 202, 205
        homemade, 205–207
tree bark, protection for, 181–82
tree guards, 182
    sources for, 184
trees
    beneficial to wildlife, 249–52
    protecting from wildlife, 181–84
    suitable for growing close to water, 73
trilliums, growing around pools, 71
trip-toe, as wild fruit, 263
trout-lily, growing around pools, 71

true bog, makeup of, 70–71
trumpet honeysuckle, to attract wildlife, 32
tupelo. *See* sour gum
turkey vulture. *See* vultures
turtle, snapping, footprints of, 151
turtles, in garden pool, 80
twelve-spot skimmer, 75. *See also* dragonflies

ultrasonic transmitters, as wildlife scare tactic, 213

viceroy, 92. *See also* butterflies; caterpillars
food plants for, 252
Virginia bluebell, growing around pools, 71
Virginia ground cherry, as wild fruit, 262
vultures, 115–17

wall, masonry, 186–87
walnuts. *See also* nuts
black, 260
Carpathian, 260
English, 260
heartnut, 260
Japanese, 260
wasps, 120–22. *See also* bees
water
construction of permanent pool for, 62–63
natural sources of, 64
as wildlife attractant, 60–83
water beetle, 75. *See also* beetles
water fowl, footprints of, 152
water lily, 70
water-milfoil, as oxygenating water plant, 69
water mocassin. *See* cottonmouth
water-shield, as oxygenating water plant, 69
water snake, 80, 110–11. *See also* snakes
water-stargrass, as oxygenating water plant, 69
water strider, 75–76. *See also* water beetle

water-weed, as oxygenating water plant, 69
weasels, 247–48
footprints of, 151
weeds
controlling spreading of, 30
desirable, 27
weed seeds, as bird food, 36
weedy plants
control of, 69–70
whirligig, food for, 75. *See also* water beetle
white admiral, food plants for, 253. *See also* butterflies; caterpillars
white-lined sphinx, food plants for, 254. *See also* caterpillars; moths
white mulberry, as wild fruit, 262
white oak, as source for nuts, 259–60. *See also* nuts
white peacock, food plants for, 253. *See also* butterflies; caterpillars
white tail, 75. *See also* dragonflies
wild apples
for attracting wildlife, 249
as wild fruit, 261
wild aster
as butterfly lure, 71
as nectar source for butterflies, 255
wild blackberry, as wildlife food, 252
wild black cherry, as wild fruit, 262
wild black currant, as wild fruit, 262
wild blue flag, growing in pools, 70
wild carrot, as nectar source for butterflies, 255
wild cherry trees, as food for birds, 250
wild gooseberry, as wild fruit, 262
wild grapes, 137. *See also* berries
for attracting wildlife, 251
as wild fruit, 264
wildlife
beneficial trees for, 249–52
birds, housing for, 46–54
brush piles as housing for, 57
controls, 208–13
dead trees as housing for, 40–41
droppings, 148
holes, 152
housing for, 39–54

identification of, 148–52
keeping records of, 15–19
observation of, 160
     optical aids for, 160–64
sounds of, 146
stalking of, 153–56
tree stumps as housing for, 58
wildlife controls
     poisons, 195–97, 201
     protective shields and barriers,
          195–210
          plant covers as, 208–209
     repellents, 209–12
          attractants, 210–11
          big game repellent (BGR),
               209
          human hair, 209
          manure, 209–10
     scare devices as, 209–10, 211–13
          animal recordings, 212
          electronic vibration of
               sound waves, 213–14
          horse fiddles, 211–12
          scarecrows, 209
          Tomco clapper, 212
          ultrasonic transmitters, 213
     traps, 200–202, 205–207
wildling recipes, 141–44
wild plants, remedies from, 132–33
wild raisin, as wild fruit, 264

wild raspberries, as food for wildlife,
     252
wild sweet cherry, as wild fruit, 262
wild weed flowers, as nectar source
     for butterflies, 255
wild yarrow, as nectar source for but-
     terflies, 255
wineberry, as wild fruit, 263
winter cress, preparation of, 131
winter grape, 137. *See also* berries
     as wild fruit, 264
wintergreen, as wild fruit, 261
wire fencing, 187–93
     installation of, 189–93
wolfberry. *See* silverberry
wolf spider, 120. *See also* spiders
woodbine, as food for wildlife, 252
woodchucks, 248
woodcock, 222–24
wood frog, 79. *See also* frogs
wood strawberry, as wild fruit, 261
wood turtle, 80
worm snake, 111. *See also* snakes

yellow jacket, 121–22. *See also* wasps

zebra swallowtail, food plants for, 94,
     254. *See also* butterflies; caterpillars
zinc phosphide, as wildlife poison, 21

GENE LOGSDON is the author of seventeen books, including *You Can Go Home Again* (also from Indiana University Press), *The Contrary Farmer,* and *A Contrary Farmer's Invitation to Gardening,* hundreds of magazine articles, and a weekly newspaper column. He writes and farms near Upper Sandusky, Ohio, where he lives with his family.